THE NHL
100 YEARS
IN PICTURES & STORIES

BOB DUFF &
RYAN DIXON

FULLY UPDATED FOR THE NHL'S 100TH SEASON

FIREFLY BOOKS

A FIREFLY BOOK

Published by Firefly Books Ltd. 2017
Copyright © 2017 Firefly Books Ltd.
Text Copyright © Hockey Hall of Fame
Images Copyright as listed on this page

First printing

Publisher Cataloging-in-Publication Data (U.S.)

Names: Duff, Bob, author. | Dixon, Ryan, author.
Title: The NHL : 100 Years in Pictures & Stories / Bob Duff & Ryan Dixon.
Description: Richmond Hill, Ontario, Canada : Firefly Books, 2017. | Second Edition. | Includes index. | Summary: This is a fully-updated history of the NHL on the occasion of its centennial anniversary.
Identifiers: ISBN 978-1-77085-970-8 (paperback)
Subjects: LCSH: National Hockey League -- History. | Hockey – Pictorial works. | BISAC: SPORTS & RECREATION / Hockey. | BIOGRAPHY & AUTOBIOGRAPHY / Sports.
Classification: LCC GV847.8.N3D844 |DDC 796.96264 – dc23

Library and Archives Canada Cataloguing in Publication
A CIP record for this title is available from Library and Archives Canada

Published in the United States by
Firefly Books (U.S.) Inc.
P.O. Box 1338, Ellicott Station
Buffalo, New York 14205

Published in Canada by
Firefly Books Ltd.
50 Staples Avenue, Unit 1
Richmond Hill, Ontario L4B 0A7

Additional writing and research: Eric Zweig
Cover and interior design: Matt Filion

Printed in China

Canada

We acknowledge the financial support of the Government of Canada.

Previous Spread: Detroit's Gordie Howe is impeded while in pursuit of the puck by Montreal's Doug Harvey.

Page 5: Two Original Six superstars show mutual respect as Bobby Hull shakes Jean Béliveau's hand, likely after a playoff match up in the mid-1960s.

On the Cover: NHL greats Mario Lemieux, Wayne Gretzky, Gordie Howe, Alex Ovechkin and Bobby Orr are joined on the cover by Edmonton's Connor McDavid — the first-overall pick in the 2015 draft — who is leading the NHL's newest generation of stars into the league's next 100 years.

PHOTO CREDITS
Roth and Ramberg Photography: 218

Hockey Hall of Fame
Graphic Artists: 55T, 60, 65 T, 97, 99, 102, 103, 108, 110, 116, 120, 123, 129, 131, 151
Paul Bereswill: 65 B, 138, 139, 141, 145, 146 T, 148, 149, 153, 154, 156, 157, 158, 159, 162, 170, 174 R, 179, 192, 223
Studio Alain Brouillard: 2-3, 62, 75, 80, 172
Michael Burns Sr.: 49, 50, 77, 84
HHOF: 13, 18, 19, 26, 33, 35, 43 M, 43 R, 47, 72, 78, 87, 127, 130, 133, 136, 180, 199
Imperial Oil–Turofsky: 15, 20, 22, 23, 27, 28, 29, 30, 32, 37, 38, 39, 41, 42, 43 L, 45 T&B, 52, 55 B, 58, 64, 68, 69, 71, 79, 83, 88, 91, 95
Fred Keenan: 106-107
David E. Klutho: 82 T, 100, 160
Hannu Lindroos: 146 B
James Lipa: 175
Doug MacLellan: 173, 174 L, 176, 177
Matthew Manor: 16, 48, 63, 74, 76, 85, 90, 119, 121, 164, 167, 171 R, 172
Mecca: 124, 142, 147
O-Pee-Chee: 118, 161, 166, 191, 202 B
Portnoy: 104, 140
Frank Prazak: 5, 7, 10 34, 51, 61, 82 B, 86, 94, 98, 101, 113, 114, 115
Chris Relke: 11, 168
Hall Roth: 12, 17, 25, 53, 183, 189
Al Ruelle: 135
Dave Sandford: 89, 186, 187, 204, 206
Robert Shaver: 132
Roger St. Jean/La Presse: 57
Le Studio du Hockey: 67 T&B
James Welch: 171L

Library of Congress Archives
LC-DIG-ds-01290, 14

Associated Press
Paul Chiasson: 184 R
Julio Cortez: 184 T
John Crouch/CSM: 224
Kevork Djansezian: 163
Andre Forget: 201
Rich Graessle: 222
Ann Heisenfelt: 210
Mark Humphrey: 200, 227, 229
John Locher: 216, 219
Pablo Martinez Monsivais: 9
Gene Puskar: 185, 202 T, 203
Rich Schultz: 205
Lynne Sladky: 213
Matt Slocum: 194-195, 209, 212
Chuck Stoody: 197 T
Mike Wulf: 207, 208
Adrian Wyld: 197 B

Icon Sportswire
John Crouch: 228
Adam Davis: 225
Bob Frid: 221
Mark Goldman: 217
Marc Sanchez: 226

Cover:
Top (L–R): Steve Babineau/Hockey Hall of Fame Paul Bereswill/Hockey Hall of Fame
Frank Prazak/Hockey Hall of Fame
Minas Panagiotakis/Icon Sportswire
Graphic Artists/Hockey Hall of Fame
Bottom: Bob Frid/Icon Sportswire via AP Images

Back Cover:
Top: Frank Prazak/Hockey Hall of Fame
Middle: Hall Roth/Hocket Hall of Fame

CONTENTS

Ken Dryden makes a kick
save against the Buffalo
Sabres in the early 1970s.

CONTENTS

Braden Holtby makes a
blocker save against the
Pittsburgh Penguins in 2016.

INTRODUCTION

In 2017 the NHL celebrated its centennial — that's 100 years of big-league hockey. In that time, nearly 8,000 players have taken the ice, and almost 350,000 goals have been scored, which adds up to a lot of triumphantly raised fists. Countless is the number of hot dogs and glasses of beer fans have consumed.

The league has expanded, contracted and expanded again and again over those years. Fans used to lean over the boards to see the action down at the far end of the rink, and now they can watch the action on big-screen HD scoreboards. Wooden sticks gave way to aluminum, and aluminum gave way to composite sticks. Goalies used to play bare-faced and nobody wore a helmet. The game has certainly changed, as has anything good enough to last for 100 years.

The NHL: 100 Years in Pictures and Stories delivers the seminal moments in league history. In a circuit with such a colorful past and enduring legacies, there are, of course, many, many moments, events, stars and anecdotes that couldn't be covered in this book. Wayne Gretzky's records alone would take up more than half the pages.

Gretzky, to be sure, is covered in depth, and so are the biggest names of the game, including Howie Morenz, Maurice Richard, Gordie Howe, Bobby Orr and Mario Lemieux. But players like Mel "Sudden Death" Hill and Manon Rhéaume also share the spotlight for their contributions to the game.

A 100th anniversary couldn't arrive without a few warts, and the dark days of the league are also recounted for all to read. From the Hamilton Tigers staging the first ever player strike to Montreal's riots following Clarence Campbell's suspension of Maurice Richard to the lockouts of the modern era and the deaths of enforcers Derek Boogaard, Wade Belak, Rick Rypien in 2011, the league has suffered black eyes and crippling blows. Yet it has survived and adapted and thrived.

Remaining relevant through two World Wars and the Great Depression was a feat in

Mario Lemieux faces off against the Vancouver Canucks in the 1990s. At left, the Toronto Maple Leafs battle the New York Rangers in Madison Square Garden in the 1960s.

itself — and led directly to the creation of the Original Six, which gave the league the stability it needed to prosper. Expanding into the American Sunbelt was another decision ripe with risk that paid off for the NHL and its fans.

The NHL: 100 Years in Pictures and Stories shares the moments that have forever shaped the league and underscores how great the game of hockey really is. From the madcap early days to the 31-team elite professional sports machine that it is today, there's no other game quite like NHL hockey.

Happy birthday, old-timer!

Steve Cameron,
Editor

WORLDS CHAMPIONS 1922-23

CHAMPIONS OF THE WORLD 1920-21

The NHL's first MVP, Frank Nighbor, wore these Ottawa Senators sweaters. The Senators claimed three of the NHL's first six championships.

1917

THE BIRTH OF THE NHL

"Pro hockey on last legs" reported the November 6, 1917, edition of the *Toronto Globe*. It seemed that, with the First World War raging in Europe, sport had become a secondary obsession. Many of hockey's top stars heeded a higher calling and enlisted with the armed forces, while those at home focused on assisting the war effort and on the news coming in from the front lines.

Sure enough, four days later the *Globe* proclaimed the National Hockey Association had disbanded. "The public want first-class hockey and unless we can furnish it for them, we will reserve the ice for skating purposes only," noted E.D. Sheppard, president of the Montreal Arena Company.

Pro hockey wasn't dead though. In fact, it was about to be reborn.

Two days after the November 10th demise of the NHA, the *Toronto Globe* reported there was "something doing in pro hockey." Speculation revolved around a new league being formed with NHA secretary Frank Calder assuming the presidency.

As would soon become clear, the NHA franchise owners were simply using the war and the league dissolution as an excuse to rid themselves of bombastic Toronto owner Eddie Livingstone, who was so difficult to deal with that disbanding and reforming was seen by the rest of the owners as the best solution to their problem. As Ottawa owner Tommy Gorman put it, "He was always arguing about everything. Without him we can get down to the business of making money."

Shortly after the NHA folded, another meeting was cobbled together by the owners of the Ottawa and Quebec City franchises,

both Montreal teams — the Canadiens and the Wanderers — and a new group representing Toronto interests called the Toronto Arena Company.

While it took until November 26th for an official announcement to be made, the new loop — the National Hockey League — was formed and Calder was indeed named president.

The original NHL could have been a five-team league with the Canadiens, Wanderers, Ottawa Senators, Quebec Bulldogs and Toronto. However, Quebec decided at the meeting not to ice a team, and in January the Montreal Arena burned down, forcing the Wanderers to cease operation. Toronto would go on to claim the league's first championship.

Livingstone filed suit against the new Toronto franchise and eventually, after years of courtroom battles, was awarded a $10,000 settlement in 1926.

THE PHANTOM MENACE

YOU DON'T GROW a league without stars, and Joe Malone was the first to illuminate the NHL.

In fact, he did so on opening night. In a 7–4 victory at Ottawa, Montreal Canadiens center Malone put five pucks past Senators goalie Clint Benedict, a Habs road record that still stands today.

Enshrined in the Hockey Hall of Fame in 1950, Malone was known as "The Phantom," and he

certainly was a menace to NHL netminders. In 1917–18 he scored 44 times in 20 games, a league mark that would stand until Montreal's Maurice Richard netted 50 goals in 1944–45. Three times that season, Malone netted five goals in a single game. No player since has ever produced more than one five-goal game in a single season.

Malone's average of 2.2 goals per game in 1917–18 remains the NHL single-season record.

Red Cross emergency influenza crews at the ready in 1918.

1919

SPANISH FLU CANCELS STANLEY CUP

In the spring of 1919, the Montreal Canadiens traveled west to meet the Pacific Coast Hockey Association champions, the Seattle Metropolitans, for the Stanley Cup. It was a rematch of the 1917 final (the last Cup final before the formation of the NHL), which had seen Seattle become the first U.S.-based team to win the Stanley Cup.

Seattle looked to be the better club in the early going, taking a 2–1 series lead and outscoring Montreal 16–6 over the first three games. Without Newsy Lalonde, who had scored all of his team's goals in the Canadiens' 4–2 win in Game 2, Montreal could easily have been down 3–0 in the series.

The fourth game of the set ended scoreless after PCHA officials misinterpreted the NHL rulebook and halted the game after two fruitless overtime periods. The Canadiens then rallied in Game 5 from a 3–1 deficit to win 4–3, knotting everything up 2-2-1 heading into the winner-take-all Game 6. Then, the series was abruptly canceled.

The Spanish Influenza epidemic that would take nearly 20 million lives worldwide also claimed the Stanley Cup. Five Montreal players — Joe Hall, Jack McDonald, Louis Berlinquette, Newsy Lalonde and Billy Coutu — as well as manager George Kennedy were bedridden with flu, Hall and McDonald so seriously ill that they were hospitalized.

Kennedy suggested the Habs could borrow players from the Victoria PCHA team to finish the series, but Seattle declined. The Metropolitans would also not accept Lord Stanley's mug via forfeit, so for the first time in its 26-year history, there would be no Stanley Cup winner.

"This has been the most peculiar series in the history of sport," PCHA president Frank Patrick said. "Precedent after precedent has been broken. There never was another series of games like the present one.

"We are sorry that the Seattle fans could not witness the deciding struggle . . . but the circumstances were such that it would have been impossible to play the game."

HE WASN'T A BAD JOE

ENTERING HIS 17TH season of big-league hockey, 38-year-old Montreal defenseman Joe Hall was in a spry mood.

"A fellow is just as old as he feels and right now I feel I am good for at least 10 more years of hockey," Hall said.

Hall led the NHL in penalty minutes in each of the league's first two seasons, topping the century mark during both campaigns even though he played just 21 and 16 games respectively. That pugnacious approach earned him the nickname "Bad" Joe Hall, though hockey people insisted it was a misnomer.

"Off the ice, he was one of the jolliest, best-hearted, most popular men who ever played," PCHA president Frank Patrick said.

As the 1919 Stanley Cup final series between Seattle and Montreal lingered on, Hall wore down, but his age had nothing to do with it. Afflicted with the Spanish Flu, Hall would never recover. Hospitalized March 31st, pneumonia gripped his body, and he died on April 5th in Seattle's Columbus Sanitarium.

"He was quarantined and nobody could go see him," longtime friend Cyclone Taylor recalled in his book *Cyclone Taylor: A Hockey Legend.* "He died all alone, and for a man like Joe who loved to have people around him, this was a particularly sad thing."

Hall was inducted into the Hockey Hall of Fame in 1961.

1923

HOCKEY HITS THE AIRWAVES

Foster Hewitt at the microphone in his famous gondola at Maple Leaf Gardens.

Originally, the man credited as the father of the hockey play-by-play would have much rather the title be given to another: "If It had been left up to me, it would have been my first and last broadcast," Foster Hewitt claimed of his February 16, 1923, live call of the third period and overtime of a Kitchener–Toronto OHA intermediate game for CFCA radio.

Calling the action via a telephone mouth-piece from a cramped 4-by-4-foot glass enclosure at ice level, conditions weren't exactly ideal for these pioneers of sports broadcasting. "I started to suffocate because

it had no air holes," Hewitt told CBC of his first live call.

Contrary to popular belief, Hewitt wasn't hockey's first play caller. Eight days earlier, fellow *Toronto Star* reporter Norm Albert had called the final period of a North Toronto–Midland OHA intermediate game. He had also provided the play-by-play of the third period of an NHL game between the Ottawa Senators and the Toronto St. Patricks on February 14th; Toronto's Jack Adams scored the first NHL goal ever to be described live on the radio as the St. Pats won 6–4.

The broadcasts were a smash hit, and the mantle of calling more games was handed to Hewitt, not Albert. By the 1930s, Saturday night had become *Hockey Night in Canada*, and Hewitt's legend was born. His calls of Toronto Maple Leafs games were carried coast to coast, and he was every bit as famous and popular as the players, known for his signature sign in of "Hello Canada and hockey fans in the United States."

Elected to the Hockey Hall of Fame in 1974, the broadcasting excellence award the Hall presents annually bears Hewitt's name.

1925 — HAMILTON TIGERS GO ON STRIKE

Last place had proven to be the personal property of the Hamilton Tigers in each of their first four NHL campaigns, but something changed during the 1924–25 season.

Led by their explosive forward line of Billy Burch between the Green brothers, Red and Shorty, and backstopped by acrobatic netminder Jake Forbes, the Tigers soared to first place in the NHL standings.

There was just one problem. Owner Percy Thompson reneged on his promise to pay

games they had played, so the players walked out in protest right before they were to play the Montreal Canadiens in the NHL final.

"Professional hockey is a money making affair," Shorty Green said. "The promoters are in the game for what they can make out of it and the players wouldn't be in the game if they didn't look at matters in the same light."

NHL president Frank Calder disagreed, suspending the entire Hamilton team, fining each player $200 and awarding the NHL title

The Tigers got little sympathy from the rest of the hockey world. "Fine time to pull a trick like that" quipped Victoria Cougars goalie Hap Holmes, whose team defeated the Canadiens in the 1924–25 Stanley Cup final.

Beyond the lost chance at a Stanley Cup, the strike proved fateful for the NHL in Hamilton. The franchise was sold to New York interests that summer and began the 1925–26 season as the New York Americans. Hamilton, despite its best efforts, has never

1926

10-TEAM NHL TAKES CONTROL OF STANLEY CUP

Heading into its 10th season, in 1926, the NHL looked nothing like the four-team league that had started with clubs in Ontario and Quebec in 1917. They had added the Boston Bruins and Montreal Maroons in 1924, and the following season the Pittsburgh Pirates joined the fray and the Hamilton Tigers became the New York Americans. But before the puck dropped on the 1926–27 season, big changes were afoot.

From the NHL's first year, it had competed with the Pacific Coast Hockey Association and the Western Canada Hockey League during the season-ending Stanley Cup playoffs. But as the NHL was adding teams in 1924, times were getting tough in the smaller markets out west.

The two western leagues had merged in 1924 (forming the Western Hockey League), but it wasn't enough to save elite pro hockey in the West. On May 3, 1926, the Patrick brothers, Lester and Frank, who ran the league, shut down operations and sold all of their players' contracts to the NHL for $258,000, leaving the NHL as the only league with teams that could vie for the Stanley Cup.

"It is a regrettable situation so far as the smaller Canadian centres are concerned," admitted Lloyd Turner, owner of the WHL's Calgary Tigers. "In the larger American cities, they are prepared to pay higher prices. It is a situation that I felt would arise as soon as the United States took up hockey."

Quickly, new franchises sprung up across the United States. Detroit interests purchased the Victoria Cougars roster for $100,000, and the Detroit Cougars, who'd eventually become the Red Wings, were born. In Chicago, the Portland Rosebuds were purchased for a similar fee and became the Black Hawks. The New York Rangers pieced together a roster comprising top amateur stars and key western players, such as Frank Boucher and the Cook brothers, Bill and Bun, who'd form the NHL's most productive forward line.

Now with 10 teams, the NHL was divided into divisions for the first time. The Rangers, Black Hawks and Cougars were joined by the Bruins and Pirates in the American Division, while the New York Americans were placed with the Montreal Maroons, Montreal Canadiens, Ottawa Senators and Toronto St. Patricks in the International Division.

By more than doubling in size in the span of two years, the NHL had truly become a major league.

Lionel Conacher wore this Montreal Maroons sweater during the 1936–37 season, his last in the NHL.

GONE BUT NOT FORGOTTEN: PRE-1967 NHL TEAMS THAT FADED FROM EXISTENCE

MONTREAL WANDERERS (1917–18)
• Won only one game. Folded after arena burned down on January 2, 1918.

OTTAWA SENATORS (1917–34)
• First NHL team to win back-to-back Stanley Cups, in 1919–20 and 1920–21.

QUEBEC ATHLETICS (1919–20)
• Joe Malone scored an NHL single-game record of seven goals during a January 31, 1920, game against Toronto.

HAMILTON TIGERS (1920–25)
• Posted a shutout victory in their first NHL game.

MONTREAL MAROONS (1924–38)
• Became first NHL expansion franchise to win Stanley Cup, in 1925–26.

PITTSBURGH PIRATES (1925–30)
• In 1926, became first American-based team to qualify for NHL playoffs.

NEW YORK AMERICANS (1925–42)
• Played 17 seasons in league and never reached Stanley Cup final.

PHILADELPHIA QUAKERS (1930–31)
• Posted an NHL-worst .136 winning percentage during it's only season of operation.

ST. LOUIS EAGLES (1934–35)
• Roster included Syd Howe and Bill Cowley, both of whom would retire as NHL all-time scoring leader.

Lester Patrick is shown here guarding New York's net.

1928

RANGERS BECOME FIRST AMERICAN NHL TEAM TO WIN CUP

When the NHL expanded to 10 teams in 1926, the first group to be awarded an expansion franchise was the New York Rangers.

Backed by super promoter Tex Rickard and with Madison Square Garden ready to house the team, they became known as Tex's Rangers and were admitted to the NHL on April 18, 1926. Though they would share their home with the New York Americans, the Rangers quickly became the sexier of the two franchises and were a hit from the get-go.

They posted a 1–0 shutout win over the Stanley Cup–champion Montreal Maroons in their opener, and they made the playoffs in each of their first nine seasons, winning two Cups and appearing in four finals.

Rickard's hockey man, Col. John Hammond, hired Conn Smythe (who gained greater fame as the architect of the Toronto Maple Leafs) to manage his team. Smythe mixed a group of top amateurs — including goalie Lorne Chabot, forward Paul Thompson and American defenseman Taffy Abel — with veteran professionals Frank Boucher and the Cook brothers, Bill and Bun, to build a deep, talented roster.

As the Rangers' first season (1926–27) drew near, Hammond feared that Smythe, who constantly butted heads with both him and Rickard, might be too inexperienced to run an NHL club. So Lester Patrick, former owner of the Western Hockey League as well as a seasoned team owner and former player, took over the operation.

The Rangers finished atop the American Division by 11 points that season. Bill Cook led the NHL in scoring, and the following season, New York beat the Maroons to become the first American-based NHL team to capture the Stanley Cup.

It was Patrick, however, who became the unlikely star of that fabled first championship.

He began the day of Game 2 of the 1928 Stanley Cup final by lobbying the officials about the interference tactics of the Montreal Maroons. He finished the evening in the hot seat.

Early in the second period, a high backhand shot by Maroons star Nels Stewart struck Rangers goalie Chabot directly in the left eye, and he was immediately rushed to Montreal's Royal Victoria Hospital. The Rangers did not have a backup goalie, and

Maroons manager Eddie Gerard refused to let New York use Ottawa Senators goalie Alex Connell or minor-league goalie Hugh McCormick, who were both in attendance.

Then Patrick's players suggested that the former All-Star defenseman take up the net.

Patrick, then 44, agreed, and while he'd previously donned the pads in a pinch for the Montreal Wanderers and Victoria Cougars, he was never going to be confused with an NHL goalie.

His netminding style was unique, to say the least. On angle shots he used his pads and stick to parry drives, but for straight-on shots he dropped his stick, fell to his knees and scooped the puck with his gloves like a baseball infielder.

Aided greatly by his team's shot-blocking efforts, Patrick made 17 saves and was beaten just once: a Stewart goal that sent the game into overtime, where Boucher scored to win it 2–1 for the Rangers.

The next day the team borrowed Joe Miller from Niagara Falls of the Canadian Pro League, and he played the final three games as the Rangers won the best-of-five series 3–2.

1929

NEW RULES OPEN UP SCORING

It was an innocuous game toward the end of the NHL's 1928–29 season, but what happened on the ice on March 17, 1929, between the Pittsburgh Pirates and New York Rangers would forever influence the way the game is played.

During the contest, won 4–3 by the Rangers, players were permitted to kick the puck and make forward passes in all three zones.

"The experimental rules produced the effect for which they were designed," reported the Associated Press. "There was wide-open action and plenty of it all the way through. The verdict of the fans was almost unanimously in favor of the change."

Defensive play had come to dominate the NHL, peaking during the 1928–29 campaign, when there were 120 shutouts posted in 220 games. The Chicago Black Hawks, the league's most goal-stricken club, were blanked in eight successive games. Total goals per game for the league hit an all-time low of 2.9.

The radical changes implemented for the 1929–30 season, namely that you could pass the puck forward in all zones, did increase scoring. Goals per game jumped to 5.9, while shutouts plummeted to 26. Boston's Cooney Weiland recorded an NHL-record 73 points, 22 more than Howie Morenz's prior NHL mark of 51. Eighteen players scored 20 goals and nine collected 50 points during the 44-game season.

In fact, NHL officials realized early that they may have swung the pendulum too far, and on December 16, 1929, they made it illegal for attacking players to proceed the puck across the opposing blue line, implementing the offside rule as it is enforced today.

1930

GEORGE HAINSWORTH BLANKS 'EM

George Hainsworth in the Montreal net in the early 1930s.

Shutouts and George Hainsworth went together like skates and ice. In 1928–29 the Montreal Canadiens netminder posted an NHL-record 22 shutouts. The following spring, Hainsworth would add to his zero-sum legacy.

At 15:34 of the first period during Montreal's opening Stanley Cup semifinal game against the New York Rangers, Murray Murdoch whipped a close-in shot past Hainsworth for a 1–0 advantage.

Armand Mondou later tied the score, and it wasn't until 8:52 of the fourth overtime that rookie Gus Rivers won Game 1 for the Habs.

Hainsworth went on to block 21 more shots in a 2–0 Game 2 win, propelling Montreal to the Cup final, where they'd face the Boston Bruins. Backed by their steady goaltender, the Canadiens posted a 3–0 win in the series opener.

"He's as cool as an iceberg," wrote W.E. Mullins in the Boston Herald. "It's icewater instead of blood which runs through his veins."

Finally, at the 16:50 mark of the second period of Game 2, Bruins defenseman Eddie Shore put a high shot into the Montreal net.

Hainsworth's 270:08 without allowing a goal set a Stanley Cup record, though for several decades, Detroit's Normie Smith, who went unbeaten for 248:32 during the 1936 playoffs, was given credit for the mark. It wasn't until 2004 that research revealed Hainsworth to be the true record holder.

Perhaps it was Hainsworth's unassuming brilliance and technically sound but seemingly disinterested play that made him easy to overlook. "I can't jump on easy shots and make them look hard," Hainsworth said.

Side profile of Ace Bailey, showing the scar from the operation that saved his life.

1933

THE BRUTAL END OF ACE BAILEY'S CAREER

When the Boston Bruins and Toronto Maple Leafs met, blood generally boiled over. It started at the top, where Boston coach Art Ross and Toronto manager Conn Smythe were constantly feuding. On the ice, Boston's Eddie Shore and Toronto's Red Horner took up the cause with their take-no-prisoners brand of hockey, and Leafs defenseman King Clancy could chirp with the best of them.

Toronto forward Ace Bailey was not among the usual combatants, but on the night of December 12, 1933, at Boston Garden, he became the innocent victim of a hockey tragedy that nearly resulted in his becoming the first on-ice fatality in NHL history.

In the second period, Shore was taken hard into the boards in the Leafs' end by Horner and was slow to get up. Elsewhere, Bailey was tangling with Boston's Red Beattie and was also slow to exit the zone.

Rising to his feet and seeing Bailey, Shore figured he was the Leaf who'd just flattened him, so to exact revenge he flipped Bailey's legs out from under him.

Bailey's head hit the ice with a dull thud that was heard throughout the rink, and immediately his body began writhing in convulsions. Horner took umbrage at Shore's cheap shot and decked the Boston defender, whose head also struck the ice hard, and a pool of blood formed under the unconscious Shore. The entire Bruins team went after Horner with the exception of Vic Ripley, who, seeing that Bailey was in peril, filled the role of peacemaker.

Bailey was taken to the dressing room, where the color was draining from his body and he was turning a hue of blue, leaving attending physicians to fear he was dead. After 10 minutes of working on him, house physician Dr. C. Lynde Gately was able to revive Bailey, and the Leafs forward was rushed to the hospital.

Suffering from a fractured skull, Bailey underwent a delicate operation in order to save his life and, in fact, some Boston papers mistakenly ran his obituary. Bailey fought for his life for days and eventually won the battle, but he would never play hockey again.

Shore, who was interviewed by Boston homicide detectives and who would have faced manslaughter charges had Bailey died, insisted their collision was an accident.

"There was no ill feeling between us," Shore told the Associated Press. "We have been friends for some time. It was purely accidental.

"I went to the dressing room to see Bailey. I said, 'Ace, I'm sorry this happened. I assure you it was not intentional.' He replied, 'That's all right, Eddie. It's all in the game.'

"I did not strike him with a stick. I had no malice."

Acting NHL director Frank Patrick agreed and gave Shore a lenient 16-game suspension.

Bailey continued in hockey by coaching the University of Toronto Varsity Blues hockey team between 1935 and 1940 and then again after the Second World War, from 1945 to 1949. During his coaching tenure, the U of T Blues won three Canadian Interuniversity Athletics Union championships. In addition, from 1938 to 1984, Ace continued his ties with the Maple Leafs and the NHL by serving as timekeeper at Maple Leaf Gardens.

1934

FIRST NHL
ALL-STAR GAME

MAPLE LEAFS and ALL STARS
TORONTO FEB. 14th 1934
NATIONAL LEAGUE BENEFIT GAME for "ACE" BAILEY
SCORE — LEAFS 7 STARS 3

With his career ended by a fractured skull suffered when hit by Boston's Eddie Shore, former Toronto forward Ace Bailey contemplated filing suit against the NHL. The league, however, came up with a compromise: they would hold an All-Star Game at Maple Leaf Gardens between the Leafs and an assembled team of stars from the other seven NHL teams, and all the proceeds of the game would go to Bailey.

The game was slated for February 14, 1934, and the Leafs players actually picked up the visiting stars at the train station and

drove them to the rink. Shore ended up catching a ride with Toronto defenseman Red Horner, who'd knocked Shore unconscious with a punch moments after he'd leveled Bailey on that fateful night.

"Eddie knew he'd done a bad thing and he was sorry," Horner explained.

Prior to the start of the game, Bailey dropped the ceremonial first puck, handed out medals to all the participants and then shook hands with Shore. That moment, and every moment during the game when Shore touched the puck, was greeted with thunderous applause.

"They sure warmed my heart," Shore told the Canadian Press. "Please thank Toronto fans for those cheers. I appreciated them more than any others I ever received."

The Leafs hammered the NHL All-Stars 7–3 in a wide-open, freewheeling affair that raised $20,090 for Bailey.

"It wasn't much of a game," grumbled the rugged Horner.

The All-Star Game model didn't become an annual affair for some time, but games were staged in times of need, when an amalgamation of stars sure to draw a good gate was used to raise money for a worthy cause.

1934

CHARLIE GARDINER DIES

Chicago's Charlie Gardiner, pictured in 1934 at the Ace Bailey Benefit Game.

They called him Bonny Prince Charlie, and perhaps no NHLer carried on a more joyous love affair with life than Chicago Black Hawks netminder Chuck Gardiner.

There was the 1933 night in Toronto when Gardiner was pummeled with 66 shots and an overzealous Leafs fan fired his derby out onto the Maple Leaf Gardens ice surface. The affable Gardiner playfully scooped up the hat, donning it for the remainder of the game.

There was also the afternoon during an early spring snowstorm in Chicago when Black Hawks defenseman Roger Jenkins joyfully pushed a wheelbarrow with Gardiner as its payload through the downtown streets, paying off a bet after Gardiner had guaranteed the Hawks would win the 1933–34 Stanley Cup.

"He was the greatest goalkeeper in the world," Jenkins said.

Earlier that season, as the Black Hawks were battling toward the franchise's inaugural Cup win, Gardiner was struck with a serious case of tonsillitis. Eschewing medical attention until season's end, Gardiner continued stopping pucks so well that he won the Vezina Trophy.

As the Black Hawks moved through the playoffs, pain began to escalate throughout Gardiner's body, and outwardly people noticed a change in his deportment. He was no longer the happy-go-lucky, jovial fellow whom everyone loved to be around and had grown withdrawn, even melancholy.

Uncharacteristically, after Detroit's fourth goal of a 5–2 Game 3 victory in the Cup final, Gardiner stalked to the Chicago bench, engaging teammate Johnny Gottselig in an argument, shaking his first in Gottselig's face and causing the Chicago Stadium crowd to boo their goaltender.

Two nights later on the same ice, Gardiner — sometimes clutching the net with his hand for balance while enduring the searing pain — made 39 saves in a 1–0 double-overtime win that gave the Black Hawks the right to lift Lord Stanley's mug for the first time.

"It was probably the best game of his eventful career," Chicago defenseman Lionel Conacher told the *Border Cities Star*.

It would also be his last.

Doctors advised Gardiner to return to his Winnipeg home for complete rest. Instead, he maintained his busy schedule, trapshooting at the gun club (he was an expert marksman) and taking singing lessons to sharpen his smooth tenor voice. He even went on that wheelbarrow ride.

By early June, however, Gardiner was bedridden, diagnosed with neuritis of the stomach and kidneys, and on June 13, 1934, he lapsed into a coma and was rushed to Winnipeg's St. Boniface Hospital. As a steady rain came down outside the building, within its walls, Gardiner, 30, was pronounced dead, the victim of a brain hemorrhage brought on by uremic convulsions.

1937

—

THE DEATH OF HOCKEY'S BIGGEST STAR

With his electrifying speed and dynamic rink-length rushes, Howie Morenz was instrumental in making the NHL a world-class spectacle. "He was to hockey in the 1920s what Babe Ruth was to baseball," suggested his son Howie Morenz Jr. in a 2009 interview.

It's difficult to debate Morenz's legacy. The three-time Hart Trophy winner was the Wayne Gretzky of his era. Known as the "Stratford Streak" for his brilliant skating, Morenz was an instant success with the Montreal Canadiens' Flying Frenchmen, and his dazzling rushes would lift spectators from their seats and carry hockey to places pucks hadn't previously been chased by professionals.

When Morenz joined the Montreal Canadiens in 1923, the NHL was a four-team, all-Canadian league with one franchise in Quebec and three in Ontario. Within a year of his arrival, the league had expanded into the United States, and by 1926 it was a thriving two-division, 10-team outfit.

Morenz helped Montreal to three Stanley Cup titles, but in 1934, fearing their star was slowing down, the Habs dealt him to Chicago. A further trade to the New York Rangers followed, but Morenz's numbers plummeted, and it appeared his best days were done.

Then in 1936, Canadiens manager Cecil Hart made a bold move. He acquired Morenz and reunited him with old linemates Aurel Joliat and Johnny Gagnon. Emboldened by a return to familiar surroundings, Morenz, 34, seemed to find the fountain of youth and roared up among the NHL scoring leaders once again.

He sat with 20 points in 29 games as the Habs welcomed the Chicago Black Hawks to the Forum for a January 28, 1937, contest. During the first period, Morenz burst down the right wing, seeking to beat bruising Chicago defenseman Earl Seibert to a loose puck along the end boards, but he lost his balance and his left skate got wedged into the boards just as he collided with Seibert. The impact shattered Morenz's tibia just above the ankle.

Morenz was stretchered from the ice and taken to Montreal's St. Luke's Hospital. The Forum crowd fell silent, and players on both sides struggled with their emotions.

"It's sure a tough break for Howie when he was going so well," Chicago forward Paul Thompson told the *Montreal Gazette*.

After the game, Chicago coach Clem Loughlin handed $10 to Montreal reporter Baz O'Meara and said, "Get some flowers for

The sweaters worn by the home side (red) and visiting side (white) at the Howie Morenz Memorial Game.

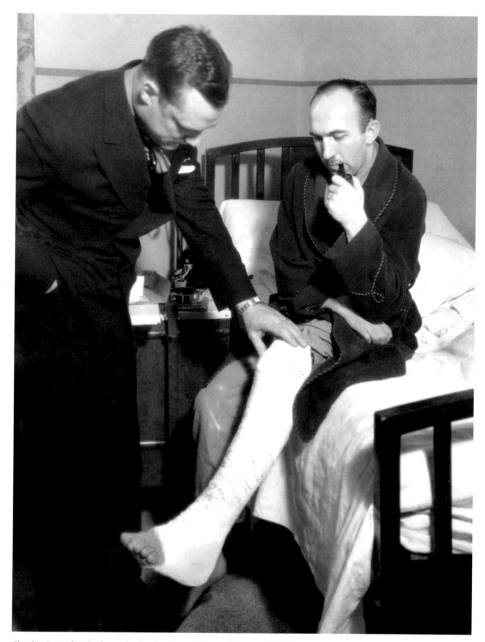

Charlie Conacher looks at the broken leg of Howie Morenz in 1937.

Howie, will you, and tell him how sorry I am to hear of his bad luck."

Expected to miss six weeks, the next day, Morenz tried to put a positive spin on his severe injury: "Don't count me out yet," Morenz told the Canadian Press. "It took 14 years to get me and they got me good."

Then Morenz took on a more philosophical tone: "Perhaps the old leg will come around and I'll be as good as new. Perhaps it won't, and well. . ."

It wouldn't. In fact, things would only get worse.

On March 8, 1937, the hockey world awoke to the shocking news that Morenz had died in hospital. Three days later, his funeral was held at the Montreal Forum, his casket at center ice.

Joliat, his longtime linemate and friend, suggested that Morenz, realizing his career was at an end, died of a broken heart. In fact, the cause of death was a pulmonary embolism.

"So his heart gave out on him," suggested Montreal Maroons defenseman Stew Evans. "Well he had a great one. There was never better."

Former NHLer Leo Bourgault summed it up succinctly: "Hockey has suffered its greatest loss."

IN ONE SENSE, Howie Morenz Jr. could have been viewed as the luckiest boy at the Montreal Forum the night of November 2, 1937. He was out on the ice, skating with the world's best hockey players, but tragic circumstances had put him there — the death of his father, Canadiens superstar Howie Morenz.

The younger Morenz was invited to skate with the Montreal All-Stars in the warm-up and sit on their bench during the Howie Morenz Memorial Game.

"I remember scoring a goal on [Montreal Maroons netminder] Bill Beveridge," Morenz Jr. once recalled. "I also remember being disappointed they gave me a white sweater to wear.

"I wanted a red one."

A game that featured 17 future Hall of Famers saw the NHL All-Stars edge the Montreal All-Stars, comprising players from the Canadiens and Maroons, by a 6–5 count.

The night raised $20,000 for the Morenz family.

1939

"SUDDEN DEATH" HILL AND THE BEST-OF-SEVEN FORMAT

Mel Hill as a member of the Pittsburgh Hornets in the mid-1940s.

The NHL's new playoff format would make a hero out of Boston Bruins forward Mel Hill.

After the Montreal Maroons franchise was suspended prior to the 1938–39 season, NHL governors voted to end the league's two-division format and go with one seven-team division. This also led to restructuring the league's playoff format, and the best-of-seven series that are commonplace today were introduced on a regular basis. (The NHL had a one-off best-of-seven series in 1919, which was decided in Game 5.)

It was determined that six of seven teams would qualify for the playoffs, with the top

two finishers during the regular season meeting in a best-of-seven set, with the winner advancing directly to the Cup final.

The other four teams would partake in best-of-three quarterfinals and semifinals to determine the second Cup final participant. The two finalists would then complete a best-of-seven series to decide who would lift Lord Stanley's mug.

The 1938–39 season ended with the Boston Bruins and the New York Rangers taking the top two spots and thus clashing in a best-of-seven series. It was a thriller.

Boston's Hill scored in triple overtime to win Game 1, and the Bruins won Game 2 on

another Hill overtime marker. Hill didn't score the winner in Game 3, but Boston won all the same. New York then rallied for three straight wins of their own to deadlock the gripping series.

Game 7 was a close checking affair and was tied 1–1 after regulation — a trip to the Cup final would be decided in overtime. For the third time in the series, Hill, on a feed from Bill Cowley, scored the OT winner.

Boston would beat Toronto 4–1 in the final, but hockey's love affair with the best-of-seven series started with Boston–New York. And for his heroics, Hill would be forever known as "Sudden Death" Hill.

1940

—

DICK IRVIN LAUNCHES HOCKEY'S BIGGEST RIVALRY

Dick Irvin drove the Toronto Maple Leafs to great heights, but he struggled to push the club to claim hockey's ultimate prize.

In charge as coach of the Maple Leafs from 1931 to 1940, Irvin won 216 games and had a .575 winning percentage. He did guide the Leafs to one Stanley Cup victory, but his six series losses in the Stanley Cup final earned him a reputation in Toronto as a coach who couldn't get the most of his charges.

Critics blamed Irvin for the Leafs playoff failures, insisting he wasn't a tough enough coach, but former Leafs defenseman Red Horner put the blame on the players: "We should have won more than one Cup [under Irvin]," Horner once explained. "We had a very fine offensive team and we had a fun-loving bunch, but we didn't swear off the fun when the playoffs began."

After losing three straight Cup final series from 1938 to 1940, Leafs' manager Conn

Smythe, knowing he'd be leaving the Leafs to help the Canadian effort in the Second World War, feared the team would grow only softer with Irvin in complete control. He therefore allowed the Montreal Canadiens to sign Irvin as coach-GM on April 17, 1940, just four days after losing the Cup final to the New York Rangers.

The day that Irvin was hired, the *Montreal Gazette* boldly noted that Tommy Gorman, director of the Canadian Arena Company, owners of the team, had been given carte blanche to pursue a big-name coach.

Smythe played the magnanimous role as Irvin departed: "We hated to see Irvin go," Smythe claimed, "but we felt that the sorry condition in which the Canadiens had found themselves wasn't doing any team in the league any good."

No one was buying Smythe's act, however, and it would later be determined that the Leafs owner had decided Clarence "Hap" Day

would be his coach for the 1940–41 season prior to Irvin's departure.

Irvin, as it turned out, also knew he was done: "The day after our last game . . . Dick came to me and said, 'I want my skates and other stuff to take home,'" related Leafs trainer Tim Daly. "I knew then that something was up, for he had never done that before."

The change would prove beneficial for both teams, and for the NHL as a whole.

Under Irvin, the Canadiens, who'd fallen on hard times in the late 1930s, would win four Stanley Cups and appear in nine finals. Meanwhile, Day would finally turn the Leafs into a team capable of rising to the occasion, capturing five Stanley Cups in the 1940s.

More significantly, the move ignited a rivalry between the two legendary franchises, who had yet to meet in the playoffs. Between 1942 and 1949, the Leafs and Habs combined to win seven Stanley Cups and faced each other in a trio of playoff series.

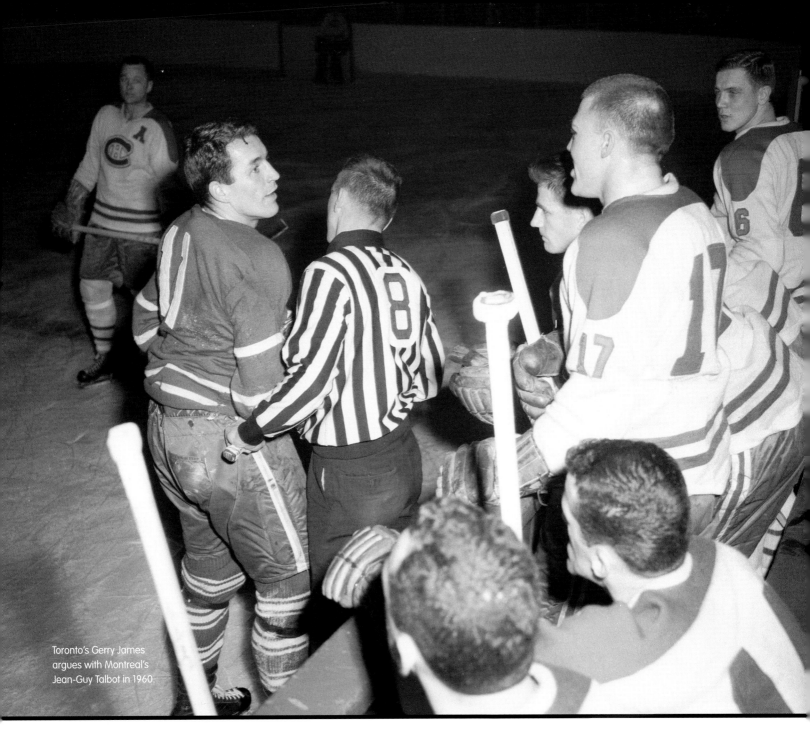

Toronto's Gerry James argues with Montreal's Jean-Guy Talbot in 1960.

SELKE FUELS THE FIRE

IF DICK IRVIN'S move from Toronto to Montreal ignited the rivalry between the Maple Leafs and the Canadiens, Frank Selke's 1946 decision to leave Toronto for Montreal to take over as managing director of the Habs created a blazing inferno.

Selke had been Conn Smythe's lieutenant from almost the moment he had taken over the Leafs in 1927, but he had grown weary of Smythe's pettiness and the way he demeaned others. In the summer of 1946, when Smythe won a power struggle to gain control of the franchise, Selke

knew his days were numbered and jumped at the chance to take charge of the Canadiens.

Immediately, the bad blood between the two men boiled over. "No wonder there is a shortage of pulp and paper in the country, [the] Canadiens have called in all the woodchoppers," Smythe told the Canadian Press early into the 1946–47 season, critical of Montreal's stickwork.

Selke countered that the Leafs held so much he was considering suiting up wrestler Yvon Robert, who'd be able to break the holds.

As it turned out, the Leafs would have been wise to hold onto Selke. The Toronto team he'd assembled while Smythe was away fighting in the Second World War won five Stanley Cups between 1945 and 1951, but then the Leafs would go without a Cup until 1962.

Meanwhile, Selke built a dynasty in Montreal that played in 10 straight Cup final series between 1951 and 1960, winning six times, including a record five in a row from 1956 to 1960.

Toronto's Syl Apps carries the "stovepipe" Stanley Cup in 1942.

1942

LEAFS STAGE GREATEST COMEBACK OF THEM ALL

The Toronto Maple Leafs were in dire straits. Heavily favored and in their first Stanley Cup final appearance under new coach Hap Day, it was as though Toronto was still being led by Dick Irvin, Day's predecessor, who had had an awful time getting the Leafs to win when it mattered most, going one for seven in Stanley Cup bids.

In the 1942 Cup final, the underdog Detroit Red Wings had raced to a 3–0 lead over Hap's Leafs and needed just one more victory to claim the title.

"We ought to wind it up soon," Detroit manager Jack Adams predicted.

"They are unbeatable," suggested Leafs goalie Turk Broda. "They're too hot. They can't seem to do anything wrong."

Heading into the fourth game of the series, Day shook up his lineup. He benched veteran defenseman Bucko McDonald and forward Gordie Drillon — the 1937–38 NHL scoring champ — and inserted youngsters Ernie Dickens on defense and Don Metz and Gaye Stewart up front.

"I don't remember there being any panic," recalled Stewart, 18 at the time and making his NHL debut. "Everyone — Hap Day, [manager] Conn Smythe — were very businesslike in their approach."

The moves paid immediate dividends. Metz set up his older brother Nick for the Game 4 winner as the Leafs rallied from 2–0 and 3–2 deficits for a 4–3 win. Afterward, Adams and Detroit players Don Grosso and Eddie Wares got into a disagreement with referee Mel Harwood, and Adams struck Harwood, earning a suspension for the remainder of the series.

With that, the tide turned. The Leafs routed the Wings 9–3 in Game 5, and Broda blanked them 3–0 in Game 6. Detroit took a 1–0 lead into the third period of Game 7, but Sweeney Schriner tied it just as a penalty to Wings defenseman Jimmy Orlando expired. Pete Langelle netted the Cup winner in Toronto's eventual 3–1 decision, completing the most amazing comeback in sports history.

"We did it the hard way," shrugged Day.

STANLEY CUP PLAYOFF COMEBACKS FROM 3-0 DEFICITS

1942 FINAL: Toronto Maple Leafs 4, Detroit Red Wings 3 (only team to accomplish this in a Cup final series)

1975 QUARTERFINAL: New York Islanders 4, Pittsburgh Penguins 3 (Isles also rallied from 3–0 down to Philadelphia in semis but lost Game 7)

2010 EASTERN CONFERENCE SEMIFINAL: Philadelphia Flyers 4, Boston Bruins 3 (Flyers used three goalies — Brian Boucher, Johan Backlund and Michael Leighton — in series)

2014 WESTERN CONFERENCE QUARTERFINAL: Los Angeles Kings 4, San Jose Sharks 3 (Kings became only team to lose first three playoff games and win Cup)

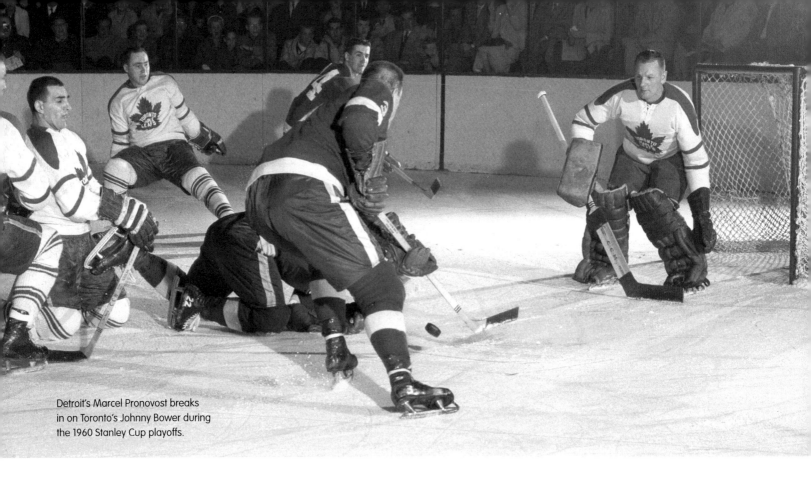

Detroit's Marcel Pronovost breaks in on Toronto's Johnny Bower during the 1960 Stanley Cup playoffs.

1942

—

ORIGINAL SIX GIVES RISE TO HOCKEY'S GOLDEN ERA

In point of fact — and often a point of contention among hockey historians — the NHL never consisted of an "original six" set of franchises. Hockey's Golden Era, however, certainly consisted of six teams, and this is how the name Original Six came to be.

By the summer of 1942, there were over 90 NHL players enlisted in the armed forces, as the Second World War raged. When the

NHL board of governors gathered for league meetings on September 24, 1942, the future of the league seemed uncertain.

The Great Depression had already cost the league three teams: the Pittsburgh Pirates had moved to Philadelphia in 1930 and folded a year later; the Ottawa Senators had shifted to St. Louis in 1934 but disbanded within a year; and the Montreal Maroons had departed the scene in 1938. Now, at

the governors meeting, Lyle C. Wright, commissioner of the minor league American Hockey Association, announced his loop was disbanding due to lack of players.

With so many good young players entering military service, the NHL had quickly become an industry lacking raw materials.

The Brooklyn Americans were hit particularly hard. Last-place finishers in 1941–42, 16 members of the Amerks enlisted in the military when the season concluded, leaving the team with just four players. Speculation was that the Americans would be dropped from the league, and on September 25, 1942, the NHL announced the franchise would be suspended for one year.

"There was no question about it being unanimous," NHL president Frank Calder told the Canadian Press. "There was nothing else we could do.

"We knew that manager Red Dutton couldn't carry on with what he had, and he realized that, too."

The cut to a six-team league may have been necessitated by war, but it would prove to be the best thing to happen to the NHL.

The league that emerged from those meetings was a six-team loop featuring the Boston Bruins, Chicago Black Hawks, Detroit Red Wings, Montreal Canadiens, New York Rangers and Toronto Maple Leafs. It would stay that way for the next quarter-century, the longest continuous run in NHL history without a single franchise change or relocation. Some of the game's most legendary stars — Gordie Howe, Maurice Richard, Ted Lindsay, Bobby Hull, Glenn Hall, Terry Sawchuk and Jacques Plante — emerged between 1942 and 1967, which would be branded hockey's Golden Age.

"We had the best players in the world split between six teams and hockey was always worth the money," Toronto owner Conn Smythe proclaimed to writer Trent Frayne.

All of a sudden, finding a job in the NHL was difficult, especially for netminders. With no backup goalies, it left just six available NHL positions for puckstoppers.

"I began to wonder several times while I toiled in the minors if I'd ever get a chance at the NHL," said Hall of Fame goalie Johnny Bower, who didn't make it to the NHL for good until 1958, when he was 33.

Keeping a job in the NHL was almost as daunting a task as getting one.

THE AMAZIN' AMERKS

THE 1942 DEMISE of the Brooklyn Americans ended one of hockey's most colorful, albeit unsuccessful runs.

The Amazin' Amerks, as they came to be known, existed from 1925 to 1942 but never won a Stanley Cup — they never even played in a Cup final. Even with their spectacular star-spangled uniforms (pictured above in 1926–27), the Americans were always overshadowed by the exploits of their more successful co-tenants at Madison Square Garden, the New York Rangers.

"Those were wonderful days," said Hall of Famer Red Dutton, speaking of his time with the Americans to New York sportswriter Arthur Daley in 1961.

Dutton played defense for the Americans from 1930 to 1936 and then coached and managed the franchise.

"I don't think there ever was a team as beloved as the Amerks," Dutton said. "Not only the fans, but even the ushers worshipped us.

"If I could have won with them, I'd have chased the Rangers out of Madison Square Garden."

But he couldn't win with them. No one could. And nothing they tried worked. The Americans made the playoffs just five times and posted only three winning seasons.

The problems with the Americans started right at the top. The franchise owner was Bill Dwyer, a New York mobster who made his fortune as a Prohibition-era bootlegger in partnership with such notorious gangsters as Owney Madden and Frank Costello.

Dwyer sought to launder his money by purchasing racetracks, nightclubs and sports franchises. He paid $75,000 to acquire the Hamilton Tigers and moved them to New York in 1925.

Dwyer soon got out of the bootlegging business after serving a prison term, but going legit didn't work out well for him. His money rapidly disappeared, and in 1935 he was arrested on gambling charges. The charges didn't stick, so the government came after him for tax evasion, and he was forced to sell off all of his possessions.

The Americans were taken over by the NHL in 1937, and Dutton was placed in charge of the franchise.

"I liked and admired Dwyer," Dutton said, "even though he did owe the Internal Revenue Service eight million dollars. He was always in financial trouble and paid salaries with post-dated checks."

Doing whatever he could to keep the team afloat, Dutton tried bringing in NHL superstars toward the end of their careers as drawing cards, acquiring the likes of Charlie Conacher, Hap Day, Hooley Smith and Nels Stewart. In 1941, the team was renamed the Brooklyn Americans, even though they continued to play their games in Manhattan at MSG.

None of it worked, and in the fall of 1942 the Americans were finally put out of their misery.

So when we talk of the Original Six, it's important to remember that it took the demise of a unique franchise to make it happen.

Montreal's Henri Richard stickhandles away from the poke check of New York's Eddie Giacomin.

"As a young player, I remember Ted Lindsay telling me to play through hurts, because there's another guy sitting out there waiting to take your job," former NHL forward Johnny Wilson recalled.

In 1949, the league increased the schedule to 70 games, meaning every team would play each other 14 times during the regular season.

With that much competition, both internal and external rivalries grew to epic proportions. "You had to play tough in those days, or they'd run you out of the building," Lindsay said.

Teams traveled via train, and if it was a home-and-home set and both clubs occupied the same train, they would wait until they pulled into a station to go to the dining car rather than walk through the opposition to get there.

"You didn't associate with the other players back then," Hall of Fame right-winger Andy Bathgate recalled. "You'd get to the All-Star Game and Ted Lindsay would walk by and grunt.

"That's the only words you'd get out of him."

Three teams dominated this era — the Canadiens finished first 12 times and won 10 Stanley Cups, the Wings were first overall in 10 seasons and five-time Cup winners, while the Leafs lifted Lord Stanley's mug on nine occasions.

The people in charge of the teams vociferously protected what they had, and the league's governors rebuffed expansion bids from both Philadelphia and Cleveland during the 1950s. Appearing on the CBC as Cleveland was bidding for an NHL club in 1953, Smythe, Toronto's head honcho, made no effort to hide his disdain for any thought of league growth: "This is the greatest game in the world and these are the greatest teams," Smythe bellowed. "Only a moron would want to change it."

Eventually the money would win out, and on February 9, 1966, the NHL announced it would add six new teams: the California Seals, Los Angeles Kings, Minnesota North Stars, Philadelphia Flyers, Pittsburgh Penguins and St. Louis Blues.

The reason for the move was simple, according to NHL president Clarence Campbell: "Television is the new box office for every sport," Campbell told Dink Carroll of the *Montreal Gazette*. "We can't sell more tickets."

The Original Six era would officially come to an end on May 2, 1967, when the Leafs downed the Canadiens 3–1 in Game 6 of the Stanley Cup final to claim the championship.

Today's fans may be certain that the current game is better, but don't try convincing Lindsay of that.

"We had great skaters," he said of those Original Six days. "We had great puckhandlers. A lot of people think we were all old fogies back in those days who couldn't skate. We had guys who could skate with anybody today."

Amen.

The 1927 NHL champions, the Ottawa Senators.

THE NHL'S FIRST DYNASTY

BEFORE THE TORONTO Maple Leafs and Montreal Canadiens became the NHL's dominant forces in the 1930s and 1940s, another Canadian team was the league's first superpower.

During the 1920s, the Ottawa Senators were the scourge of the NHL. Loaded with future Hall of Famers such as goalie Clint Benedict, defensemen Sprague Cleghorn, King Clancy and Eddie Gerard, and forwards Frank Nighbor, Punch Broadbent and Cy Denneny, the Senators were the first NHL team to win back-to-back Stanley Cups, in 1919–20 and 1920–21. They won again in 1922–23 and once more in 1926–27. They also finished first overall in the league seven times during that span.

Success on the ice, however, wasn't paralleled with success off the ice, in the team's coffers. Even during their Cup-winning campaign of 1926–27, the club reported $50,000 in losses.

The bloom was already off Ottawa's rose when the NHL expanded into the United States, leading to a rapid increase in salaries and other expenses related to running a team. This put the Senators, a small-market team with a tiny arena compared to the palaces in other NHL cities, into a desperate downward spiral that they would

never escape. The bad situation got worse when the Great Depression hit.

"There weren't the people [to support the team]," former Senators forward Frank Finnigan explained to the *Ottawa Citizen* in 1989. "[The population was] only 110,000, 120,000 at the most back in the 1920s, up into the 1930s. There wasn't a whole lot of money and not too much industry in Ottawa or [nearby] Hull [Quebec] at the time. It was just the government that was the big employer."

To survive, the Senators began selling off their assets — namely, their star players. First to go was forward Hooley Smith, star of Ottawa's 1926–27 Cup-winning squad, who brought $22,500 from the Montreal Maroons in October 1927. Three years later, all-star defenseman King Clancy was auctioned off to the Leafs for $35,000.

The revenue kept them afloat, but only for a brief time. The Senators began switching home games to the visiting team's rink in order to garner a larger gate. But the drawback to selling off their best players was that the Senators plummeted from perennial contenders to annual doormats.

They finished in last place in 1930–31, and after opting to take a year off from the NHL, they returned in 1932–33 and finished last again in each of the next two seasons before deciding to call it quits.

Noting the team had to borrow $60,000 to operate in its two prior seasons, team president F.D. Burpee informed the *Ottawa Citizen* on April 6, 1934, that the Senators would relocate to another city.

"We are now convinced that owing to the small population in the Ottawa territory, which is many times smaller than that of the average city in the National Hockey League, we cannot succeed in getting the necessary revenue, even with a winning team," Burpee said. "The cost of running a National Hockey League team does not differ by more than a few thousand dollars if it is run in Ottawa instead of a city like New York.

"It is therefore apparent that we must try to move the Ottawa Senators to some very large city which has a large rink."

They opted for St. Louis, but after one season, that team folded. Ottawa would not return to the NHL until 1992.

1943

HOCKEY HALL OF FAME ESTABLISHED

A plan was afoot to honor the greats of the game, and, almost immediately, the battle was on to see which city would be the location for the new hockey shrine.

On September 10, 1943, Kingston, Ontario, was announced as the proposed site for the new Hockey Hall of Fame, but there was consternation in both Montreal and Halifax, two cities that, like Kingston, claimed to be the birthplace of hockey.

E.M. Orlick of Montreal's McGill University stated that those selecting the Hall's location "were the victims of the greatest hoax ever perpetrated in the annals of Canadian sport."

On May 1, 1945, the inaugural inductees into the Hall were announced, selected by a committee that included Lester Patrick, Art Ross, Red Dutton and OHA president W.A. Hewitt. The list of luminaries included Howie Morenz, Georges Vezina, Charlie Gardiner, Eddie Gerard and pre-NHL stars such as Tom Phillips, Frank McGee, Hod Stuart, Harvey Pulford and Hobey Baker, the only American in the group.

Three builders were announced as part of the original group of inductees in October 1945, Lord Stanley of Preston, Captain James T. Sutherland and Sir Montagu Allan.

When progress on a building to house the Hall was slow to develop, Montreal Canadiens GM Frank Selke was appointed to do something about it. Later that year, a location on the grounds of Toronto's Canadian National Exhibition was selected. The Hockey Hall of Fame was officially opened on August 26, 1961. Canadian prime minister John Diefenbaker and United States ambassador Livingston T. Merchant presided over the opening. In its first year of operation, the Hall drew 750,000 visitors.

In 1993, the Hall relocated to its current location at the corner of Front and Yonge Streets in Toronto.

CLAPPER OFF, CLAPPER IN

DIT CLAPPER STEPPED off the ice and into the Hall of Fame.

When the veteran Boston Bruins defenseman announced his retirement after becoming the NHL's first 20-season man in 1947, he was immediately welcomed in the Hall during on-ice ceremonies prior to a game at Boston Garden on February 12, 1947, the first player to have the mandatory waiting period waived.

"The Hall of Fame has been honored by the addition of its only living player," NHL president Clarence Campbell said.

While Eddie Shore was the face of the Bruins, the steady, quiet Clapper was Boston's heart and soul and, at the time, the only NHLer to be named an All-Star at both forward and defense.

"There is no player who could have been more faithful, loyal, or more of a credit to the game," Bruins owner Charles Adams said.

1943

INTRODUCTION OF RED LINE OPENS UP GAME

When the NHL allowed forward passing in all three zones in 1929, it opened up the game. However, as with any innovation, coaches eventually devised a way to derail the excitement.

By the late 1930s, forechecking systems in which teams would dump the puck into the defensive zone beyond the defense and then swarm the zone were crushing creativity. Since players weren't permitted to pass from the defensive zone over the blue line and into the neutral zone, it was difficult for teams to clear their defensive zone, and multi-player scrums for possession had become commonplace.

Working with Canadian Amateur Hockey Association president Cecil Duncan, New York Rangers coach Frank Boucher came up with a solution to once again open up the game. A center red line that divided the neutral zone in half was introduced along with a rule permitting the puck to be passed all the way to the red line. This allowed defenders more options to clear the zone as well as the potential to spring forwards for breakaway chances.

The plan worked, and flow and offense returned. Four of the six NHL teams scored 200 goals during the 1943–44 campaign, Boston's Herb Cain scored a record 82 points and Toronto defenseman Babe Pratt collected 57 points, an NHL mark for rearguards that would stand until 1964–65.

1944

RICHARD NETS FIVE IN A GAME

Montreal's Maurice Richard in 1950.

During the early part of Maurice Richard's career, all signs pointed to the Montreal Canadiens winger never living up to his potential as a scoring star. Then came the night he was the one and only star, and the questions that had dogged him disappeared forever.

If the 1943–44 regular season was a coming out party for "The Rocket," the playoffs that spring demonstrated just how far he could go. In helping the Montreal Canadiens win their first Stanley Cup in 13 years, Richard registered one of the most notable games in postseason history, notching five goals in a single game versus the Toronto Maple Leafs in the league semifinal. The night went from memorable to magical when Richard was named first, second and third star of the game, lending some fairy dust to the tale of a man poised to become the face of his team and league.

As a sophomore NHLer in 1943–44, Richard had much to prove. A string of injuries — including a broken leg in his rookie year — had earned him a reputation as a fragile player, and many observers doubted his ability to score consistently in the big league. That all changed when Montreal coach Dick Irvin shifted the left-shooting Richard to right wing and paired him with center Elmer Lach and left-winger Toe Blake, forming what soon became known as the Punch Line. The result was a top trio capable of carrying a Canadiens team that had been in a funk for more than a decade. For his part, the 22-year-old Richard netted 32 goals in 46 games.

Richard's huge night in Game 2 of the best-of-seven semifinal, however, was as much due to the Punch Line as it was due to coach Dick Irvin's savvy. After Richard

Maurice Richard charges hard at Toronto's Harry Lumley during the 1953–54 season.

had a quiet night in Game 1 thanks to the blanket coverage provided by Toronto's Bob Davidson, Irvin shortened his bench, using just eight forwards and skating with all three of his lines at different times. This tactic, combined with Montreal getting the last change by virtue of being the home team, meant Toronto coach Hap Day couldn't figure out when Richard was coming on the ice, making it impossible for him to counter with Davidson.

By the 2:05 mark in the second period of Game 2, Richard had scored two goals in a 17-second span. He put one more past Toronto goalie Paul Bibeault before the end of the period, giving him a hat trick with 20 minutes still to play.

Richard again came racing out for the

third, netting his fourth goal of the contest before the final stanza was a minute old. He then tied the playoff mark set by former Canadien Newsy Lalonde in 1919, with his fifth goal of the contest at 8:54. No other Habs player found the net during the 5–1 win, prompting the delightful decision to award Richard all three stars.

"There were games when I felt every shot would go in," Richard told the Associated Press. "On some nights, if I touched the puck, I knew I would score."

Since that night, three other players have equaled the record of five goals in a postseason game, but those occasions are harder to remember thanks to the little gimmick that gave Richard a lasting legacy.

BLAKE GETS A BOOST

SIX YEARS ELMER Lach's senior and nine years older than Maurice Richard, Hector "Toe" Blake was 31 and a nine year NHL veteran when the Punch Line was formed. During the unit's first season together, in 1943–44, Blake notched his best scoring total to date with 24 goals. During each of the next two years, Blake notched 29 goals.

After some very lean years, he also experienced enormous playoff success, scoring a league-leading 18 points in nine contests while earning his first Cup with the Canadiens, in 1944. He then paced the 1946 playoffs with seven goals in nine games to win another ring before calling it quits after the following season.

RICHARD SCORES 50 IN 50

As time on the clock waned, so too did the hopes of the Montreal Canadiens faithful. Fans of the team had hoped to witness history, and it seemed they would be denied that opportunity. But if Maurice Richard had proven anything during his brief NHL career with the Montreal Canadiens, it's that the man they called "The Rocket" had a flare for the dramatic. And when the door opened a crack, Richard seized the moment, setting a new magical mark that instantly became ingrained in hockey lore.

Scoring 50 goals in a season has been the goal of every top sniper since Richard proved it could be done in 1944–45. In Richard's case, though, the schedule dictated he had just 50 games to hit the half-century mark, and he did so while playing the Boston Bruins in the final contest of the year. Habs fans had a new reason to cheer their ascendant star that night, as Richard continued to burrow his way into the hearts of Montreal's passionate supporters.

By the fall of 1944, Richard had already demonstrated big-time potential as an NHL goal-scorer. The year prior, as a second-year player, Richard had distanced himself from nagging questions about his inability to stay healthy by netting 32 goals in 46 games then adding a league-leading 12 — including five in a single game — during Montreal's run to its first Stanley Cup in more than a decade.

Armed with more confidence and thriving as a left-shooting right-winger on a line with center Elmer Lach and Toe Blake, the 23-year-old Richard took his game to another level in his third season. That was never more obvious than on December 28, 1944. Initially, Richard was hoping to skip the Canadiens home game that night versus the Detroit Red Wings because he'd spent much of the day moving his family from one apartment to another. But coach Dick Irvin insisted, and a weary Richard suited up.

Just a couple of minutes into the affair, Richard was already on the board with a goal. In the second period, he netted two markers just eight seconds apart, and by the end of 40 minutes, No. 9 had registered four goals and a pair of helpers for six points. The final frame brought another goal and assist, allowing Richard to set a new NHL mark with eight points in one evening.

As the season wore on, Richard's goal-scoring exploits continued. Beyond possessing a great shot, Richard had a burning desire to get to the net, and he established a reputation as the most dangerous player on the ice once he crossed the opponent's blue line.

When Richard netted his 45th tally of the campaign, he notched a new single-season NHL record for goals, surpassing Canadiens forward Joe Malone, who set the mark in the NHL's first season of 1917–18.

"I am happy that my record was broken by such a fine young player." Malone said at the time. "[Richard] is one of those players that comes along every once in a while, and I hope he goes on to even greater feats."

With the previously unthinkable 50-goal plateau within reach, the fiery star was about to do just that. In his second-last game of the season, Richard watched referee King Clancy disallow a potential score that would have been his 50th. With that, the stage was set for the final outing of the year, as Montreal visited Boston.

Close checking resulted in a low-scoring affair, as the clubs finished the first two periods knotted 1–1. In the third, Boston took the lead, and, increasingly, it appeared Bruins supporters would get to revel in being the spoiler. With just over two minutes left, however, Richard buried a puck behind Bruins goaltender Harvey Bennett, tying the game and giving hockey a new, sparkling phrase: 50 in 50.

When that shot beat Bennett, Richard started transitioning from beloved athlete to folk hero. And though he never again hit the 50-goal mark in his career, the fact that he was the first to ever do it remains an enormous part of Richard's lasting legacy.

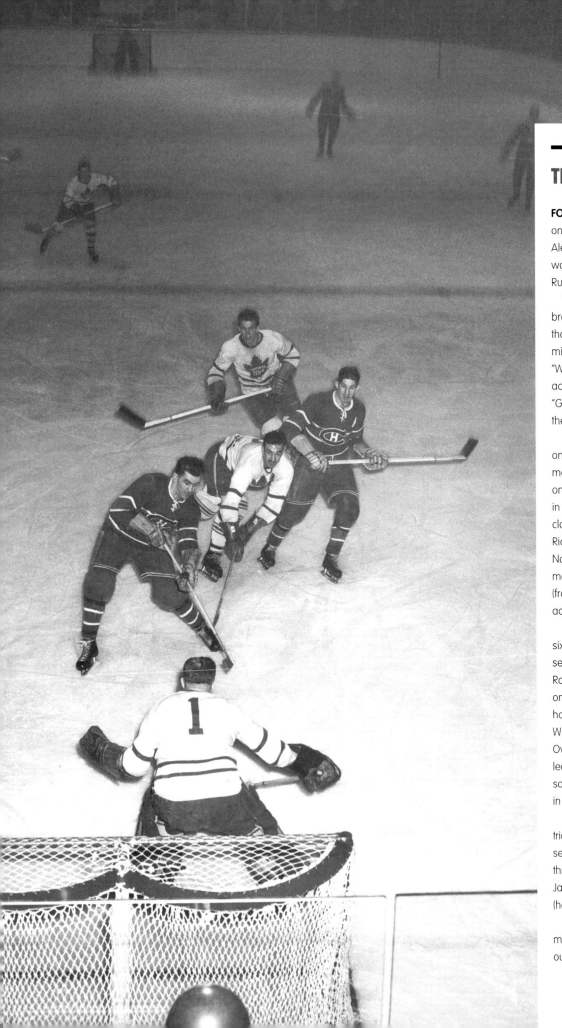

THE MODERN ROCKET

FOR A PLAYER who is often pilloried as a one-dimensional coach killer, Washington's Alex Ovechkin certainly didn't sound that way on the night he became the top-scoring Russian in NHL history.

When asked to comment on his record-breaking 484th goal, Ovechkin graciously thanked his team before lamenting his club's missing out on two points in the standings: "Without my teammates I would never accomplish that." Ovechkin told NHL.com "Good moment, but unfortunately we lost the game."

Ovechkin's goal against the Dallas Stars on November 19th, 2015, broke his tie with mentor and friend Sergei Fedorov. It was also one of the 50 goals the superstar scored in the 2015–16 season, during which he claimed his fourth straight Maurice "Rocket" Richard Trophy as the league's top scorer. Not since Wayne Gretzky scored the league's most goals in four consecutive seasons (from 1981–82 to 1984–85) had anyone accomplished the feat.

Ovechkin has led the league in goals six times in his career, through the 2016–17 season, which is one more than the original Rocket, and it puts him in elite company, as only Phil Esposito (six) and Bobby Hull (seven) have led the league as many or more times. With his record-setting season in 2015–16, Ovechkin also became the third player in league history to notch seven 50-goal seasons, joining Wayne Gretzky and Mike Bossy in that exclusive club.

His march to 50 in 2015–16 came via a hat trick against the St. Louis Blues in Washington's second-last game of the season. The 15th three-goal game of his career, it tied him with Jaromir Jagr for the most by an active player (he now sits first with 17).

"Obviously, it's nice," Ovechkin said of the milestone 50th. "The guys tried to find me out there."

Clarence Campbell presents Maurice Richard with the Stanley Cup in 1960.

1946

CLARENCE CAMPBELL NAMED NHL PRESIDENT

The man who would reign over the NHL's greatest era of growth was caught by surprise when he was asked to lead the league on September 4, 1946.

"Today's developments were much more rapid than I anticipated," said Clarence Campbell, a Rhodes Scholar and Edmonton lawyer who had just returned to Canada after serving first in the Canadian Army and then as part of the Canadian War Crimes Unit, participating the Nuremburg Trials. He'd been filling the role as assistant for interim league president Red Dutton since late summer, and Dutton had lobbied NHL owners to ensure they would name Campbell his successor.

Dutton had reluctantly been on the job since 1943, when he had stepped in for previous president Frank Calder, who had died following a heart attack at a league meeting early in the year.

The only former NHL player to run the league, Dutton remained around the game in the hopes of reviving the suspended New York Americans franchise that he'd run before the war effort thinned his club to the point that they were forced to suspend operations. When it became clear the Americans would never return, he stepped down as president, but only after ensuring Campbell would be his successor.

Before Campbell's appointment as Dutton's assistant, and before he had enlisted in the military, he had served as an NHL referee from 1936 to 1940.

"I am not exactly a stranger to the National Hockey League nor its governors and I am hopeful that I will be able to make a real contribution," Campbell said. "I have unbounded confidence in the future of hockey, not only in Canada and the United States but throughout the whole world. In my opinion, there is no limit to its expansion."

In fact, under Campbell's leadership the league tripled in size, from six to 18 teams by the time he retired in 1977. His reign also saw the NHL develop a pension plan and negotiate national television contracts in Canada and the United States.

Campbell was elected to the Hockey Hall of Fame in 1966.

1948

A GAMBLING SCANDAL ROCKS THE NHL

Boston's Don Gallinger and Billy Taylor (pictured while playing with Toronto), in the 1940s.

In early March 1948, rumblings began to surface about NHL players who had wagered money on their own team to lose. In reality, the league had begun its investigation a month earlier into allegations that James Tamer, a known Detroit gambler, had worked with Boston Bruins players to get insider information on games.

The allegations came to light after Tamer was arrested in Michigan on a parole violation in February 1948.

On March 4, 1948, syndicated columnist Walter Winchell named Bruins forward Don Gallinger as one of the players, and at first Gallinger seemed stunned by the allegation.

Approached by *Montreal Gazette* columnist Dink Carroll after a Canadiens–Bruins game, Gallinger admitted he knew Tamer but denied all involvement in the illegal wagering.

NHL president Clarence Campbell begged to differ and, following his initial investigation, announced the indefinite suspension of

Gallinger and the life suspension of New York Ranger, and former Bruin, Billy Taylor for known associations with gamblers.

Taylor, like Gallinger, admitted knowing Tamer but insisted, "I never have been asked to bet on the outcome of a game."

Campbell stated that the league had proof that Taylor had wagered on the Chicago Black Hawks in a February 18, 1948, game against the Bruins that Boston won 4–2.

Upon further investigation, Campbell determined that Gallinger had wagered $1,500 against the Bruins in the same game against the Black Hawks. The evidence was irrefutable, as a Detroit police wiretap on Tamer's phone had captured the calls.

Eventually, Gallinger confessed his guilt to Campbell, and for decades he fought for reinstatement, but it wasn't until August 28, 1970, that both players' lifetime bans were lifted.

Taylor landed a job as an NHL scout, but Gallinger never returned to hockey.

THE BABE'S PRATFALL

BABE PRATT WAS a rollicking, gregarious sort who loved to sample all that life had to offer, but in 1946, the Toronto Maple Leafs defenseman took his taste for excitement across a line that nearly ended his NHL career.

When NHL president Red Dutton confirmed that Pratt had been gambling on games involving his own team, he had no choice but to expel the 1943–44 Hart Trophy winner.

"I haven't any proof that Pratt bet against his own club and that's why there is no scandal attached to this case," Dutton explained to the *Montreal Gazette*. "But we are determined to keep our game clean."

NHL governors reinstated Pratt, who immediately admitted his guilt and apologized profusely for his actions, having sat out a nine-game suspension.

"Babe didn't feel he was doing anything wrong in gambling on hockey results," Toronto coach Hap Day said. "I know he has felt pretty terrible since he was expelled."

Pratt was elected to the Hockey Hall of Fame in 1966.

1949

THE NHL'S FORGOTTEN DYNASTY

The first NHL team to win three straight Stanley Cups seldom gets mentioned these days, having long been overshadowed by the Montreal Canadiens' successive five Cup wins (1955–56 to 1959–60). But the Toronto Maple Leafs who won three times from 1946–47 to 1948–49 were unique both in their accomplishment and in the method by which they achieved each championship.

The Leafs certainly didn't begin their Stanley Cup quest in record-breaking fashion. After missing the playoffs in 1945–46, the Leafs opened the 1947 Cup final on the wrong side of a 6–0 score against the Canadiens in Montreal.

"How did these guys get in the playoffs?" Montreal goalie Bill Durnan quipped to *Montreal Herald* sports editor Elmer Ferguson.

Big mistake.

The Leafs netted four power-play goals in Game 2 at the Forum for a 4–0 win. Back in Toronto, they recorded 4–2 and 2–1 triumphs to gain at 3–1 stranglehold on the series. Montreal won Game 5 on home ice by a 3–1

count, but in Game 6, tallies by Vic Lynn and Teeder Kennedy overcame a first-period marker by Montreal's Buddy O'Connor in a 2–1 victory that gave the Leafs the Cup.

Off to a middling 3-2-2 start in 1947–48, Leafs GM Conn Smythe engineered a blockbuster deal with Chicago, trading an entire forward line — the Flying Forts of Gaye Stewart, Bud Poile and Gus Bodnar, so called because all hailed from Fort William, Ontario — as well as defensemen Bob Goldham and Ernie Dickens for Black Hawks center Max Bentley, the NHL scoring champ in 1945–46 and 1946–47, and seldom-used forward Cy Thomas.

"I feel it's quite a gamble but that it's worth it because we're getting the league's scoring leader," Smythe explained.

With captain Syl Apps and Bentley as a one-two punch down the middle, the Leafs rolled to an NHL-best 32-15-13 regular-season mark. In the playoffs, Toronto won eight of nine games, sweeping Detroit in the Cup final series.

And just as no one expected big things in

the 1946–47 season, a three-peat wasn't on the minds of hockey watchers heading into the 1948–49 campaign. With the announcement of captain Syl Apps' retirement, Toronto won just three of its first 12 games without their anchor at center. In early February, the injury-riddled Leafs sat fifth in the standings, out of the playoff picture. But they rallied to finish fourth, albeit with a 22-25-13 mark.

The Leafs stunned second-place Boston in the first round, needing only five games to dispatch the Bruins. But that was nothing compared to what was to come. For the second straight Cup final series, Toronto swept Detroit, the highest-scoring team in the league, outpacing them on the scoreboard 12–5 over the four games. Going back to the final game of the 1947 playoffs, the Leafs set a record by winning nine straight Stanley Cup final games.

"None of us were worried about finishing in fourth," Leafs forward Howie Meeker claimed. "We knew we'd come out smelling sweet."

Syl Apps tests Frank Brimsek during the 1948 Stanley Cup final.

BRODA WAS MONEY AND HE KNEW IT

WITH GEORGE HAINSWORTH nearing the end of his Hall of Fame career, Toronto Maple Leafs GM Conn Smythe set out in search of a replacement. Scouting the 1936 International League final between Windsor and Detroit, Smythe had traveled to look at Windsor goalie Earl Robertson, but it was the guy in the Detroit net who caught his eye. Later that spring, Smythe handed $8,000, a record amount for a minor-league goalie, to the parent Detroit Red Wings for Turk Broda.

"I think the boy is a high-class goaltender," Smythe told the *Windsor Star*.

The Wings would rue their decision for most of the 1940s.

It started in 1942 when, with Broda in goal, the Leafs rallied from a 3–0 deficit to beat the Wings and win the Stanley Cup in an unprecedented comeback. Six years later, Broda and the Leafs swept Detroit in the final, a performance they repeated in 1949.

In all, Broda backstopped Toronto to five Stanley Cup titles in nine years. The first NHL goalie to appear in 100 playoff games, Broda posted 21 wins and four shutouts in Stanley Cup final play and a career playoff goals-against average of 1.98.

"He's terrific, simply terrific," Smythe said. "And what I like about him is he is generally that way when the chips are on the line."

"He's the greatest playoff goalie of them all. In Turk Broda we've got the greatest money goaltender in hockey."

The fabulous fat man, as the pudgy Broda was known, was inducted into the Hockey Hall of Fame in 1967.

1950

—

LINDSAY STARTS A STANLEY CUP TRADITION

Maybe he was caught up in the emotion of the moment. Perhaps it was simply his nature taking control.

The 1949–50 Stanley Cup final, after all, was one that you couldn't blame someone for getting worked up about. It was the first Cup ever decided in sudden death of the seventh game, and the winning goal by Detroit's Pete Babando is famous in its own right for that reason. It was also a series in which New York and Detroit didn't play a single game in Madison Square Garden, the Rangers having been pushed out of their building by the circus that was already booked. Detroit also won the Cup without their dependable star winger Gordie Howe, who had been in serious condition in hospital just weeks prior. It was also Detroit's first Cup since 1943.

But Lindsay had simpler reasons for what he did. After watching Wings captain Sid Abel put the Cup back on the table at center ice after the official presentation to the team by league president Clarence Campbell, "Terrible Ted" swooped in, scooped up the Cup and set off on a jaunt.

"[My teammates] probably thought, 'That Lindsay is off on another tangent,'" said Lindsay, who wasn't looking to make history, just to give thanks to the people who made it possible for him to earn a living as a hockey player.

"When they presented the Cup, I just went over and picked it up," Lindsay said. "I knew who paid our salaries and I wanted the fans to see what we were playing for; to let them see some of the names on it. I just went around the ice and showed the people."

Carrying the Cup around on the ice in celebration has become a ritual of hockey springtime, but Lindsay was only trying to show the paying customers what all the fuss was about.

"I wasn't looking to start a tradition but apparently I started a tradition," Lindsay said.

HOWE NEARLY A FATALITY

TO SAY THERE was bad blood between the Detroit Red Wings and Toronto Maple Leafs would be an understatement. The Leafs had beaten the Wings in the Stanley Cup final four times between 1942 and 1949, so when the two teams were slated to meet in the 1950 Stanley Cup semifinals, all eyes were on the series.

Late in Game 1, Detroit star Gordie Howe set his bombsights on Toronto captain Teeder Kennedy, but Kennedy saw him at the last moment and tried to sidestep the check.

Howe glanced off Kennedy and stumbled awkwardly headfirst into the boards, falling to the ice in a motionless heap, blood quickly pooling under him.

Howe was rushed to hospital, and his list of injuries included a fractured cheekbone, broken nose, lacerated right eyeball and severe concussion. He underwent surgery that night at Detroit's Harper Hospital. They bored a hole through his skull to drain blood and relieve pressure on his brain. Howe's parents rushed to Detroit from their Saskatoon home, fearful their son wouldn't make it through the night.

Amazingly, Howe quickly recovered, and by the time Detroit was facing the New York Rangers in Game 7 of the Cup final series, he was among the Olympia Stadium crowd, watching the Wings win the title.

As the Wings celebrated, fans chanted Howe's name and he joined his teammates on the ice, his head still wrapped in bandages.

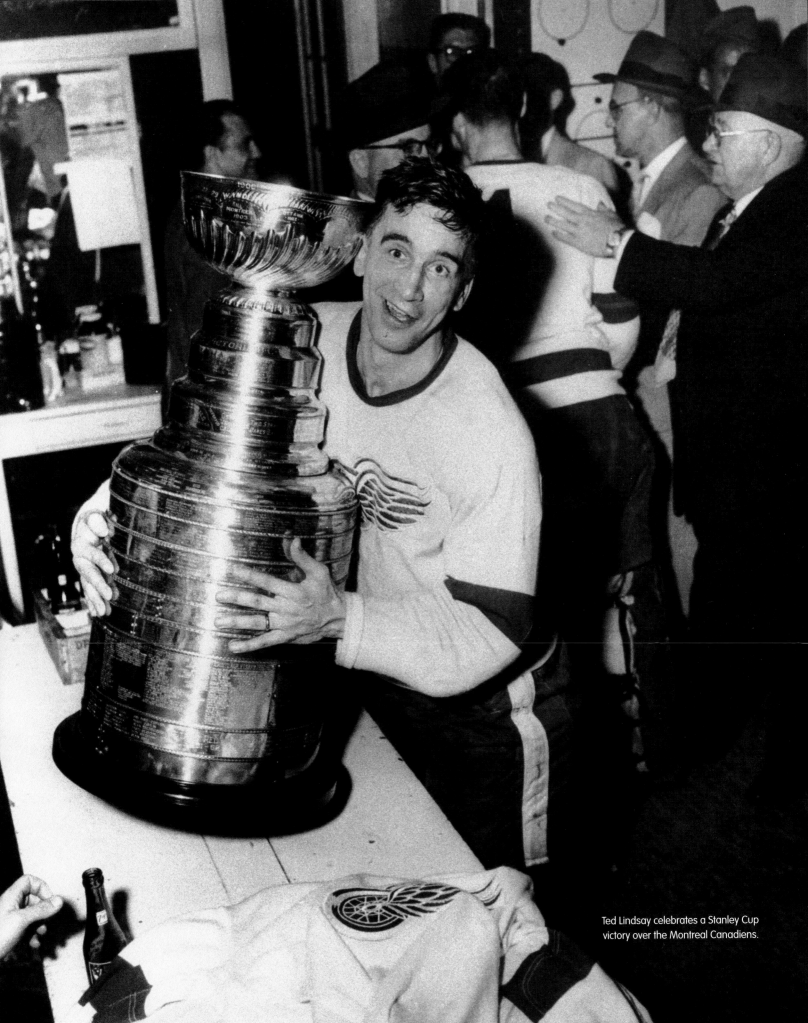

Ted Lindsay celebrates a Stanley Cup victory over the Montreal Canadiens.

Toronto's Bill Barilko, celebrating at right, scored the 1951 Stanley Cup winner with this puck; it was the last goal he ever scored.

1951

—

BARILKO'S FAREWELL GOAL WINS CUP FOR LEAFS

As the 1951 Stanley Cup playoffs got underway, there were rumors that Toronto Maple Leafs defenseman Bill Barilko would be dealt to the Montreal Canadiens in the off-season.

"I don't admire his methods, but I'd rather have him on our side than against," answered Montreal GM Frank Selke when approached regarding the trade talk surrounding Barilko.

Known more for his punishing hits than his prowess with the puck, Barilko had fractured the collarbone of New York Rangers forward Jackie McLeod with one of his checks that season, but he frequently rode the bench due to his penchant for taking costly penalties.

In the Stanley Cup final that spring, Barilko would hand out the ultimate penalty to the Canadiens.

A fascinating Stanley Cup final series between the Leafs and Habs saw each of the first four games go to overtime, Toronto winning three of them.

Trailing Game 5 by a 2–1 count, the Leafs pulled goalie Al Rollins in the dying seconds of regulation time, and the move paid off when Tod Sloan scored at 19:28, forcing yet another overtime session.

It didn't last long. Barilko pinched down from the point, pounced on the rebound of a Howie Meeker shot and, falling forward as he struck the puck, drove a 15-foot slap shot high into the net past sprawling Montreal goalie Gerry McNeil just 2:53 into the extra session. The Cup belonged to Toronto.

Jubilant teammates Cal Gardner and Bill Juzda lifted Barilko up on their shoulders

Cal Gardner and Bill Juzda hoist overtime hero Bill Barilko in 1951.

and carried him around the ice in celebration.

Four months later, Barilko, 24, would be gone forever.

Barilko and bush pilot Dr. Henry Hudson set out in Hudson's plane for a late-summer fishing trip in northern Ontario. They never came back, disappearing on August 26, 1951, during their 236-mile return flight from Rupert House, on James Bay, to Timmins. A massive search effort costing upward of $250,000 and involving 1,345 hours of flying by 17 RCAF aircraft came up empty.

Nearly 11 years would pass before the mystery would be solved. On June 7, 1962, a helicopter crew from the Ontario Department of Lands and Forests came across an airplane wreck in the bush. Inside, the skeletons of the two men were found, still strapped in the seats of their yellow Fairchild-24 airplane.

Barilko's No. 5 was retired by the Leafs in his memory.

DUFF'S GOAL ENDS BARILKO CURSE

AFTER THEIR 1951 Cup triumph, the sixth by the franchise since 1942, the Toronto Maple Leafs would hit the skids.

The Leafs would go eight years without appearing in a Cup final series. They'd miss the playoffs three times during that span and go through four coaches.

Leafs fans began referring to it as the curse of Barilko. Bill Barilko, scorer of Toronto's 1951 Cup-winning goal, was lost in a plane crash that summer and his body had never been found.

Under Punch Imlach, the Leafs finally returned

to the Stanley Cup final, albeit in losing efforts against Montreal in 1959 and 1960. But in 1962, the Leafs were back again, this time to face the defending-champion Chicago Black Hawks.

Deadlocked 2–2 in the series, things looked grim for Toronto. Goalie Johnny Bower was lost to a hamstring injury, but with backup Don Simmons, the Leafs won Game 5 on home ice 8–4. Trailing 1–0 in Game 6 at Chicago Stadium, Bob Nevin tied the score at 10:29 of the third period.

Chicago's Eric Nesterenko went off for holding at 13:27, and that was the opening the Leafs

needed. Toronto defenseman Tim Horton drove a hard shot into traffic in front of the Black Hawks net, and the rebound shot out to Dick Duff about 10 feet in front of the cage. Without hesitation, Duff whipped a high shot past Chicago netminder Glenn Hall for the Cup winner in a 2–1 verdict.

"I knew if we got a goal we could get two," Toronto forward Frank Mahovlich said.

Just 46 days after the Cup victory, a helicopter pilot spotted the wreckage of the missing plane containing Barilko's remains. The curse was forever lifted.

1951

—

HOWE WINS FIRST
SCORING TITLE

Gordie Howe puts the puck past
Johnny Bower in 1960.

Just months after his life had nearly
ended, Detroit Red Wings right-winger
Gordie Howe came into his own.
Since his arrival in the NHL in 1946, many
insiders had considered Howe hockey's next
great thing. His steady progression then
exploded into superstardom during the
1950–51 season, as he won the first of his six
NHL scoring titles and the first of his four
consecutive Art Ross Trophies.

Still suffering from headaches and
occasional bouts of dizziness, he had to wear
a helmet as a precautionary measure after
suffering a near-fatal head injury during the
first game of the 1950 Stanley Cup playoffs.
Despite these apparent limitations, Howe
stood head and shoulders above his peers,
setting a new NHL single-season points
mark with 86. Just 22, he also led the NHL
with 43 goals and 43 assists, becoming
the first player since Howie Morenz of the
1927–28 Montreal Canadiens to top the NHL
in all three major offensive categories (goals,
assists and points) during the same season.

All three totals were new Red Wings club
standards.

Howe was teamed with center Sid Abel
and left-winger Ted Lindsay on Detroit's
aptly named Production Line, and the trio
had finished one, two, three in scoring in
1949–50, with Lindsay followed by Abel
and Howe. However, the man who would
become known simply as "Mr. Hockey"
would take the league by storm during the
1950–51 campaign.

"Howe has looked immense against us,"

GORDIE'S SECOND ACT

AS THE ONLY man to play big-league hockey in five different decades, Gordie Howe — a.k.a. "Mr. Hockey" — built a massive memory bank of exceptional moments.

"But the day I first stepped on the ice professionally with the boys had to be the biggest thrill," Howe recalled in a 1977 interview, adding, "There is no way I can possibly relate to people how it felt."

The chance to play for the Houston Aeros alongside Marty and Mark, his two eldest sons, in the World Hockey Association's second season of 1973–74 pulled Howe out of a two-year retirement, which seemed premature even at the age of 43.

Two years before retiring he had scored 103 points with the NHL's Detroit Red Wings, but recurring wrist problems had forced him to move from the ice to the team's front office in 1971. His career in Detroit saw him win four Stanley Cups, six Hart Trophies and six Art Ross Trophies, and he posted a phenomenal run of 20 straight seasons in which he finished no lower than fifth in NHL scoring. Howe was almost universally regarded as the best to have ever played the game, but he felt that he was being underused and underappreciated by the Wings after his retirement.

Howe had wrist surgery in order to play with his sons on the Aeros, and the team immediately became one of the league's flagship franchises. Houston won two league championships in the trio's first two seasons, and Gordie registered 31 goals and 100 points his first year in Texas to be named league MVP. Mark, meanwhile, was the Rookie of the Year.

Howe had 369 points in four years with Houston before the family moved to the New England Whalers in 1977–78 for the final two years of the WHA. After the Whalers were included in the WHA's 1979 merger with the NHL, Howe, now 51, played his final NHL season, scoring 15 goals and 41 points nine years after he had originally retired from the league.

said Joe Primeau, coach of the Toronto Maple Leafs.

The debate as to who was the best right-winger in the game — Howe or Montreal's Maurice "Rocket" Richard — was officially underway.

"I would have to take Richard over Gordie Howe if I had my choice of either for a single game," New York Rangers GM Frank Boucher said. "Over the season? Well, Howe is the better all-around player, and should do more to help his team."

Howe made his own statement about the rivalry on February 17, 1951, during Rocket Richard Night at the Montreal Forum: he scored his 100th career NHL goal as Detroit beat the Canadiens 2–1.

As for the helmet, Howe doffed it not long into the campaign. "It makes me sweat," he complained.

However, Howe found the crown on his head as the NHL's greatest player much more comfortable, and he would wear it for the next two decades.

1952

HOCKEY NIGHT IN CANADA DEBUTS

Foster Hewitt is often mistakenly credited as the first radio voice of the NHL, when in fact it was Norm Albert who called the action as the Ottawa Senators and Toronto St. Patricks battled on February 14, 1923.

Likewise, Hewitt wasn't the first voice to bring the televised version of *Hockey Night in Canada* into the nation's living rooms.

That honor went to French-language play-by-play legend René Lecavalier, who called the action of a Montreal Canadiens–Detroit Red Wings game on October 11, 1952.

Montreal Gazette columnist Dink Carroll explained to his readers how the newfangled technology would work: "Television pictures of tonight's NHL game, the first to be broadcast in Montreal, will go underground before they take to the air. To link the Forum with the CBC studios, a video circuit has been installed by the Bell Telephone Company. The video path is provided by special wires in regular telephone cables which run beneath the city's streets. The pictures from the television cameras will travel through other underground Bell cables to the mountaintop transmitter."

It wasn't until November 1, 1952, that Hewitt would be at the microphone of his first televised NHL broadcast, as the Toronto Maple Leafs hosted the Boston Bruins.

These early televised games were joined in progress, usually midway through the second period, in the hopes that the inability to watch the entire match would encourage people to still buy a ticket to see the action in person rather than catch it at home. It wasn't until 1968 that entire games were broadcast.

NHL president Clarence Campbell originally wasn't a fan of the broadcasts. He blamed television for declining attendance in both Chicago and New York and decried the small screen as "the greatest menace of the entertainment world."

"Fights, injuries, boarding and other rough tactics are the easiest to catch on television," president Campbell told *The Hockey News*. "On the other hand, the fast end-to-end rushes, the skillful, attractive features of the game are most difficult to portray because of TV's limited field of view. This is not a proper representation of the overall action and certainly can't be doing the game any good.

"This is especially important, since all the surveys taken so far have shown hockey to be one of the most popular forms of TV entertainment. But, if the television fans are going to get the impression hockey is made up only of fights and injuries, the game will suffer."

Noting how hard it was to get a seat at a Montreal home game, Dink Carroll was among those who disagreed with Campbell's fears: "Several hockey fans who would be glad to buy season tickets if they were available wonder why Canadiens' home games aren't broadcast in total, arguing that it wouldn't keep anyone away from the Forum, which is always packed," he wrote.

It turned out that the NHL had nothing to worry about. The television broadcasts introduced people to the game who otherwise wouldn't have seen it, especially in the United States, paving the way for the 1967 expansion that would add six U.S. cities and double the NHL's size to 12 teams.

It also became hockey's number-one revenue generator — almost immediately. In 1952, Toronto owner Conn Smythe sold sponsorship rights to Leafs games to Imperial Oil for $100 per game. The next year, the two sides agreed on a three-year deal that would pay the Maple Leafs $450,000.

Terry Sawchuk in the
Hockey Night In Canada
studios in the late 1960s.

HOW TELEVISION CHANGED THE GAME

TO MAKE HOCKEY on television more palatable for viewers, the NHL introduced a number of aesthetic changes.

In 1949, the league began painting the ice white, the contrast making it easier to spot the black puck as it whizzed around the rink. In 1951, the NHL introduced a rule whereby the home team was required to wear white uniforms and the visiting team dark colors so the two teams wouldn't be difficult to distinguish from one another on the small screen.

In 1957, another alteration saw the solid center red line replaced with a checkered line, to differentiate it from the two blue lines on black-and-white TV sets. Officials went from wearing white sweaters to black and white stripes, allowing them to be easily recognized from the players.

A major technological change also helped usher in the television era. In 1949, California inventor Frank Zamboni developed the first ice-resurfacing machine, which bears his name.

The Zamboni arrived to the NHL in 1954, allowing for quick cleaning of the ice between periods, creating the short intermissions required to adhere to tight television schedules.

1952

—

THE ROCKET AND SUGAR JIM SHAKE HANDS

If the combination of Marilyn Monroe, a white dress and a blast of air from a subway vent created the most celebrated pop culture photo of the 1950s, the image of a bloody Maurice Richard shaking hands with goalie "Sugar" Jim Henry was the most iconic sports snap of the decade. And while Monroe was hamming it up for the cameras, the exchange between Henry and Richard couldn't have been more authentic.

Two years before Monroe made love to the camera in 1954, the Boston Bruins and Montreal Canadiens had played a grueling seven-game semifinal series in the 1952 playoffs. The decisive contest occurred at the Montreal Forum, and when it was over, photographer Roger St. Jean caught the unique exchange between Richard and Henry not long after the former had bested the latter for the game-winning goal.

Along with a clear mutual respect, the picture also captures a slight bow from Henry, seemingly in deference to a man who would stop at nothing in pursuit of victory.

The seventh game was necessary only after the Canadiens avoided elimination in Game 6 with a double-overtime victory. In that contest, Henry had his nose broken by a slap shot from Canadiens defender Doug Harvey, while Richard — who had been forced out of the lineup for much of the regular season with injuries — sustained a bruised knee. But everybody was counted on to be back in action for the final showdown in Montreal.

During the middle frame of the winner-take-all match, Richard tried to burst between two Boston blue-liners and wound up striking his head on the ice. The Rocket was out cold and bleeding. Long after being carried from the playing surface, Richard remained in a fog, clearly concussed from the blow. He didn't return until well into the third period and, even then, was struggling to maintain his mental focus.

Scoring goals, though, was about muscle

memory for No. 9, and with the game knotted 1–1 and the teams playing four aside, Richard went to work. Taking a pass from Butch Bouchard, Richard blasted by one Bruins defender then drove toward Henry. With a full head of steam, Richard cut through the crease and stuffed the puck inside the far post. The Forum went nuts. A man who, about an hour prior, was lying motionless on the ice had just provided the home team with the lift it needed.

"I didn't remember how I scored the goal," Richard told the CBC in 1977. "A few days later I saw the movie of it and then I remembered. I was just like a boxer when

he's groggy. I didn't know which way to go. I knew that there was the color of the Boston Bruins on one side. I was trying to skate away from all the guys. I went around the defenseman and I put the goalkeeper out of his net and I scored that goal."

Billy Reay's empty-netter made it a 3–1 Canadiens win, giving Montreal the series. It was then, during the traditional handshake line, that Richard and Henry — the goalie's eyes still blackened from the shot he had taken in Game 6 — came together. Thankfully St. Jean was there to make a sure a special moment between two proud warriors could be displayed for the world to see.

MONTREAL HAD BOSTON'S NUMBER

THE 1952 PLAYOFFS marked the third time since 1946 that Boston and Montreal met in the postseason. The Canadiens won all three matchups — as well as the next 15. In an almost unthinkable run of dominance, Montreal claimed 18 consecutive postseason series with Boston during a 41-year run that stretched to 1987. The Bruins finally broke the Canadiens' streak in 1988. In all, the two clubs have contested 34 playoff series — the most in North American pro sports.

Detroit captain Sid Abel battles with Toronto's Cal Gardner in the early 1950s.

1952

RED WINGS GO 8-0 IN PLAYOFFS

To paraphrase Franklin Delano Roosevelt, the only thing the Detroit Red Wings had to fear was themselves.

Rolling to their second straight 100-point regular season — the first and at that point the only team in NHL history to ascend to the century plateau — the Wings just kept on winning in the playoffs, sweeping both the Toronto Maple Leafs and Montreal Canadiens to become the first team to win the Stanley Cup in the minimum eight games then required.

"For balance, for depth, for anything you want to call it, this is the best Red Wing team I have ever had," said GM Jack Adams, who'd been running Detroit's show since 1927.

"We win the playoffs in eight straight. We score 201 points in regular play in two seasons. I will let those figures speak for themselves, and let any other club in the league try to match them."

He got no argument from the vanquished Canadiens: "The present Detroit club is one of the best balanced, if not the very best, I have ever seen," Habs GM Frank Selke said.

The Wings dominated the hardware chase. Right-winger Gordie Howe won the Art Ross and Hart Trophies, Terry Sawchuk earned the Vezina Trophy and Sawchuk, Howe, left-winger Ted Lindsay and defenseman Red Kelly were all named to the NHL's First All-Star Team.

Adams suggested the linchpin of their

success was veteran captain Sid Abel, center of Detroit's legendary Production Line between Lindsay and Howe.

"He's a take-charge guy," Adams told the *Montreal Gazette*'s Dink Carroll. "He needles Howe and Lindsay into giving it everything they've got.

"Guys like him come along about once every 10 years."

As it turned out, the Cup decider would be Abel's last game as a Wing. He took over as player-coach of the Chicago Black Hawks in the summer.

The eight-win sweep of the playoffs is also the postseason when Detroit first saw an octopus fly over the glass. Eight tentacles for eight wins, so the story goes…

SAWCHUK BARS THE DOOR

A FEW MONTHS after their 1949–50 Stanley Cup victory, the Detroit Red Wings stunned the hockey world by shipping goalie Harry Lumley to the Chicago Black Hawks as part of a record nine-player deal.

Jack Adams knew he could give up Lumley, a future Hockey Hall of Famer, because the Wings had another goalie waiting in the wings, Terry Sawchuk.

Adams' decision proved to be prophetic when Sawchuk won the Calder Trophy in 1950–51,

posting 44 wins and 11 shutouts, but the best was yet to come.

Finishing the 1951–52 season with 44 wins, 12 shutouts, a 1.94 GAA and the Vezina Trophy, Sawchuk turned into an absolute brick wall in the playoffs. He won all eight games, allowing just five goals for a minuscule 0.63 GAA. His save percentage was .977. Sawchuk didn't allow a goal on home ice the entire postseason, collecting four shutouts at Olympia Stadium.

Sawchuk's four shutouts tied the playoff single-season mark shared by Frank McCool of the 1944–45 Toronto Maple Leafs, Dave Kerr of the 1939–40 New York Rangers and Clint Benedict of the 1925–26 Montreal Maroons, but Sawchuk was unimpressed.

"I wasn't worried about equaling the playoff shutout record," Sawchuk insisted after the Cup-clinching win against Montreal. "All I wanted to do was get the series over with."

1953

MONTREAL FINALLY GETS "LE GROS BILL"

Montrealers can be dismissive of Quebec City. The larger and more cosmopolitan metropolis has often looked down its collective nose at its smaller counterpart. But in the early 1950s, Quebec had something Montreal wanted so bad it couldn't possibly hide its envy.

Jean Béliveau had the size and skill to be a force unlike any other in the NHL. Fully aware of that fact, Montreal Canadiens GM Frank Selke pushed hard to get the 6-foot-3 burgeoning talent in the Canadiens lineup. But Béliveau, the object of huge affection while skating for the Quebec Aces of the Quebec Senior League, was in no hurry to join the Habs. Finally, Selke simply opened the vault, and so began one of the most storied careers in NHL history.

Béliveau had actually played a handful of games with the Canadiens following his junior career, which was also spent in Quebec, with the Citadels. In the spring of 1951, he dressed for two contests with Montreal, netting a goal and an assist. He also played a game for the Aces that year, and when fall came around, the 20-year-old Béliveau opted to stick with the Aces rather than give in to Selke's overtures and sign with the Canadiens, who owned his NHL rights.

"I stayed in Quebec first and foremost out of a sense of obligation to the people," Béliveau explained in his book *My Life in Hockey*.

Selke spearheaded a campaign to have the NHL and CAHA implement a rule that stated any player on an NHL team's negotiation list could be forced to sign with that NHL team before being assigned to play senior hockey. It was mockingly referred to as "the Béliveau rule" because it was so blatantly obvious that the Canadiens GM was trying to force Béliveau to sign with the Habs.

Jean Béliveau, pictured at left in the 1960s, signs autographs for his adoring fans as a member of the Quebec Aces in the early 1950s.

Jean Béliveau races New York's Andy Bathgate for the puck in his rookie season, 1953–54.

The rule was not passed, and after scoring 45 goals and 83 points in 59 games for Quebec during the 1951–52 campaign, Béliveau again raised eyebrows by returning to the Aces for the 1952–53 season rather than join the big boys in the NHL. Quite simply, he loved playing in Quebec City, where Aces fans feted him as a hero. The team also paid him handsomely, and he earned more than many star NHLers. He also fell in love in Quebec City with his future wife, Élise Couture.

"Financially at least, I had nothing to lose by staying in Quebec," Béliveau explained. He was paid $10,000 a season to play for the Aces, whereas the average NHL salary of the day was $7,000.

By the summer of 1953, though, Selke was putting on a full-court press, especially after Béliveau had played three more games for the Canadiens at the end of the preceding season

and scored a stunning five goals. Naturally, the public outcry to get Béliveau in red, white and blue was nearly deafening.

To make it happen, Selke offered "Le Gros Bill" a five-year $105,000 contract, the most lucrative offer ever seen in the NHL. With a gaggle of sportswriters on hand to cover the event, Béliveau arrived at the Forum on October 3, 1953, to put his name on the deal. With that, Montrealers could breathe a huge sigh of relief — and finally stop being so jealous of their provincial rivals.

Béliveau never regretted his decision to delay his NHL debut: "It was perhaps the wisest course I chose," he said. "I was able to mature on and off the ice at more or less my own pace.

"The Jean Béliveau who arrived in Montreal in 1953 was much better prepared for the demands of NHL stardom."

OLD CONTRACTS

LONG BEFORE THE draft democratized the process by which young players are assigned to teams, prospects had a much more restrictive path to the NHL. During the Original Six era, teams signed amateur players to either an A, B or C Form. The terms of these documents heavily favored the teams, giving the clubs enormous control over a player's salary should he make the top squad as well as dictating what junior or minor-pro teams a player could suit up for if he didn't make the NHL. By the time expansion rolled around in 1967, the old, oppressive system was crumbling, and the amateur draft — and later the entry draft — became the means by which players joined the league during the 1970s.

1955

—

BÉLIVEAU'S BIG NIGHT LEADS TO "CANADIENS RULE"

Two minutes. It's a small portion of an entire 60-minute NHL contest, but when it came to facing the Montreal Canadiens power play during the 1950s, the two minutes a player spent in the penalty box could feel like an awful eternity for the club forced to play a man short.

By the 1955–56 season, the Canadiens were an emerging power. In addition to veteran stars like Maurice Richard and Doug Harvey, Montreal also featured up-and-coming gunners Jean Béliveau (pictured above with Bert Olmstead), Bernie "Boom Boom" Geoffrion and 19-year-old Henri Richard. As such, Montreal was absolutely deadly with the man advantage, as was witnessed on November 5, 1955.

The events that evening at the Montreal Forum became the symbol for why league president Clarence Campbell was soon looking to alter the rule book and create the "Canadiens rule," which allowed a player to leave the box while serving a minor penalty if his team was scored upon.

During the game in question, the Boston Bruins' Cal Gardner was sent to the penalty box late in the first period, and teammate Hal Laycoe joined him there just 16 seconds into the second. Down 2–0 and with a two-man advantage, Montreal went to work.

The first Canadiens tally came when Bert Olmstead found Béliveau's stick for a redirection past goalie Terry Sawchuk. The two men hooked up again just 26 seconds later, as Béliveau tied the score with his second

goal of the power play. Big No. 4 then completed the hat trick, all three goals coming within a 44-second span.

Of the six NHL teams, only the Canadiens had voted against Campbell's proposed rule change, but NHL moguls scoffed at the notion that it was directed specifically at the Montreal club. "That's nonsense," Boston Bruins GM Lynn Patrick said.

"Only the Canadiens voted against it and that's why it's being said the rule was aimed at wrecking their power play," added New York Rangers GM Frank Boucher.

"I think it's all right," Canadiens star Maurice Richard told the *Montreal Gazette* of the rule change, which was implemented the following season. "How many times do you think we scored more than one goal

Gordie Howe presents Jean Béliveau the Hart Trophy in 1964.

while the other team was a man short? I think if you checked back, you'd find it didn't happen very often."

The new rule may have made serving penalties potentially less costly, but it didn't slow down the Canadiens much. They won the Stanley Cup at the end of the 1955–56 campaign and won it again the next four springs. They led the league with 222 goals during the 1955–56 season and led the league during each successive championship season, only once dipping below their goal total from 1955–56, recording 210 in 1956–57.

The offensive breakout also keyed a career-best season for Béliveau, who, in his third NHL campaign, registered 88 points in 70 games to win both the Art Ross Trophy as scoring champion and the Hart Trophy as league MVP.

OILERS FORCE FOUR-ON-FOUR CHANGE

The Montreal Canadiens weren't the only team to force the league's hand when it came to goal scoring and penalty-related rules. The Edmonton Oilers of the early 1980s were so swift and deft with the puck that they didn't even require a power play to experience a distinct advantage.

Prior to 1985–86, when players took coincidental minor penalties, teams played four players aside. The extra space afforded by having two less players on the ice heavily favored the Oilers (led by speedsters Wayne Gretzky and Jari Kurri, seen at right) as they blew past opponents in the open ice. Some went so far as to suggest Edmonton exploited the coincidental penalty rule by provoking opponents so that it might land a friendly four-on-four scenario. That compelled the league to keep playing five-on-five whenever two players went to the box at the same time. Years later, when scoring began to drop around the league, the NHL reverted back to the four-on-four model.

1955

RICHARD RIOT

Believe it or not, when the trouble started, the time was 9:11.

The visiting Detroit Red Wings were at the Montreal Forum to face the Canadiens on March 17, 1955, with first place in the NHL on the line, but somehow, everyone knew the game would be a secondary story that night.

Earlier in the day, Canadiens superstar Maurice "Rocket" Richard had been suspended for the remainder of the NHL season, and Montreal was a city on edge.

"There was a feeling before the game that something could happen," recalled Marcel Pronovost, a Red Wings' defenseman from 1950–51 to 1964–65.

Richard's suspension stemmed from an incident during a March 13th game at Boston. Angered when cut on the forehead by the stick of Boston's Hal Laycoe during a melee, Richard went after the Bruins' player, swinging his stick and connecting twice with Laycoe's head. Linesman Cliff Thompson attempted to intervene and was punched twice by Richard and felled by a wicked right-hander.

Richard was assessed a match penalty, accompanied by an automatic $100 fine. It was his second major incident of the season. On December 29th, he had been fined $250 after slapping linesman George Hayes with his gloved hand.

This time, Richard's problems were just beginning.

On March 17th, after a hearing at his Montreal office, the NHL president announced that Richard was suspended for the remainder of the regular season and the entire Stanley Cup playoffs.

"The time for probation or leniency is passed," Campbell said. "Whether this type of conduct is the product of temperamental instability or wilful defiance of the authority in the game does not matter. It is a type of conduct which cannot be tolerated from any player — star or otherwise."

Richard was stunned: "A thing like this doesn't make you feel like carrying on in hockey," he told *Montreal Herald* sports editor Elmer Ferguson.

Fans were angered. The phones at the NHL offices rang off the hook with death

A fan confronts Clarence Campbell (top) on March 17, 1955. The encounter kick-started the riot that required Maurice Richard (bottom) to take to the airwaves to plead with protesters to relent.

Hal Laycoe, the recipient of Maurice Richard's scorn, which led to his riot-inciting suspension.

AN UNQUIET BEGINNING TO THE QUIET REVOLUTION

IT'S SPECULATED BY many Quebec historians that the Richard Riot was the night that Quebec went from being a province into a nation unto itself.

The night is viewed by some as the birth of Quebec's Quiet Revolution, the first howl of rage from the French-Canadian people, which led to the separatist movement of the 1970s.

Others aren't as certain that the connection is so straightforward.

Author Charles Foran argues the former point, believing that Montreal Canadiens captain Richard was the face of the Québécois people: "I think there was an acknowledgement that this man, who dealt with his own limitations, had willingly carried the weight of a people," Foran wrote in his biography of Richard. "He'd accepted all these responsibilities and burdens, and he'd done so with enormous grace."

Montreal historian Nick Auf Der Maur begged to differ in a 1987 piece he wrote for the *Montreal Gazette* about the riot: "I don't at all remember it having an English-French connotation. There was probably an element of nationalism involved, just as there probably was an element of class conflict. But that certainly wasn't the entire story.

"Richard was everybody's idol, our Babe Ruth, a man we all intensely identified with. In that sense, Richard was Everyman.

"And it seemed Campbell was punishing us all."

threats for Campbell. He was warned not to take up his usual seat that night at the Forum as Montreal hosted the Detroit Red Wings.

Campbell, a lawyer who had brought down Nazi war criminals at the Nuremberg trials following the conclusion of the Second World War, wasn't about to back down. When the puck dropped, he was there, seated as always in the southeast end of the rink.

At first, only verbal taunts were hurled in his direction. Then people began hurling garbage at the NHL president.

A fan approached Campbell with the pretense of shaking his hand. Instead, he slapped Campbell twice in the face. As he was taken away by police, the man tried to kick Campbell. That's when the trouble escalated. A tear gas bomb landed near the goal judge at the south end of the Forum. Panic set in as spectators rushed toward the exits.

Detroit, leading 4–1 at the time, was awarded the win by forfeit. The game was

over, but the riot was just getting underway. Fans leaving the rink joined in with demonstrators outside the Forum. It was estimated that the mob grew to 10,000, amassed along St. Catherine Street. Windows were shattered, cars overturned, trolley cables pulled down, phone booths toppled and stores looted.

When it was all done, there was $100,000 in damages along a 15-block stretch of the city, 70 people were arrested and nearly 30 injured, including a dozen Montreal police officers.

The next day, seeking to quell the anger, Richard took to the airwaves, begging people to "do no more harm."

They listened and things quieted down, but the ultimate damage would be done in April, when the Canadiens, minus Richard, lost the Stanley Cup final in seven games to the Red Wings.

1956
—
REFEREE HAND
SIGNALS INTRODUCED

You could say that Bill Chadwick had a hand in hockey history. He never could recall specifically when he first did it — but when he did, he forever changed the way referees would call penalties, even if the NHL took forever to officially adopt his innovative idea.

"Somewhere around 1943 or 1944 would be fairly accurate," former NHL referee Chadwick told author John Halligan regarding when he first began using hand signals to indicate penalty calls.

"I know it was during the Stanley Cup finals. There was so much noise that I had difficulty communicating with the penalty timekeeper.

"I began using a kind of sign language."

Chadwick would touch his leg to indicate tripping and his elbow to signify elbowing, and before long he had developed a complete system of hand gestures that are now used by officials worldwide.

But it wasn't until 1956, a season after Chadwick retired from officiating, that the NHL moved to make the hand signals a standard part of their referees' repertoire.

Amazingly, the Manhattan, New York–born Chadwick worked as an NHL arbiter for 16 seasons despite losing the sight in his right eye in a 1935 hockey game. He was the league's first American-born on-ice official.

"I really don't know if any of the players really knew about it," Chadwick told writer Stan Fischler. "But this much I do know; in all the years I refereed ... nobody said anything to me about my eye."

In 1964, Chadwick became the first U.S.-born official inducted into the Hockey Hall of Fame.

1957

—

TED LINDSAY ORGANIZES NHLPA

Ted Lindsay can't explain what led him to spearhead the organization of the NHL's player association: "Don't ask me why I did it," Lindsay said. "I was one of the better hockey players in the world and I was having one of my best years as a Red Wing at the time."

Lindsay the player was enjoying success, but Lindsay the man couldn't stomach the way he saw his fellow players being treated by those in charge of the game.

"I felt a responsibility, because I saw fellows being sent down," Lindsay explained. "The clubs could send you home — they could send me home — and they didn't owe you five cents."

Announcing the organization of their association on February 11, 1957, Lindsay listed their objectives as "to promote, foster and protect the best interests of National Hockey League players."

Lindsay felt the NHL could improve the pension plan for the players. Launched in 1947, the plan paid a player with two years of service $15 per month beginning at age 45. Increased payments were received on a graduating scale based on experience. For example, a 10-year veteran could receive as much as $300 per month if he didn't touch his pension until the age of 65.

"Actually, we don't have many grievances," Lindsay told the Associated Press. "We just felt we should have an organization of this kind."

Other NHLPA officers elected by the players were Montreal's Doug Harvey, Boston's Fernie Flaman, Chicago's Gus Mortson, Toronto's Jim Thomson and the New York Rangers' Bill Gadsby.

It didn't take long for battle lines to be drawn.

That summer, after posting a career-best 85 points, the Wings dealt Lindsay to the woeful Chicago Black Hawks, and he was sure the move had everything to do with his efforts to organize the NHLPA.

"A series of rumors about my attitude as well as derogatory statements about myself and my family showed me that the personal resentment of the Detroit general manager [Jack Adams] toward me would make it impossible for me to continue playing hockey in Detroit," Lindsay told the AP.

In October 1957, the NHLPA filed a $3 million lawsuit against the NHL, charging that since 1926 club owners had "monopolized and obtained complete domination and control and dictatorship" of professional hockey.

Almost as quickly, the association's resolve began to wane. A month after the suit was filed, Red Kelly announced that the Wings had voted to drop out of the NHLPA because their consent was not sought before the lawsuit was filed.

In December, a petition filed by Lindsay to include the Boston Bruins in the NHLPA was refused for faulty procedure by the Massachusetts State Labor Relations Commission, which stated the petition failed to show interest by 30 percent of Boston players.

Following a February 5, 1958, meeting in Palm Beach, Florida, rather than recognize the NHLPA as the bargaining agent for players, the league agreed to form a player-owner council to deal with future issues.

Gains made by the players included a $7,000 minimum salary and an agreement that the owners would match the $900 annual contribution made by the players to the pension fund. Playoff bonus money was also increased.

Although this attempt to organize the players eventually failed, it paved the way for the birth of the current NHLPA a decade later.

PAYING THE PRICE

AS THE 1956–57 NHL regular season wound to a close, Toronto Maple Leafs captain Jim Thomson called a press conference to announce that he would never play for the team again.

"I want to play hockey in the NHL again, but certainly not with the Leafs because I feel my loyalty has been questioned," the 12-season Toronto defenseman said.

Leafs president Conn Smythe was critical of Thomson, who was Toronto's NHLPA rep.

"I find it very difficult to imagine that the captain of my club should find time during the hockey season to influence young players to join an association that has no specific plans to benefit or improve hockey," said Smythe, who felt it caused a distraction for his team, which missed the playoffs.

During the summer, Thomson was dealt to Chicago. As for the other player reps, Chicago shipped Gus Mortson to the minor leagues in 1957, and Detroit's Red Kelly and New York's Bill Gadsby were traded for each other in 1960, but the deal fell through when Kelly refused to report. He was then traded to Toronto, and a year later Gadsby was again traded to the Wings.

Boston's Fern Flaman was sent to the minors in 1961, the same year that Montreal traded Doug Harvey to the Rangers.

SPORT REVUE

Le magazine sportif des Canadiens-Français

Novembre 1957   25 CENTS

Comment Ivan
a dérobé un
plan au Détroit

500

1957

ROCKET NOTCHES 500th GOAL

Everyone in the Montreal Forum knew the pass was coming. Sitting on 499 goals, Maurice "Rocket" Richard parked himself in the high slot during a Montreal Canadiens power play in the first period of a home game versus the Chicago Black Hawks on October 19, 1957. He'd entered the 1957–58 season with 493 goals, and in the sixth game of the campaign he was poised to make history.

Surrounded by puck-moving masters, Richard, as the best marksmen always do, found a quiet little piece of ice and waited. When Jean Béliveau found Richard's stick with a pass, No. 9 wasted no time firing home goal No. 500. And with that, a man who had already inspired near God-like reverence from his followers added another magical milestone to his incredible career.

"I knew that he wouldn't miss," Béliveau told the *Montreal Gazette*.

As a 23-year-old in 1945, Richard had done the unthinkable when he netted 50 goals in 50 games, becoming the first player in league history to reach the plateau in a single season. Twelve years later, as a 36-year-old on the last leg of his run, Richard gave players everywhere another signature record to shoot for when he netted his 500th goal, becoming the first NHLer ever to reach the mark (in fact, since scoring his 325th goal in 1952 to surpass Nels Stewart's NHL record, every goal he had scored was a new benchmark). By the end of his career, the numbers 50 and 500 were as synonymous with Richard as the famous No. 9 he wore on his back.

"I've been nervous since August when they started all that talk about the 500th goal," Richard told the *Gazette*. "But I hope I keep on being nervous until the end of the season if it will help me to score goals."

Though his most impressive individual achievements came in the first half of his career, Richard continued to experience all kinds of success in his second and third acts. At 32, he led the league in goals with 37 in 1953–54, and then he followed up with 38 the following season to tie teammate Bernie "Boom Boom" Geoffrion for top spot in the NHL. And while Richard's most prolific goal-scoring years happened before his 30th birthday, he also won five Stanley Cups in the final five years of his career, after claiming a relatively paltry three during his first 13 seasons.

Richard's 500th goal provided an occasion for Montreal fans to shower him with appreciation, and indeed the game stopped for roughly 10 minutes after Richard beat Chicago goalie Glenn Hall while the Forum faithful remained in full throat. Unfortunately, the Rocket missed the vast majority of that season battling injuries, as was frequently the case during his final two seasons in the league, before his retirement in 1960. But when, almost 40 years later, the league decided to finally institute a trophy to honor the top goal-scorer of the season, there was no doubt who it would be named after.

Numerous players have gone on to score more goals than Richard's career tally of 544, but nobody is more linked to the act of burying a puck in the net than the man who captured the imagination of hockey fans and players everywhere, first with 50 and then with 500.

TOP-10 FASTEST TO 500 GOALS

WAYNE GRETZKY	575 games
MARIO LEMIEUX	605 games
MIKE BOSSY	647 games
BRETT HULL	693 games
ALEX OVECHKIN	801 games
PHIL ESPOSITO	803 games
JARI KURRI	833 games
BOBBY HULL	861 games
MAURICE RICHARD	863 games
MARCEL DIONNE	887 games

1958

STANLEY CUP TAKES ON ITS PERMANENT SHAPE

Unquestionably the most famous and easily recognizable trophy in sports is hockey's Stanley Cup. And like the sport itself, the cherished mug has undergone significant design changes since it was first introduced in 1893.

It began life as a bowl, and it wasn't until the 1906–07 Montreal Wanderers that the names of all players on the winning team were engraved on the Stanley Cup. As the Cup filled with names over the years, tiered rings and bands were added, followed by long, narrow bands beginning in 1928, causing the Stanley Cup to take on a long, cylindrical shape, becoming known as the "stovepipe Cup" (see page 30).

"If we add another story to it, it'll topple over," suggested NHL president Red Dutton. "We may have to start a new Cup."

As it grew too long to hold, the trophy was altered in 1948 to take on a tiered shape with a barrel of wider rings, providing a more ample base. It was also two separate pieces, with the cup coming apart from the barrel (see page 80).

In 1958, Lord Stanley's mug acquired its modern shape of a bowl, three tiered bands, a collar and five barrel or uniform bands, each filled with the names of championship-winning clubs and their members. The first winning captain to lift the new version of Lord Stanley's mug was Maurice Richard of the Montreal Canadiens following their triumph over the Boston Bruins in the 1957–58 Cup final.

The last blank space to be filled on the barrel of the 1958 design was the entry for the 1991 Cup-winning Pittsburgh Penguins. With no room left to add new teams, it was decided a barrel would be removed from the top and new one added to the bottom, ensuring the Cup kept its iconic shape; the first band removed contained the winning names from 1927–28 through 1939–40. This cycle was repeated in 2004, with the winning names from 1940–41 through 1952–53 being removed. The retired bands are on display, along with the Cup, at the Hockey Hall of Fame.

The current Stanley Cup, topped with a copy of the original bowl, is made of a silver and nickel alloy. It is 89½ inches (89.54 cm) tall and weighs 34 pounds (15.5 kg).

Willie O'Ree, No. 22, skates in his first NHL game, on January 18, 1958.

1958

WILLIE O'REE IS THE NHL'S FIRST BLACK PLAYER

Today he's called the Jackie Robinson of hockey, but Willie O'Ree's arrival in the National Hockey League wasn't exactly front-page news.

"I can't recall any big deal being made," said O'Ree, who became the NHL's first black player when he suited up for the Boston Bruins on January 18, 1958, at the Montreal Forum against the Canadiens.

"The fact that we beat the Canadiens 3–0 in the Forum, now that was big news."

Born in Fredericton, New Brunswick, O'Ree played two games for the Bruins in 1957–58 and made it back to the big leagues for another 43 games in 1960–61, amassing a less-than-stellar line of four goals and 10 assists for 14 points.

A solid left-shooting winger, O'Ree had a hard time keeping his spot in the notoriously competitive six-team NHL. After his time in Boston he played for more than a decade in the Western Hockey League with Los Angeles and then San Diego. He potted a league-high 38 goals in 1964–65, one of six seasons he hit the 30-goal plateau.

O'Ree was 32 when the NHL expanded to 12 teams in 1967, and he wondered what might have happened had he been a few years younger.

"There was the expansion and then when the WHA came to San Diego in 1975, I used to go to all their games," O'Ree said. "I felt I could have played for that club, but they never approached me and I wasn't about to beg for a tryout."

Today O'Ree is involved with the NHL's diversity task force, helping spread the message that hockey is for everyone, regardless of ethnicity. And as for breaking hockey's color barrier, O'Ree says, "I'm getting more attention now than I ever did when I was playing in the NHL."

EARLY BLACK HOCKEY LEAGUES

IT'S NOT ENTIRELY surprising that the NHL's first black player came from Canada's East Coast, given that people of color were playing hockey in Canada's Maritime provinces long before the formation of the NHL.

The Coloured Hockey League of Maritimes in Nova Scotia was formed in 1894, 22 years before the NHL. The first all-black hockey league included more than a dozen teams and over 400 African-Canadian players who were from Nova Scotia, New Brunswick and Prince Edward Island.

In 1928, unlike major league baseball, NHL president Frank Calder declared that there would be no color barrier in his league: "Pro hockey has no ruling against the colored man, nor is it likely to ever draw the line," Calder said.

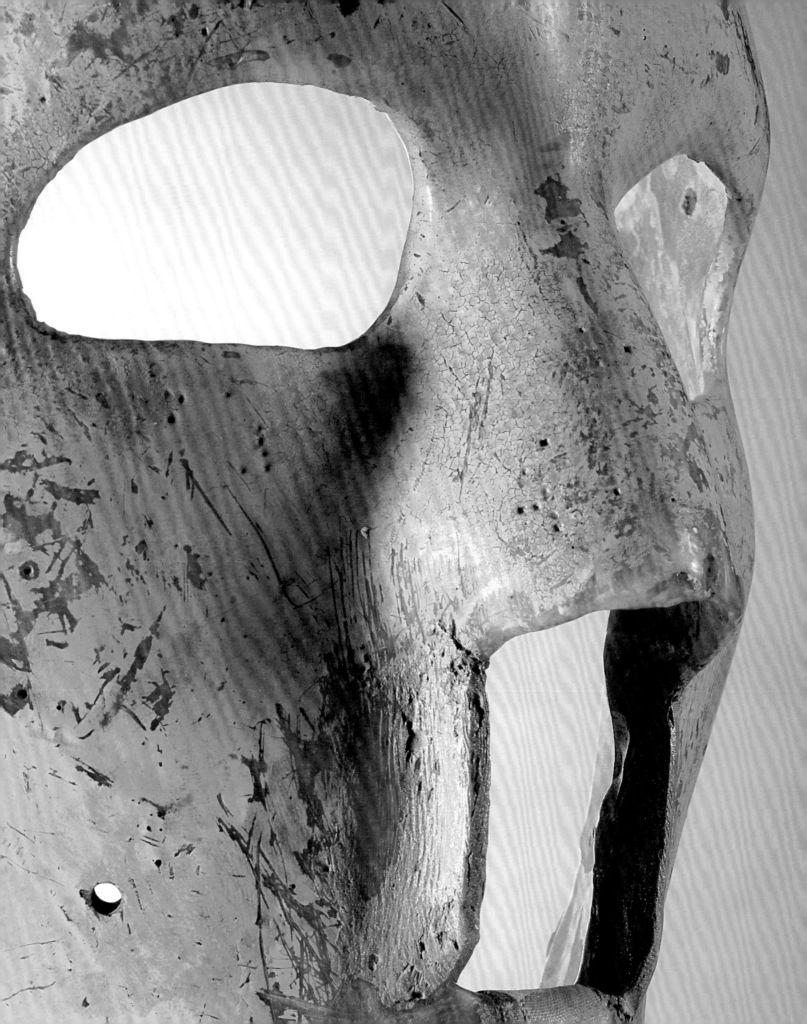

1959

JACQUES PLANTE PUTS ON HIS MASK

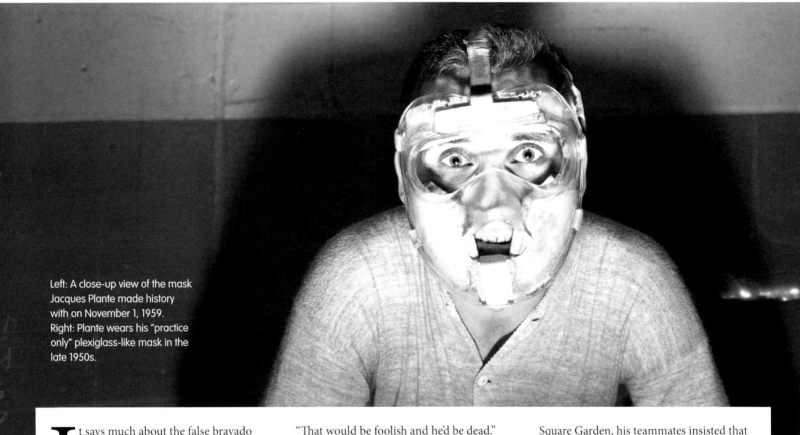

Left: A close-up view of the mask Jacques Plante made history with on November 1, 1959.
Right: Plante wears his "practice only" plexiglass-like mask in the late 1950s.

It says much about the false bravado of the era that the man who sought to protect himself from harm was considered the one to be off his rocker. Yes, the prevailing opinion at the time Montreal Canadiens goaltender Jacques Plante became hockey's first masked man was that a goaltender who wore a mask had lost his nerve.

"Should a parachute jumper jump without a parachute to show that he's not afraid?" Plante asked Al Nickelson of the *Globe & Mail*.

"That would be foolish and he'd be dead."

Steadfast and cocksure — and an innovator at heart — Plante had the perfect personality to go up against the hockey traditionalists.

"I've had both my cheekbones and my nose broken," Plante explained. "That's why I'm all for the mask."

After a shot from the stick of New York Rangers forward Andy Bathgate ripped open Plante's nose and upper lip for seven stitches in a November 1, 1959, game at Madison

Square Garden, his teammates insisted that Plante was delighted.

"Plante was the happiest guy in the rink that he got cut," Montreal defenseman Bob Turner said. "He was waiting for the opportunity [to wear his mask during a game]."

Plante had been experimenting with a variety of masks in practice and finally felt he'd hit on a design that would protect him without inhibiting his ability to stop the puck.

BENNY THE INNOVATOR

GOALIE CLINT BENEDICT was always seeking an edge on the competition. His creative interpretation of the rules while playing with the Ottawa Senators in the NHL's first season of 1917 was born of necessity. The rules of the day forbade goaltenders from leaving their feet to make a save, but that wasn't a practical way to stop the puck.

Nicknamed "Tumbling Benny" by writers, Benedict developed a knack for flopping to stop pucks while making his sprawling act appear accidental, leaving referees in a quandary as to whether they should penalize the Ottawa puckstopper.

"What you had to be was sneaky," Benedict explained to *Montreal Gazette* writer George Hanson in 1976. "You'd make a move, fake losing your balance or footing and put the officials on the spot — did I fall, or did I intentionally go down?"

The frustration level of opponents and officials alike boiled over, and on January 9, 1918, in the midst of the league's inaugural season, NHL president Frank Calder announced he was changing the rule and goalies could now leave their feet to stop the puck.

A dozen years later, Benedict again shook the foundation of the game.

Playing for the Montreal Maroons, he suffered a broken nose and cheekbone when struck in the face by a shot from Montreal Canadiens superstar Howie Morenz.

After a 14-game absence, Benedict returned for a February 20, 1930, game at Madison Square Garden against the New York Americans, appearing in net wearing a crude face mask.

"It was leather and wire with a big nosepiece," Benedict said.

He wore it for five games and then was injured again while wearing the mask and missed the remainder of the campaign. He played one more pro season the next year, but never played in the NHL again.

Though it would be nearly three decades before Jacques Plante made the mask commonplace, Benedict had opened the door.

Doug Harvey poke checks a Ted Hampson shot in front of Jacques Plante on December 30, 1959.

When Plante returned wearing his fiberglass mask and blocked 29 out of 30 shots in a 3–1 victory, even Montreal coach Toe Blake, who initially wouldn't allow Plante to wear the mask after he had struggled while using it during preseason play, changed his tune: "When he was wearing it in preseason training he wasn't sharp and my feeling then was that the mask was to blame," Blake explained to the *Montreal Gazette*. "But perhaps it was Jacques himself and not the mask.

"He can wear it as long as he likes, if it doesn't interfere with his goaltending."

Blake even said "It's the coming thing in the game. The time will come when they'll have an even better mask than Plante's and it'll be standard equipment for goalies."

Others weren't as supportive. Fans heckled Plante and called him a coward.

"Hey, Jacques, Halloween was two weeks ago," bellowed a Boston Garden fan during a mid-November game against the Bruins.

Writers were equally critical. Rex MacLeod of the *Globe & Mail* described it as Plante's "hideous false face."

With their masked man in goal, the Canadiens embarked on a 10-0-1 run. But when the Habs hit a 2-4-3 skid in December, Blake ordered Plante to undergo eye tests with and without the mask, an idea that left his goalie undaunted.

"I can see just as well with it as without it," Plante told the Associated Press. "I can't explain the slump, but I know the mask doesn't bother me. I can see down at my feet just the same."

Other netminders who were also experimenting with facial protection contradicted Plante, such as Marcel Paille of the New York Rangers. "It is not so good as I thought," Paille said of his new mask.

"The perspiration from my forehead drops into my eyes and I can't see so good. And when I go for low shots, my vision is blurred. It is uncomfortable, like wearing someone else's glasses."

Plante briefly gave in to his coach's complaints and doffed his mask for a March 8, 1960, game at Detroit. When Plante performed poorly in Montreal's 3–0 loss, Blake relented again.

"I play just as well with or without it and I have just as much guts whether I wear it or not," Plante said.

At the conclusion of the season, Plante had won the Vezina Trophy and the Canadiens had copped their fifth straight Stanley Cup by sweeping through the playoffs with a perfect 8–0 record.

Plante's battle was won. The mask was here to stay.

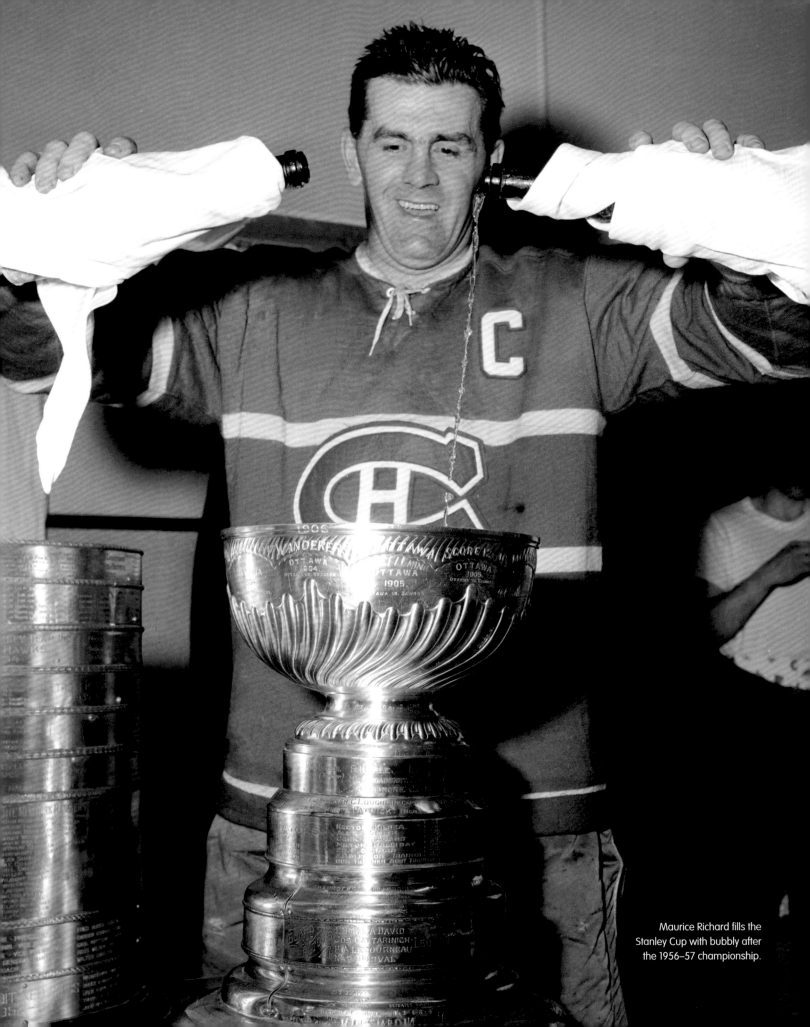

Maurice Richard fills the Stanley Cup with bubbly after the 1956–57 championship.

1960

MONTREAL MAKES IT FIVE STRAIGHT

The spring of 1955 was a time of reflection for the Montreal Canadiens organization. For the second straight season, the Canadiens had dropped a seven-game Stanley Cup final to the Detroit Red Wings. Led by Gordie Howe, Ted Lindsay and Terry Sawchuk, the Red Wings had ascended to the league throne, capturing four of the previous six Stanley Cups, while Montreal had won just a single championship in the past nine seasons. On top of that, longtime Montreal coach Dick Irvin, who had helped turn the franchise around in the early 1940s, was leaving after 15 years behind the bench.

The Canadiens were a team in transition.

While established stars like Maurice Richard, captain Émile "Butch" Bouchard and Doug Harvey helped guide the way, what really changed the Canadiens' fortunes was the contributions of talented youngsters who'd developed in the farm system set up by the man who'd also hired new coach (and former Richard linemate) Hector "Toe" Blake. General manager Frank Selke worked tirelessly to put the pieces in place, and with patience the results came — and they were magical. In Blake's inaugural year as Montreal's coach, the team registered its first ever 100-point season and won the 1956 Cup. The Canadiens went on to claim four more titles, setting a mark of five consecutive

championships that has never been equaled.

In a satisfying twist for some, the roots of Montreal's dynasty traced back to the Toronto Maple Leafs. Selke began his NHL career working under Leafs' owner Conn Smythe in the 1930s, but the two men had a falling out in the middle of the next decade. At issue was Selke's decision to acquire a player while Smythe was serving in Europe during the Second World War. The player was future Leafs captain Ted Kennedy, and the team Selke stole him from was Montreal. Nonetheless, the authoritarian Smythe was unhappy with Selke's unilateral act, and in 1946, Selke left Toronto for the GM's chair in la Belle Province.

Jacques Plante and Maurice Richard celebrate Montreal's fifth straight Stanley Cup, on April 14, 1960.

Selke's top priority when he took over the Canadiens was building the development model he'd always envisioned to churn out top NHLers. To help execute this plan, he hired an enterprising young executive named Sam Pollock, a man who eventually forged his own Habs dynasty decades later. By the early 1950s, the Canadiens farm system was paying dividends, as future stars like Jean Béliveau, Bernie "Boom Boom" Geoffrion and goalie Jacques Plante made their NHL debuts. Also joining the team in 1955–56 was Henri Richard, who, at 19, was 15 years younger than his famous older brother, the Rocket.

The Habs went 8–2 in the 1956 playoffs, downing Detroit in the final to overthrow the reigning champs who'd bested them in back-to-back Cup finals. In 1957, the Canadiens again dropped only two postseason games, defeating the New York Rangers in the semifinal before downing the Boston Bruins in the showcase series.

While Béliveau was firmly entrenched as the team's best player by 1957–58, Rocket Richard, in many ways, remained the face of the organization. And he could still play. During the 1958 playoffs, No. 9 led the league with 11 goals in 10 games as the Canadiens cruised to their third title in as many years, again over Boston. When Montreal beat Toronto for the 1959 crown, the Habs became the first team in NHL history to win four consecutive championships, eclipsing the three straight Cups the Leafs had won from 1947 to 1949.

"They are certainly the best team of this era," expressed Hap Day, coach of the three-peat Leafs teams.

Selke's Canadiens got the best of Smythe's Leafs in the final again in 1960 and finished the postseason with a perfect 8–0 record. That gave Montreal five Cups in as many years and a playoff-winning percentage of .816 from 1956 though 1960.

In the winning dressing room after the fifth straight Cup, the Canadiens' celebration was subdued, almost businesslike.

"Well," Harvey explained to the *Montreal Gazette*. "When you win 4–0 and win in four games and after four Cup titles, you don't get too excited."

The hand wringing that once surrounded the club very carefully turned itself into a handful of rings.

THE 1960S CANADIENS: THE QUIET DYNASTY

SANDWICHED BETWEEN MONTREAL Canadiens teams that won five consecutive Stanley Cups to close out the 1950s and four straight to end the 1970s is a decorated club that narrowly missed out on a huge run of its own.

The Montreal Canadiens teams that won four Cups in five seasons from 1964–65 to 1968–69 rarely get their due when it comes to talk of the best squads ever assembled. But had the favored Habs actually beat the underdog Toronto Maple Leafs in the 1967 final, they, too, would

have strung together five consecutive Stanley Cups.

The fact that Montreal lost that series to their biggest rival on Canada's 100th birthday means many people focus on that event rather than the team's successes. Montreal rebounded from the loss to down the fledgling St. Louis Blues in the 1968 (shown at right) and 1969 finals.

Some have argued that the NHL's decision to put the Original Six teams in one division and the expansion clubs in another — thus ensuring an expansion club reached the Stanley Cup

final — lessened the accomplishment. But it also meant the Canadiens had to win two tough series before even getting the chance at Lord Stanley's mug.

Montreal and Toronto shake hands
after the 1959–60 Stanley Cup final.

1962

—

CHICAGO'S MILLION-DOLLAR MAN

As the puck-drop for the NHL All-Star Game rapidly approached, there were questions about whether the defending Stanley Cup–champion Toronto Maple Leafs would be able to ice a team to face the chosen stars from the other five NHL clubs. Only two Leafs — rookie defenseman Kent Douglas and captain George Armstrong — had signed their contracts for the season.

Chicago Black Hawks owner Jim Norris sought to unburden the Leafs of their financial crisis. On the eve of the October 6th All-Star Game, at a party following the annual NHL All-Star dinner, he offered the club $1 million for left-winger Frank Mahovlich, who'd scored a club-record 48 goals for Toronto in 1960–61.

At the time, it was the largest amount ever offered for a player in pro sports. The highest purchase price on record was the $225,000 the Boston Red Sox had paid the Washington Senators in 1934 for shortstop Joe Cronin.

"I have made the offer," Norris confirmed to the Associated Press. "I have offered the Maple Leafs one million dollars for Mahovlich."

Norris handed ten $100 bills to a Toronto official at the party as a down payment, to be returned to him when the $1 million check was delivered to the Leafs.

"As far as I'm concerned, it is a deal," Norris said. "As far as I am concerned, I have bought Mahovlich."

Leafs president Stafford Smythe confirmed the reality of what Norris was saying, but he also wondered whether everyone had imbibed too much bubbly at the party: "Jim Norris made me an offer for one million dollars for Mahovlich, but I will not consider such a deal at a party," Smythe explained. "We can't consider a deal of that nature without going to the board of directors.

"If he would like to meet me at my office at noon and make the same offer, I am interested."

The next day, Chicago general manager Tommy Ivan arrived at Maple Leaf Gardens with a certified check for $1 million signed by Norris and made out to the Toronto Maple Leaf Hockey Club.

Eventually, the Leafs scoffed at the idea. "I consider this to be a publicity stunt," Smythe said. "No human being is worth one million dollars — not even Frank Mahovlich."

NHL president Clarence Campbell begged to differ. "The firm bid indicates there was an offer intended," Campbell said. "But no responsible officer of the Leafs accepted."

"That's right," Smythe agreed. "No one accepted, at least no one with authority."

Mahovlich stayed with the Leafs, signing a new four-year contract that would pay him $110,000.

Oct. 6/62

$ 1,000,000.00

One & One for Frank Mahovlich,

Lou Norris,

Accepted

A. J. Ballard

Maple Leaf
Hockey Club

No. 864
2-1
710

JAMES D. NORRIS   CHICAGO, ILL.   October 6   1962 $ 1,000,000.00
(For payment in full for player
Frank Mahovlich)

PAY TO THE
ORDER OF   Toronto Maple Leaf Hockey Club   ----- (Canadian Funds) - - - DOLLARS   D

One Million Dollars - - - - -

TO   James D. Norris
THE FIRST NATIONAL BANK
OF CHICAGO
CHICAGO, ILL.

THE ROYAL YORK
TORONTO CANADA

A hastily scrawled agreement and an un-cashed million-dollar check are all that remain of the scuttled 1962 Mahovlich-to-Chicago deal. Mahovlich, seen at left shooting on Glenn Hall, never did play for the Black Hawks.

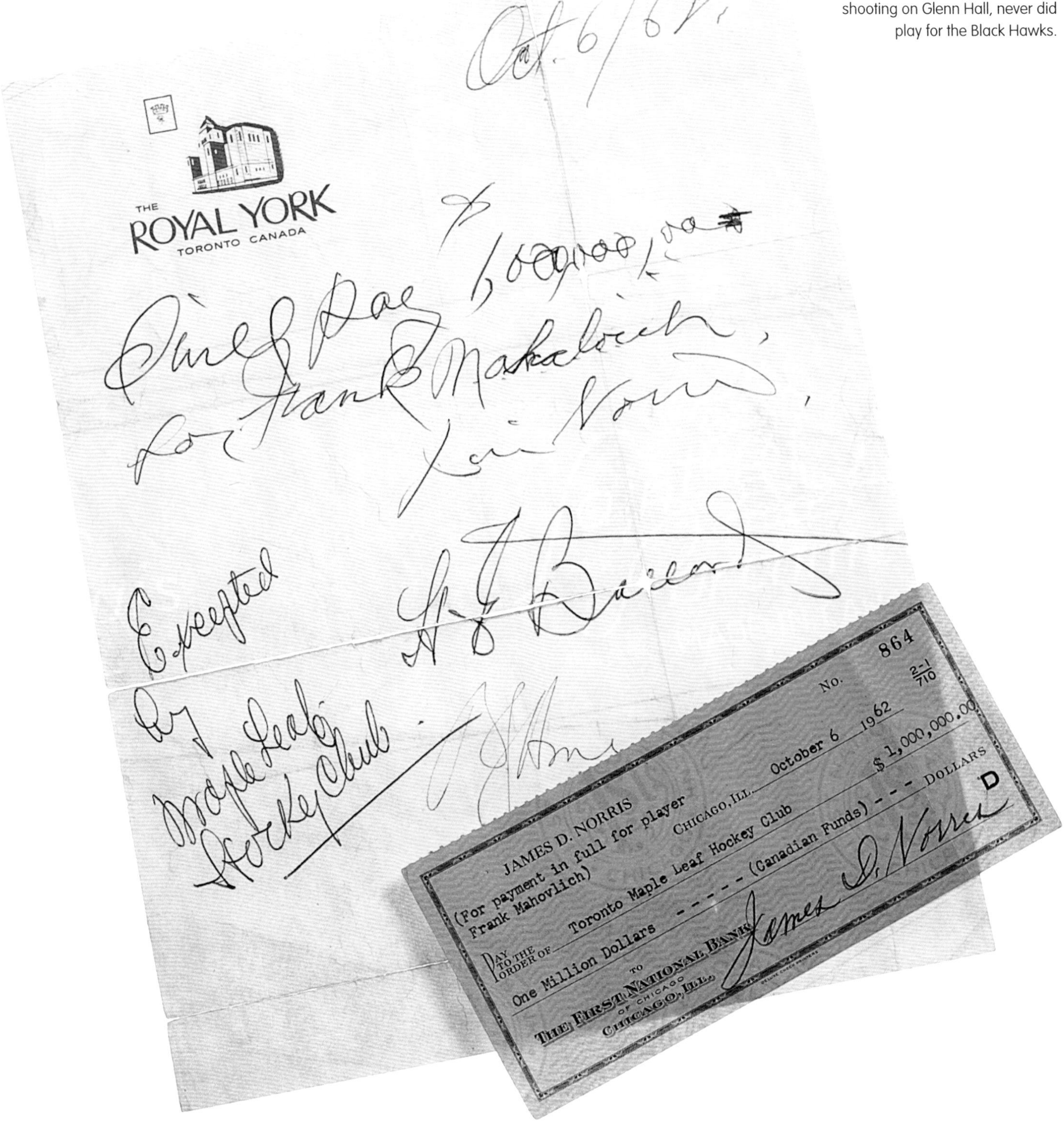

Glenn Hall makes a blocker
save during the 1960s.

1962

GLENN HALL'S STREAK

Gordie Howe's 801 goals, Terry Sawchuk's 103 shutouts, Babe Ruth's 714 home runs — all of them were thought to be unassailable records. All of them were ultimately shattered.

In hockey, there is likely only one mark that will never be touched: the 502 consecutive games played by Chicago Black Hawks netminder Glenn Hall.

In today's two-goalie system, no puckstopper will ever play 100 straight games, let alone the seven-plus straight seasons during which Hall took the starting nod.

"I've got to be proud of that string," Hall said. When you factor in playoff games, Hall's streak runs to 552 games.

Hall's streak began on October 10, 1955, when he tended goal for the Detroit Red Wings in a 3–2 loss to the Black Hawks. It would run until November 7, 1962, when Hall, ailing with a back injury, removed himself from a game against Boston when he missed a shot he felt he should have stopped: "The pain in my back made me afraid to bend down," Hall said. "I decided that it was time to get out of the game."

Denis DeJordy replaced Hall, and when he started three nights later in Montreal, the streak was done — but Hall's place in hockey history was secured forever.

"I look back fondly at it," Hall said. "This is what we always talked about — you were going to get hit, get knocked on your ass, but you got up — not because you were tough or brave, particularly, but because the guys before you always got up."

THE NHL'S CONSECUTIVE GAMES STREAK

Georges Vezina: 190 games
(Dec. 19, 1917–Nov. 28, 1925)

Murray Murdoch: 508 games
(Nov. 16, 1926–Mar. 21, 1937)

Johnny Wilson: 580 games
(Feb. 10, 1952–Mar. 20, 1960)

Andy Hebenton: 630 games
(Oct. 12, 1956–Mar. 22, 1964)

Garry Unger: 914 games
(Feb. 24, 1968–Dec. 21, 1979)

Doug Jarvis: 964 games
(Oct. 8, 1975–Oct. 10, 1987)

IRON MAN BEFRIENDED BY IRON HORSE

WHILE PLAYING FOR the New York Rangers, Murray Murdoch struck up a friendship with New York Yankees star Lou Gehrig. But hockey's iron man and baseball's "Iron Horse" never discussed their respective consecutive games streaks.

"Mostly we talked about hockey," Murdoch recalled in a 2000 interview. "He was a big Rangers fan."

Between 1926 and 1937, Murdoch played a then NHL-record 508 consecutive games and reigned as the league's iron man until 1959. Gehrig's 2,130 consecutive games was major league baseball's mark until Cal Ripken Jr. surpassed it in 1995.

Gordie Howe scores a goal in the early 1960s on his way to his record-setting 545th tally.

1963

HOWE SURPASSES RICHARD WITH 545th GOAL

The goal that gave him the tie for the record was celebrated almost as much as the goal that gave him the record.

On October 27, 1963, in front of 14,749 fans at Olympia Stadium, the largest crowd of the season, Detroit's Gordie Howe took a pass from Bruce MacGregor during a Red Wings power play and drove a shot past Montreal Canadiens goaltender Gump Worsley for the 544th regular-season goal of his NHL career, tying him with former Canadiens star Maurice "Rocket" Richard for first on the league's all-time list.

Even the Habs couldn't help but applaud Howe's milestone.

"I wish I could have played center for you," Canadiens coach Toe Blake, who played with Richard on Montreal's famous Punch Line, told Howe.

Fans showered the ice with everything that wasn't nailed down while Howe breathed a sigh of relief.

"I'm glad I got it," Howe told the Associated Press. "This should help the club. They've been out there looking for me."

As Howe looked for the goal to shoot him past the Rocket, not everyone was celebrating. Richard felt that an asterisk should be placed next to Howe's totals because the Red Wings' star had played 1,120 games as opposed to Richard's 978.

"It's like when in baseball Babe Ruth hit 60 home runs in 154 games and Roger Maris hit 61 in 162 games a few years ago," Richard said. "They left Ruth's record in the book with an asterisk."

"I missed 169 games because of injury. Howe has been luckier that way."

NHL president Clarence Campbell would hear no such talk.

"As far as I'm concerned, when Gordie Howe scores his 545th goal he will be the record holder," Campbell said. "To keep Richard's total there would destroy the image of who the record-holder actually is."

Howe, 35, would wait awhile for his record-breaking tally, going scoreless through the next five games. When he did finally break through on November 10th, it was again against the Habs at Olympia Stadium.

With Alex Faulkner off serving a high-sticking major, Howe was sent over the boards to help kill the penalty.

Marcel Pronovost started the play from the Detroit end, feeding a pass to Howe. Howe in turn passed to Bill McNeill, who was coming through the neutral zone. Bill Gadsby jumped up from defense to give Detroit a three-on-two break. McNeill passed to Howe, and Howe fired a low shot behind Montreal goalie Charlie Hodge.

The record was his, but, more than a sense of accomplishment, Howe felt a sense of relief: "That goal was probably the best pain-killing pill ever invented," Howe said. "I feel altogether different now.

"Since I tied the record, everything seemed so much harder to do. I must have lost 10 pounds in that stretch."

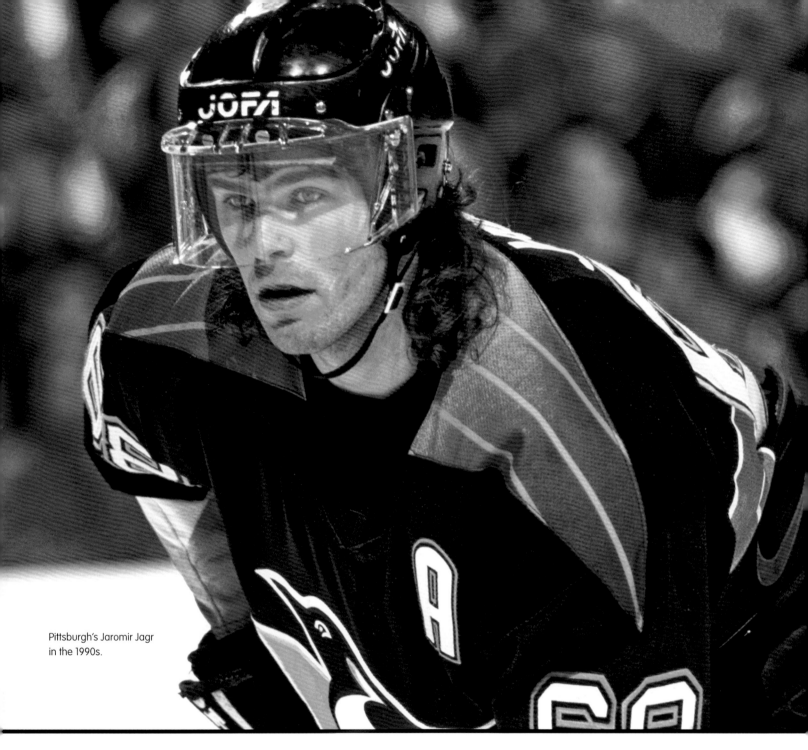

Pittsburgh's Jaromir Jagr
in the 1990s.

THE NHL'S 545-GOAL CLUB

WAYNE GRETZKY	894	TEEMU SELANNE	684	MIKE BOSSY	573
GORDIE HOWE	801	LUC ROBITAILLE	668	JOE NIEUWENDYK	564
JAROMIR JAGR	765*	BRENDAN SHANAHAN	656	MATS SUNDIN	564
BRETT HULL	741	DAVE ANDREYCHUK	640	MIKE MODANO	561
MARCEL DIONNE	731	JOE SAKIC	625	GUY LAFLEUR	560
PHIL ESPOSITO	717	JAROME IGINLA	625*	ALEX OVECHKIN	558*
MIKE GARTNER	708	BOBBY HULL	610	JOHN BUCYK	556
MARK MESSIER	694	DINO CICCARELLI	608	RON FRANCIS	549
STEVE YZERMAN	692	JARI KURRI	601	MICHEL GOULET	548
MARIO LEMIEUX	690	MARK RECCHI	577		

*As of the completion of the 2016–17 NHL season

Terry Sawchuk wore these pads during his second tour with the Detroit Red Wings (from 1957 to 1964). He is seen at right swatting a puck out of harm's way in the 1950s.

1964

—

KING OF THE ZEROS

The night Terry Sawchuk tied George Hainsworth's NHL mark of 94 career shutouts, nobody noticed. That's because on the same night, November 10, 1963, as the Detroit Red Wings blanked the Montreal Canadiens 3–0, teammate Gordie Howe tallied his 545th NHL goal to surpass Maurice Richard as the NHL's all-time goal-scoring leader.

The moody Sawchuk, who liked to deflect attention in the same manner that he turned aside pucks, probably enjoyed being an afterthought. But he'd be front and center the night of January 18, 1964, when he made 36 saves to beat the Canadiens 2–0 at the Montreal Forum and surpassed Hainsworth's shutout standard.

"I didn't give a darn about that during the game," Sawchuk told the Canadian Press of his record performance. "The win was more important."

Then he let his gruff exterior down for a moment of brevity: "Hey, do you know I stopped one of those shots with the butt end of my stick? No kidding."

Certainly, Howe's record-setting night earlier in the season was the more ballyhooed of the two events, and Sawchuk seemed to accept that reality, even if he felt it was a bit misplaced.

"It's not like Gordie's record." Sawchuk said. "But I'll tell you this: It's much harder to get. You gotta play 60 minutes to get my record."

The Canadiens did everything they could to protect Hainsworth's mark. In the second period, rugged Montreal forward John Ferguson crashed hard into Sawchuk, sending the Detroit netminder to the ice and knocking the wind out of him.

In the final moments, though they were down two goals, Habs coach Toe Blake pulled goalie Charlie Hodge and Montreal stormed the Detroit net, seeking to spoil the shutout.

Detroit defenseman Marcel Pronovost recalled that Blake's decision galvanized the Wings: "It only made us madder and we dug down deeper. At the time, it was a record that nobody ever thought would be touched, but Terry did it. We couldn't believe it."

Sawchuk's favorite victims over the years were the Chicago Black Hawks, whom he blanked 23 times. Next on the list were the New York Rangers (19), followed by Boston (18), Montreal (17) and Toronto (15). He also got three against Detroit when he was a member of the Bruins.

Sawchuk would finish his NHL career with 103 shutouts, and he reigned as the league's shutout king until being surpassed by Martin Brodeur in 2009.

1965

FIRST CONN SMYTHE TROPHY AWARDED

Five years without a Stanley Cup title might not seem like a long time for an NHL franchise, but for the Montreal Canadiens, it felt like an eternity.

When the drought finally ended in 1965, after the Canadiens blanked the Chicago Black Hawks 4–0 in Game 7 of the Cup final series and captain Jean Béliveau triumphantly lifted Lord Stanley's mug, Forum organist Leo Duplessis broke into "Happy Days Are Here Again."

For Béliveau, the happiness would continue to grow. Not long after he was presented the Cup by NHL president Clarence Campbell, it was announced that

he was the inaugural winner of the Conn Smythe Trophy as the most valuable player of the Stanley Cup playoffs.

Béliveau led all scorers in the final series with five goals and five assists in seven games. He scored three game-winners in the playoffs, including the decisive goal in Game 7 of the final, tallied 14 seconds after the opening face-off for the quickest Cup-winner in history.

Upon learning his unit would begin the game, Béliveau urged linemates Dick Duff and Bobby Rousseau to have a good start, "so that the other lines will follow the way." However, he hardly expected to score on that first shift.

It wasn't a pretty goal, with Duff's pass bouncing into the net off Béliveau's leg.

"I had my legs together, expecting to stop the pass and get my stick on the puck," Béliveau explained. "But it bounced right into the net."

The goal was a fluke, but the win was hardly that. Béliveau, who was part of Montreal's five-straight Stanley Cup wins from 1956 to 1960, was effusive in his praise of the 1964–65 club: "This is the best of the six championship teams I've been on," Béliveau said. "There's more satisfaction because no one thought we would win. But the players were more optimistic."

CONN'S GAME

CONN SMYTHE, THE man who built the Toronto Maple Leafs into a dynasty, was a wheeler-dealer at heart. He assembled the group that purchased the Toronto St. Patricks in 1927 and renamed the team the Maple Leafs. He parlayed racetrack wagers into enough cash to acquire NHL All-Star King Clancy from Ottawa. He raised the money to build Maple Leaf Gardens during the heart of the Great Depression, convincing construction workers to take Gardens shares in lieu of cash as payment.

Smythe, seen here with Max Bentley and Ted Kennedy, was also a vindictive man. His feuds with Boston manager Art Ross were legendary. During the 1939–40 season, when the Leafs visited Boston to face the defending Stanley Cup–champion Bruins, Smythe took out an ad

in the *Boston Globe* inviting fans to come to the Boston Garden that night to see a real NHL team in action, the Toronto Maple Leafs.

He fought for years to keep former Leaf Busher Jackson out of the Hockey Hall of Fame because Jackson was an alcoholic and a wife beater, and when Jackson was finally enshrined in 1971, Smythe resigned from the Hall's selection committee. He also resigned from the Gardens board when Muhammad Ali was booked to fight there. Smythe viewed Ali as a draft dodger for his stand against the Vietnam War.

A passionately patriotic Canadian, Smythe fought in both World Wars, organizing the Sportsmen's artillery during the Second World War.

In the 1940s, he had a falling out with Frank Selke, his right-hand man. Selke left for

Montreal, building the Habs into the scourge of the NHL, which lead to a bitter rivalry between Canada's two NHL teams during the six-team era. It must have galled Smythe to see his namesake trophy first go to Canadiens captain Jean Béliveau, since Smythe despised the Habs.

For all his cantankerous nature, Smythe also had a soft spot for those less fortunate, and he was a tireless worker for several charities, especially the Crippled Children's Society of Canada.

Jean Béliveau poses with the Conn Smythe Trophy as its first-ever recipient.

Bobby Hull skates for a loose puck against the Montreal Canadiens in the 1960s.

After Chicago Black Hawks left-winger Bobby Hull joined the NHL's 50-goal club in 1961–62, Chicago coach Billy Reay was certain that Hull would be the first NHLer to surpass 50 goals in a season.

"If he doesn't do it this year, he will do it next year or the year after that," Reay said.

Hull used his overpowering slap shot to become the third NHLer to reach the 50-goal plateau, joining the Montreal Canadiens pair of Maurice "Rocket" Richard and Bernie "Boom Boom" Geoffrion, who had hit 50 the season prior to Hull.

With his cover-boy looks, incredible wheels and a devastating shot, Hull was a new breed of NHL star, and during the 1965–66 season, he became the most prolific single-season goal-scorer in league history.

On March 12, 1966, facing the New York Rangers at Chicago Stadium, Hull fired a 40-foot slapper, which he claims he didn't connect well with, past Rangers goalie Ceasare Maniago on a Black Hawks power play in the third period for his 51st goal of the season, becoming the first to scale past the 50 barrier.

Play was halted for nearly eight minutes as a capacity crowd of delirious Chicago fans littered the ice with hats and other debris.

After the goal, Hull shook hands with all of his teammates and then skated to where his wife, Joanne, was seated to pose for photos.

"It felt wonderful and certainly was a load off my back," Hull told the *Montreal Gazette*. The goal tied the score at 2–2 as Chicago rallied from a 2–0 deficit for a 4–2 victory.

"I'm glad it came at a time we needed it. It was a thrill getting the goal, but the biggest thrill was that roar from the crowd."

The goal was a double record-setter, as it was Hull's 21st power-play tally of the season, shattering the NHL mark of 20 set in 1953–54 by Rangers forward Camille Henry.

It was apparent that the Black Hawks had been struggling to tally during the games as Hull inched toward the record, the players being too focused on setting Hull up for the big goal.

"I'd say the guys were bending over backwards to get me the 51st goal," Hull admitted.

It was equally apparent that Hull's punishing slapper was getting inside the heads of the NHL goalies, causing them to play head games in order to face him.

"I keep telling myself that Hull's just got an ordinary shot," Maniago said. "That it's no harder than anybody else's."

He didn't sound convinced, nor did any other puckstopper.

"He uses a stick with a curved blade," Montreal netminder Gump Worsley said. "His shot sometimes drops and you gotta watch for it."

Those assigned to shut down Hull found him equally troublesome: "He was tough to check because he's all over the ice," said Rangers forward Reggie Fleming, Hull's former Chicago teammate.

Hull wasn't done breaking records that season. He also won the Art Ross Trophy with 97 points, one better than the NHL record point total of 96 established by Montreal's Dickie Moore in 1958–59.

BOOMER'S BIG NUMBER

FOR MUCH OF the 1960–61 NHL season, all eyes were on Frank Mahovlich. The Toronto Maple Leafs left-winger scored 26 times in the first 29 games, and insiders anticipated that he'd become the league's second 50-goal-scorer.

But when Mahovlich trailed off toward the end of the season, it was Montreal's Bernie "Boom Boom" Geoffrion — so named because of his booming shot — who picked it up. Geoffrion fired 22 goals in his last 19 games and snapped a shot into the Toronto net on March 16, 1961, to join former teammate Maurice "Rocket" Richard as the game's only 50-goal snipers to that point.

The season also saw Geoffrion join Richard as the only other Canadiens to reach 270 career goals — the previous franchise high set by Aurèle Joliat in 1938. (Jean Béliveau also hit the mark toward the end of the season).

The evening before his 50th, Geoffrion had admitted he'd endured a sleepless night, but now he felt like he was dreaming: "Gee, 50 goals — it's like a dream come true," Geoffrion said.

And poor Ceasare Maniago. He was the goalie on record for both Geoffrion's 50th and Hull's 51st goals.

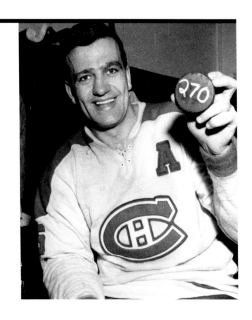

1967

EXPANSION

As the NHL's board of governors gathered on February 2, 1966, at New York's St. Regis Hotel, the league was about to undergo its most significant change in 40 years.

In 1926 the NHL had grown to its largest size of 10 teams, adding the Detroit Cougars, Chicago Black Hawks and New York Rangers to its membership. By 1942, the Great Depression and Second World War had combined to reduce the NHL's size to six teams, and for a quarter century, the league would prosper greatly during the so-called Original Six era.

But while the NHL idled, North America's other major sports advanced. Major League Baseball, the National Football League and the National Basketball Association all grew in size during the 1960s. Each league expanded to add teams on the West Coast of the United States.

NHL moguls watched this development and realized they needed to get on the bandwagon or be left behind as a big-league sport. There were also fears that if the NHL stayed a six-team loop much longer, a rival league might form in the available cities, as had happened with the American Football League and American Basketball Association.

Immediately, several groups lined up to lobby the NHL for a franchise. The NHL received 15 franchise applications from 10 different cities. Crooner Bing Crosby and George Flaherty, head of the Shasta Corporation and owners of the Ice Follies, fronted a group seeking a team for San Francisco.

There were five separate applications from Los Angeles, one headed by former Boston Bruins GM Lynn Patrick; another backed by Dan Reeves, owner of the NFL's Los Angeles Rams; a third from Metromedia Corp., owners of the Ice Capades; a fourth from Tony Owen, husband of actress Donna Reed; and, finally, one from transplanted Canadian Jack Kent Cooke, owner of the NBA's Los Angeles Lakers.

There were also two rival groups after a team for Pittsburgh, one featuring Pittsburgh Steelers owner Art Rooney, attorney Peter H. Block and Pennsylvania State Senator Jack MacGregor, and the other represented by John Gleason, a Chicago banker.

Jack Kelly, brother of Princess Grace of Monaco, was among a syndicate seeking

Philadelphia's Gary Dornhoefer fires a puck toward
Toronto's Bruce Gamble during the 1967–68 season.

Henri Richard chases a puck while former teammate Doug Harvey (No. 2) looks on during the 1968–69 season.

a team for Philadelphia that also included Jerry Wolman, owner of the NFL's Philadelphia Eagles. Max Winters, co-owner of the NFL's Minnesota Vikings, fronted a group seeking a team for Minneapolis–St. Paul.

Art Modell, owner of the NFL's Cleveland Browns, sought a team for that city, and Lamar Hunt, owner of the AFL's Kansas City Chiefs, pursued a team for Dallas. Northrup and Seymour Knox were after a franchise for Buffalo. There were also bids from groups representing Baltimore and Vancouver.

Each city was required to pay $2 million for its franchise and provide a suitable arena with a minimum seating capacity of 12,500.

On February 9th, the winning bidders were announced. Cooke, who promised to spend $7.5 million to construct a 16,000-seat arena, got the franchise for L.A., and Rooney's group was awarded the Pittsburgh club. San Francisco, Philadelphia, Minneapolis–St. Paul (to be known as Minnesota) and St. Louis were also welcomed into the fold, all to begin play for the 1967–68 season. It

was also announced that all six teams would be housed in a separate group, to be known as the West Division, with the six existing NHL teams forming the East Division and the winners of the two divisions meeting in the Stanley Cup final.

The schedule would be expanded from 70 to 74 games per team. Each team would play 10 games against the other teams in its own division and four against each team in the opposing division.

"The new teams will play against themselves

OLD FACES, NEW PLACES

WITH THE FRANCHISES and owners in place, it was time to determine how the rosters would be stocked.

On January 18, 1967, plans for the expansion draft, slated for June 6th of that year, were outlined in Montreal during the NHL's All-Star Game festivities. Each of the six new teams would be allotted 20 players, but none of the existing six clubs would lose more than five skaters and one goalie from their current roster. Each would be allowed to protect 11 players from their 20-man roster, consisting of 18 skaters and two goaltenders. Players of junior age (20 and under) were ineligible to be selected in the expansion draft.

On draft day, the expansion clubs took different approaches to stocking their rosters. Goaltenders were selected in the first two rounds, and the Los Angeles Kings opened by grabbing veteran Terry Sawchuk, who'd just backstopped the Leafs to the Stanley Cup. The Philadelphia Flyers opted for potential by selecting Bernie Parent, and then the St. Louis Blues went for experience, tabbing 10-time NHL All-Star Glenn Hall from Chicago.

The Minnesota North Stars began the skater portion of the draft by selecting forward Dave Balon from Montreal, and the California Seals followed by taking four-time Stanley Cup–winning defenseman Bobby Baun from the Leafs.

Sawchuk and Hall weren't the only future Hall of Famers to hear their names called. Pittsburgh grabbed former Hart Trophy–winner Andy Bathgate (pictured at right) and defenseman Leo Boivin from Detroit. St. Louis grabbed defenseman Al Arbour off Toronto.

A pair of Calder Trophy winners also moved to the new teams. Philadelphia grabbed Brit Selby (the 1965–66 winner) and California selected Kent Douglas (the 1962–63 winner), both from the Leafs. Montreal's Charlie Hodge, like Hall and Sawchuk a past Vezina Trophy winner, went to California with the sixth pick among goalies.

"If Charlie is only the sixth-best goalie, I'm a monkey's uncle," quipped Canadiens goalie Gump Worsley.

The Seals felt they'd done well at the draft table: "We have the ingredients of a strong club, good goaling, a solid defense and strength down the middle," said Frank Selke Jr., president of the Seals.

"We look tough on paper and we'll be tough on the ice," added California coach Bert Olmstead.

However, the only thing that proved to be tough for the Seals was surviving. They came home last in the West Division in their inaugural season.

The other clubs faired better, but not a single one of them finished their inaugural season with a winning percentage of .500. In the end, the St. Louis Blues were the West Division's entrant to the Stanley Cup final, where the Montreal Canadiens swept them in four straight.

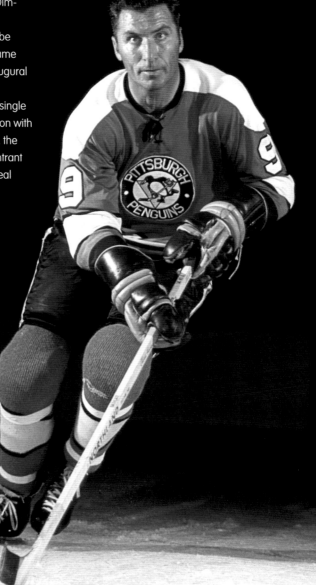

Pittsburgh's Leo Boivin is chased by Frank Mahovlich during the 1967–68 season.

until they have reached the same competitive level as the present teams," NHL president Clarence Campbell told the *Montreal Gazette*.

The shocking inclusion in this sextet was St. Louis, since no group from the Missouri city had applied for a franchise, but a little digging showed why this development should be no surprise at all: Jim Norris and Arthur Wirtz, co-owners of the Black Hawks, also owned the St. Louis Arena, and Jim Norris, in particular, was dead set against expansion.

It's believed that, behind the scenes, Norris agreed to the expansion plans in return for a

franchise for his rink. Norris and Wirtz were given until April 5, 1966, to come up with an ownership group for a St. Louis franchise, one that would be willing to purchase the St. Louis Arena from the two men.

This was hardly comforting for those cities left at the altar. Baltimore was proclaimed as first alternate should any of the six new groups drop out of the picture, with Vancouver second in line as a fill-in.

There was vitriol in Canada, since all six of the new cities were based in the United States: "No matter how vigorously they may deny it, the NHL has sold its soul to

television in exchange for the silver of expediency," wrote Jack Kinsella in the *Ottawa Citizen*.

Added Hal Pawson of the *Edmonton Journal*: "This decision is a final harsh reminder that Canada's game is no longer Canada's, that it has been Sold America."

Naturally, the politicians got in on the act. Federal opposition leader John Diefenbaker demanded that the Canadian government tell the NHL that Canada warranted greater representation, but Prime Minister Lester Pearson was unmoved: "I have a good many problems these days," Pearson said. "I hope

I don't have to take on those of the National Hockey League."

Angry Vancouverites threatened to boycott Molson beer, which sponsored *Hockey Night in Canada* and owned the Montreal Canadiens, going as far as to present a petition with 60,000 signatures to Campbell, asking that he reconsider the city for expansion.

What torpedoed the Vancouver bid was that there was no clear owner, which the NHL governors preferred to a syndicate. "Vancouver made a poor presentation," Canadiens president Donald Molson said.

When it came to Buffalo's missed opportunity, Leafs co-owner Stafford Smythe admitted he had been the one to scuttle the bid put forward by the Knox brothers, who were said to be worth $300 million: "I don't want to kill the goose that lays the golden egg," Smythe said. "They're so close [to Toronto], they scare me."

Not all old-school hockey types feared expansion, though. Former Detroit GM Jack Adams felt the new teams would be a boon for the sport: "Kids are the salvation of this game," Adams said. "And with expansion, you'll see more and more American boys coming into the game."

And on the appointed date, the St. Louis franchise had its buyer. A group headed by Sidney Salomon III stepped forward on April 5, 1966, to purchase the St. Louis Arena for $4 million and acquire the rights to the open St. Louis franchise, thus settling all debate on which city would be the home of the NHL's sixth expansion franchise.

Gump Worsley dives in desperation against Red Berenson's scoring attempt.

OPEN SEASON FOR RECORD-BREAKING

WITH MORE PLAYERS filling out the rosters for more teams than the league had ever boasted before, there was bound to be some surprises.

The first was probably St. Louis' Red Berenson. A left-shooting centerman who spent much of the early 1960s on the outside of the Montreal Canadiens main lineup, Berenson quickly became a star in St. Louis. On February 2, 1968, he added to his new luster by beating Philadelphia Flyers goalie Doug Favell six times in an 8–0 victory. It was the most goals a player had scored in an NHL game since 1944 and an NHL record for goals scored by a player in a road game.

"A couple of games before, [teammate] Camille Henry got a hat trick," Berenson recalled. "I told him, 'I wish I could get one of those,' because I'd never had one.

"I ended up getting two."

Berenson, who's best before expansion was 16 points in 69 games in 1963–64, was the first expansion team member to rate among the NHL's top-10 scorers when he garnered 82 points in 1968–69.

Other expansion surprises included Minnesota's Mike McMahon, who led all NHL defensemen in scoring in 1967–68 with 47 points. Minnesota's Danny Grant and Oakland's Norm Ferguson tied the NHL record for goals by a rookie, each scoring 34 times in 1968–69. And Phil Goyette of the Blues challenged for the NHL scoring title in 1969–70, finishing fourth with 78 points and winning the Lady Byng Trophy.

Meanwhile, the NHL establishment was shattering the record book.

Boston's Phil Esposito became the NHL's first 100-point-scorer with a goal on March 2, 1969, against Pittsburgh. He finished the 1968–69 campaign with a whopping 126 points, far exceeding the 97-point record previously shared by Chicago's Bobby Hull and Stan Mikita.

That same season, Hull eclipsed his own goal record of 54 when he came two shy of 60, and the Bruins' Bobby Orr established new standards for goals (21) and points (64) by a defenseman.

101

1968

DEATH OF
BILL MASTERTON

Bill Masterton (No. 19) during
the 1967–68 season.

After three years of minor-league hockey in the Montreal Canadiens chain, Bill Masterton, a former NCAA standout, opted to give up the game: "The Canadiens were loaded with centers," Masterton explained to the *Boston Record American*. "I never had much chance to make the grade with them."

When his rights were purchased from the Habs by the expansion Minnesota North Stars in 1967, Masterton couldn't resist the urge to give it one more try and came out of retirement: "I had to give it a try," Masterton said. "Once you're in hockey, you always wonder if you can play with the best."

Masterton's gamble initially paid off when he cracked the Minnesota roster, scoring the first goal in franchise history on October 11, 1967, against the St. Louis Blues, but the night of January 15, 1968, the same decision would cost Masterton his life.

Skating in a game against the Oakland Seals, Masterton, who'd worn a helmet in college at Denver but doffed his headgear as a pro, collided with two Seals players in the Oakland zone and fell awkwardly, striking his head hard on the ice.

"I've never seen anybody go down that way," Minnesota coach-GM Wren Blair said. "We heard him crash to the ice on the bench. He was checked hard, but I'm sure it wasn't a dirty play. He hit so hard that I'm sure he was unconscious before he fell."

A pool of blood quickly formed under Masterton, who lay prone on the ice, and he was rushed to Southdale Hospital in Fairview, Minnesota.

Masterton, 29, never regained consciousness and died in hospital 30 hours later of a massive brain injury.

It was the first direct fatality from an on-ice incident in NHL history. At the conclusion of the season, the NHL instituted the Bill Masterton Memorial Trophy to go to the player who best exemplifies the qualities of perseverance, sportsmanship and dedication to hockey. Claude Provost was the first recipient.

MASTERTON'S DEATH SPARKS HELMET DEBATE

WHEN THE NHL'S best gathered in Toronto for the 1968 All-Star Game just two days after the death of Minnesota North Stars forward Bill Masterton, debate over the use of helmets was all the talk. At the time of Masterton's death, only three percent of NHLers wore helmets.

"The reason we don't wear helmets is vanity, that's all," Chicago superstar Bobby Hull reasoned.

Others were ready to put their vanity aside in favor of safety: "I'll be wearing a helmet as soon as I can find a good one," Hull's team-mate Stan Mikita told the Canadian Press.

Others still weren't sold: "Let's face it, trouble has been if a player wore a helmet he was looked upon as an outsider," Pittsburgh's Ken Schinkel said. "If all the players wore helmets, I'd gladly wear one."

1969

POLICE INTERVENTION

Wayne Maki (pictured while playing with Vancouver) and Ted Green.

It was expected to be just another innocuous NHL preseason game when the Boston Bruins and St. Louis Blues clashed on September 21, 1969, at Ottawa's Civic Centre. Instead, it would be a game remembered forever and for all the wrong reasons.

During the first period, Blues forward Wayne Maki and Bruins defenseman Ted Green clashed. According to Boston GM Milt Schmidt, Maki speared Green in the groin, and Green retaliated by swinging his stick and hitting Maki in the head. As Green turned away, Maki swung back, his stick striking Green on the left side of the head.

"I think the whole story is this: Teddy wasn't expecting a swing in the severity it was delivered, because his swing had only been half-hearted," Schmidt told the *Boston Herald*.

Green slumped to the ice and was taken to the Ottawa General Hospital, where he underwent surgery for a depressed skull fracture. He'd recover but would miss the entire 1969–70 season.

Both players were suspended for 30 days by the NHL and were charged with assault causing bodily harm by the Ottawa police department.

Maki was acquitted of all charges, Judge C. Edward Carter ruling that he was acting in self-defense. Green's charge was reduced to common assault, and he was also acquitted.

One of hockey's toughest customers, Green was never the same player after the incident. He returned to the Bruins in 1971 and won a Stanley Cup with the club in 1972. He jumped to the WHA the following spring and finished his career with the Winnipeg Jets in 1979.

Maki also never recovered fully from the incident.

"Wayne has lost much of his aggressiveness," Blues coach Scotty Bowman told the *Boston Record American* in 1970. "He came completely apart from the business."

Maki died of a brain tumor on May 12, 1974.

THE NHL ON TRIAL

1918: Toronto's Alf Skinner and Montreal's Joe Hall are arrested and charged with common assault for a stick-swinging altercation. Charges are dropped.

1975: Boston's Dave Forbes is charged with aggravated assault after striking Minnesota's Henry Boucha with his stick. The case ends in a hung jury.

1975: Detroit's Dan Maloney does community service for an assault charge after attacking Toronto's Brian Glennie.

1976: Philadelphia's Joe Watson, Don Saleski and Bob Kelly are found guilty of simple assault for attacking Toronto fans with their sticks.

1977: Toronto's Dave "Tiger" Williams is acquitted of assaulting Pittsburgh's Dennis Owchar with his stick.

1982: Winnipeg's Jimmy Mann pleads guilty to assault charges for breaking the jaw of Pittsburgh's Paul Gardner and pays a $500 fine.

1988: The first NHLer is jailed for on-ice violence; Minnesota's Dino Ciccarelli is sentenced to one day in jail and fined $1,000 for assaulting Toronto's Luke Richardson with his stick.

2000: Boston's Marty McSorley receives a sentence of 18 months probation for assaulting Vancouver's Donald Brashear with a stick slash to the head.

2004: Vancouver's Todd Bertuzzi is given a conditional discharge after pleading guilty to assault causing bodily harm after his on-ice attack on Colorado's Steve Moore.

1970

TONY O BLANKS THEM ALL

They called him Mr. Zero and Tony O, and the NHL also called him a rookie, which made what Chicago Black Hawks goaltender Tony Esposito accomplished during the 1969–70 season all the more impressive.

Claimed by Chicago from the Montreal Canadiens in the June NHL Intra-League Draft, the younger brother of Boston Bruins shooting ace Phil Esposito, the reigning NHL scoring champion, was a stopper extraordinaire.

"I knew I wouldn't be protected by Montreal," Esposito said. "I didn't know where I was going, but I wanted it to be someplace where I'd get the chance to play."

That chance came with the Chicago Black Hawks, who'd missed the playoffs in 1968–69 and, judging from the way the season had started, figured to be postseason outsiders again.

The Black Hawks were 0-5-1 entering an October 25, 1969, game at Montreal, and that's where the magic started. Esposito turned aside all 30 shots in a 5–0 win.

With that, Esposito got on a goose-egg roll. Three times he posted back-to-back shutouts. A 1–0 win on January 17th at Boston was Esposito's 10th shutout of the season, making him the first NHL goalie to reach double-digit zeros since Detroit's Glenn Hall in 1955–56.

Another whitewash of the Bruins on March 11th in a scoreless tie allowed Esposito to equal the Black Hawks franchise-record 12 shutouts posted by Charlie Gardiner in 1930–31. Consecutive 1–0 wins on March 22nd over the St. Louis Blues and March 25th at the Detroit Red Wings pushed Esposito past the modern-day shutout mark of 13 established by Toronto's Harry Lumley in 1953–54. Finally, a 4–0 win on March 29th over the Maple Leafs left Esposito with 15 shutouts.

In NHL history, the only goalie to record more shutouts was George Hainsworth of the Canadiens, who posted 22 in 1928–29, the year before the advent of forward passing in all zones and long before the introduction of the red line, two rule changes that significantly increased offense in the game.

Esposito sought to downplay his accomplishment: "The shutouts aren't that important," said Esposito, who won the Calder Trophy as the NHL's top rookie and earned the Vezina as its best goalie.

"It's great [but] it's the whole team. We've got the trophy but it wasn't me who won it."

Behind Esposito's stellar netminding, the Black Hawks roared from last place to top spot in the East Division in one season, an NHL first, leaving Black Hawks coach Billy Reay to suggest his netminder should receive another award, the Hart Trophy as MVP of the league.

"He was instrumental in us finishing first," Reay told the *Windsor Star*.

Instead, it was Esposito who was shutout this time. Boston's Bobby Orr, the first defenseman in league history to win the scoring title, won the Hart.

"What does a guy have to do?" Reay asked of his goalie. "He had 15 shutouts. He also had 15 one-goal games.

"There's all together too much emphasis placed on scoring statistics by some of the people who pick these things."

1970

—

ORR SCORES SPECTACULAR CUP WINNER

Becoming the first NHL defenseman to record a 100-point season and win the Art Ross Trophy, Bobby Orr soared above the competition during the 1969–70 season. And he would do so quite symbolically on the Stanley Cup–winning goal that spring.

In what's been called the most famous photo in hockey history, Orr is caught horizontally in midair, his hands raised in celebration, a split second after slipping the overtime winner past St. Louis Blues goalie Glenn Hall to give the Bruins a sweep of their Stanley Cup final series and Boston's first title since 1941.

"This is the greatest day of my life," Orr said.

Bruins coach Harry Sinden proclaimed Orr to be the game's greatest player: "No other defenseman in hockey could have

made that play," Sinden told the *Boston Record American*. "He saw the opening. Derek [Sanderson] fed it to him just perfect.

"Bang. That was it."

Orr admitted that he'd gambled by diving down so low to be in front of the St. Louis net, and he wasn't certain if he'd scored: "I didn't know if it was going to get in there," Orr said. "I was flying through the air and when I pushed the puck ... it went between Glenn's legs as he came out."

When he heard the roar of the 14,835 packed into Boston Garden, Orr knew the Cup was theirs: "I don't know where the shot went," Orr said. "I just knew it was in."

Escaping from the teammates who mobbed him, Orr headed toward the Boston bench. "My father [Doug] was sitting there and I wanted to see him," Orr explained. "But he ran out because he was crying."

VANQUISHED BLUES PART OF HISTORIC HOCKEY PHOTO

THE FAMOUS PHOTO of Bobby Orr's 1970 Stanley Cup–winning goal immortalized Orr as well as the two victims on the play, St. Louis Blues goalie Glenn Hall and defenseman Noel Picard.

It was Picard who flipped Orr's legs out from under him with his stick just as this photo was taken, giving Orr the appropriate appearance of Superman flying through the air.

Whenever he makes appearances, Picard is frequently presented the photo to sign and always obliges.

"I get asked about that a lot," Picard told *St. Louis Today*. "People send me cards and pictures [to his home] in Montreal and I sign them all the time."

While Picard was a solid performer for the Blues, Hall was a future Hall of Famer known

simply as *Mr. Goalie* due to his excellence between the pipes. Even with all of his accomplishments, Hall still has the iconic photo on display at his home in Stony Plain, Alberta.

"Don't know how many times I've signed it," Hall told writer Dave Stubbs. "I've told him, 'Bobby, I had showered before you even hit the ice.'"

Bobby Orr wheels behind the net, looking up ice
before taking off on a signature drive.

1970

ORR COLLECTS RECORD TROPHY HAUL

Rare is the athlete who has the innate ability to completely transform their chosen profession. Bobby Orr is one such athlete.

The Boston Bruins knew Orr was special, and they went out of their way to acquire the rights to the wunderkind from Parry Sound, Ontario, sponsoring the teams he played on all the way up until he reached the NHL.

By 1966–67, Orr was an 18-year-old who was regularly turning the heads of NHL players, executives and fans. He played 61 games that season, recorded 41 points and was named Rookie of the Year. It was his style of play, however, that really garnered headlines. Orr was an end-to-end virtuoso, capable of starting a rush from behind his own goal line that wound through the entire team and finished with the puck in the back of the opposition's net. His offensive forays drew double and triple coverage, and the odd-numbered matchups always ensured he had a teammate open for a pass. He back-checked hard and used his great skating to keep players to the outside, making the shots easier for his goalies to handle. Quite simply,

Orr was the first to master defense by playing offense.

On March 15, 1969, Orr collected his 60th point of season to set the NHL single-season record for defensemen. In the 1969–70 season he obliterated the mark, notching 33 goals and 87 assists for 120 points. Those totals made him the first defenseman to lead the NHL in scoring and to win the Art Ross Trophy.

Orr, just 22 years old, was the unanimous choice as winner of the Norris Trophy as the league's top blue-liner and became the first defenseman since Tommy Anderson of the Brooklyn Americans in 1941–42 to win the Hart Trophy as the NHL's most valuable player. He also captured the Conn Smythe Trophy as MVP of the Stanley Cup playoffs. With that, he became the first NHL player to win four major awards in the same season.

"There are no words left to praise him," said Pittsburgh Penguins coach Red Kelly, the first winner of the Norris, who presented the trophy to Orr during the NHL awards ceremony. "He is the greatest defenseman in the league today and he can be as long as he wants to play."

Bruins GM Milt Schmidt, the 1950–51 Hart winner, summed up Orr's phenomenal impact on the game: "In my opinion he is the greatest thing I have seen in the past, the greatest in the present, and if there is anything greater in the future, I hope I am around to see him."

The next season Orr would go on to set the single-season league record for plus/minus with a plus-124 rating, as well as another new single-season points mark for defensemen with 139.

He was, however, vulnerable, and his knees gave way long before his drive did. He underwent three knee surgeries between 1966 and 1969, and an additional four between 1972 and 1977.

His last memorable moment came with Team Canada at the 1976 Canada Cup, where he was named tournament MVP, and where many marveled he was better on one leg than any other player on two.

Orr announced his retirement on November 8, 1978, and in June 1979 he became the youngest member ever enshrined in the Hockey Hall of Fame.

Phil Esposito scores on the
Toronto Maple Leafs in the 1970s.

1971

PHIL ESPOSITO SCORES 76 GOALS

The 1970–71 Boston Bruins took a wrecking ball to the NHL record book. They established 37 team and individual standards, but what was perhaps most astonishing was the way center Phil Esposito put the league's scoring marks through a shredder.

The NHL record for goals in a season of 58, set by Bobby Hull in 1968–69, was in Esposito's sights as he suited up on March 11, 1971, for a game at Los Angeles against the Kings. He was dead even with Hull when he took the ice, but after netting two goals in a 7–2 victory, both the record and the 60-goal plateau were his. So was the single-season points mark. Esposito finished the game with 128 points, two more than the record he'd established in 1968–69.

"I'm glad that's over," Esposito told writer Leo Monahan. "I knew that sooner or later, I'd get the record."

He even went as far as to speculate about how much he could increase the goals standard, but it would turn out that Esposito was selling himself short. "I'd be happy with 65, maybe 70," he said.

When Esposito put three goals past Montreal's Phil Myre in a season-ending 7–2 drubbing of the Canadiens on April 4th, his NHL-record sixth hat trick of the season, it left him sitting at 76 goals and 152 points.

Some pundits made light of Esposito's work, citing the watered-down NHL that included eight expansion teams, including the first-year Buffalo Sabres and Vancouver Canucks, as the real reason for his goal explosion.

"When the watered-down talk first started I just grinned," Esposito told the *Boston Herald*. "I had a good laugh, right? Heck, is it my fault the league expanded? Was I the one who added the teams?"

Esposito was also quick to point out that just he and teammate John Bucyk (51 goals) were able to reach the 50-goal barrier during the 1970–71 campaign: "If the league is so watered down then why aren't there more than two 50-goal guys," Esposito asked. "Don't the people on the other 13 teams have the same opportunity?"

He blamed some of the criticism on old-school hockey types, and he promised not to be such a stick in the mud when the time came and he was crossed out of the record book: "Comparisons are inevitable and records are made to be broken," Esposito reasoned. "My records, Bobby Orr's records, everybody's records will be broken someday.

"Someone will come along and when that does happen, I won't be bitter."

NHLERS WITH 76 OR MORE GOALS IN A SEASON

WAYNE GRETZKY 92
Edmonton Oilers, 1980–81

BRETT HULL 86
St. Louis Blues, 1990–91

MARIO LEMIEUX 85
Pittsburgh Penguins, 1988–89

WAYNE GRETZKY 84
Edmonton Oilers, 1983–84

ALEXANDER MOGILNY 76
Buffalo Sabres, 1992–93

TEEMU SELANNE 76
Winnipeg Jets, 1992–93

PHIL ESPOSITO 76
Boston Bruins, 1970–71

1971

KEN DRYDENS MVP DEBUT

For many great players, claiming the Calder Trophy as rookie of the year is the first notable step in announcing that they've arrived. Ken Dryden, however, managed to score playoff MVP.

The precocious Dryden was a virtual unknown when he was called up by the Montreal Canadiens from their American Hockey League affiliate late in the 1970–71 season. The 6-foot-4 goalie — he was all arms and legs in the crease — shone during a six-game stint to close out the regular season, posting a 1.65 goals-against average and .957 save percentage.

Even though Dryden had only played that handful of games on the big stage, coach Al MacNeil decided to roll with him in the postseason. The Canadiens had uncharacteristically missed the playoffs the year before and were slated to face the powerhouse Boston Bruins in the first round, so there was a little more desperation in the air than usual in Montreal.

The Big Bad Bruins were the defending Stanley Cup champions and had finished first overall with 121 points that season, 24 more than Montreal's total of 97. Boston's success was built on a high-powered offense that featured Bobby Orr, Phil Esposito, Johnny Bucyk and Ken Hodge, all of whom had scored more than 100 points. The Bruins had scored 399 goals during a year in which the second-highest scoring team — which happened to be the Canadiens — had scored just 291.

All that served as the backdrop for a first-round series that went back and forth, with the teams emerging in a 2–2 deadlock after four games.

"Cripes, the kid's got paws like a giraffe," said Phil Esposito, who had just set the NHL's single-season record for both goals and points, when asked about Dryden's puck-stopping prowess.

When Boston won Game 5 on home ice, it seemed like only a matter of time until they closed out their opponents. Even after

Ken Dryden eyes the puck while making a save in the early 1970s.

Ken Dryden strikes his familiar pose in the Montreal crease in the early 1970s.

Montreal blasted the Bruins 8–3 in Game 6 to force a decisive contest, the Canadiens were facing an uphill battle in Game 7 in the Boston Garden.

But Dryden was ready for the climb.

In the final showdown, Dryden limited Boston to just two goals as the Habs emerged with a 4–2 victory in enemy territory, notching one of the biggest and most celebrated playoff upsets in the history of the league. The mission, however, was far from over.

After knocking off the Minnesota North Stars in six games, the Canadiens faced a very formidable Chicago Black Hawks team in the final. Just as they had in the first-round versus the Bruins, the Habs fell behind 3–2 in the series and were faced with the prospect of having to win both Games 6 and 7 to claim the Cup. A narrow 4–3 victory at the Forum helped Montreal push the series back to Chicago, but the Canadiens were on the ropes quickly in the final

contest, as the Black Hawks jumped out to a 2–0 lead. Dryden, however, shut the door after that, and the Habs rallied for a dramatic 3–2 win.

When it was time to award the Conn Smythe Trophy to the postseason's most valuable player, nobody was surprised to hear Dryden's name called. Because he'd appeared in barely a handful of regular season games during 1970–71, Dryden still retained his rookie status. His fantastic play carried over as, in 64 games, he posted a 2.24 goals-against average and claimed rookie of the year honors in 1971–72.

Including the six appearances that made up his 1970–71 season, Dryden suited up for only eight NHL seasons. He sat out the 1973–74 season, spending the time off obtaining his law degree. Dryden won the Stanley Cup a staggering six times and finished with an almost unfathomable career record of 258-57-74.

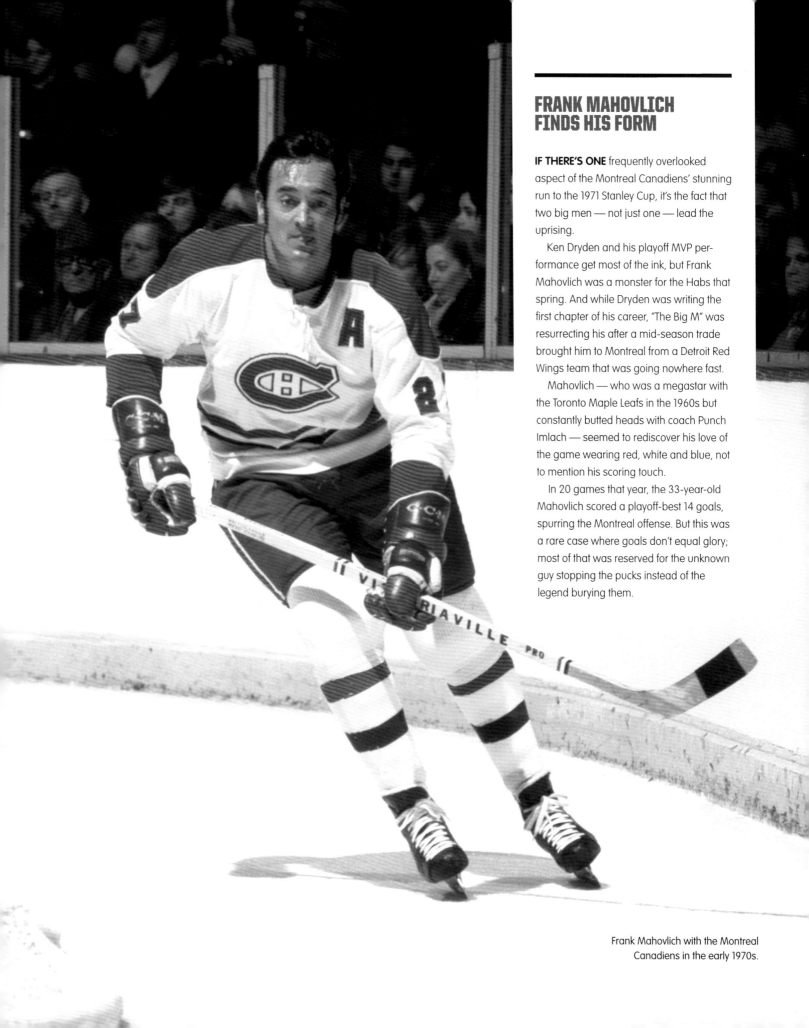

FRANK MAHOVLICH FINDS HIS FORM

IF THERE'S ONE frequently overlooked aspect of the Montreal Canadiens' stunning run to the 1971 Stanley Cup, it's the fact that two big men — not just one — lead the uprising.

Ken Dryden and his playoff MVP performance get most of the ink, but Frank Mahovlich was a monster for the Habs that spring. And while Dryden was writing the first chapter of his career, "The Big M" was resurrecting his after a mid-season trade brought him to Montreal from a Detroit Red Wings team that was going nowhere fast.

Mahovlich — who was a megastar with the Toronto Maple Leafs in the 1960s but constantly butted heads with coach Punch Imlach — seemed to rediscover his love of the game wearing red, white and blue, not to mention his scoring touch.

In 20 games that year, the 33-year-old Mahovlich scored a playoff-best 14 goals, spurring the Montreal offense. But this was a rare case where goals don't equal glory; most of that was reserved for the unknown guy stopping the pucks instead of the legend burying them.

Frank Mahovlich with the Montreal Canadiens in the early 1970s.

Bobby Hull as a member of the
WHA's Winnipeg Jets.

1972

BOBBY HULL AND THE WHA

He wore No. 9 on his back and was the 91st player signed by the World Hockey Association and the 34th with NHL experience. There can be no question, though, that when Bobby Hull put his name on the dotted line on June 28, 1972, to two WHA contracts worth a combined $2.5 million — a $1.5 million pact with the Winnipeg Jets and a $1 million personal services contract with the league — it legitimized the upstart rival loop.

A five-time 50-goal-scorer in the NHL and one of the league's most recognizable superstars, the Golden Jet sent both the Jets and the new league soaring.

"I have no regrets, no ax to grind," Hull said as he signed his deal. "The WHA is going to be as great as the NHL someday. My main concern now is to make the league go. I'm hoping a few more of the boys will come over now."

You could say that Hull built the WHA, and then they came — in droves.

"Hull gave the league instant credibility," said Dennis Murphy, cofounder of the league and commissioner of the WHA for two seasons.

Jim Niekamp of the Los Angeles Sharks wore this jersey in the WHA's inaugural season.

"He brought another 67 NHL players with him.

"To lure that many NHLers in our first year of operation was unbelievable. We changed hockey."

The first NHL star to sign a deal with the WHA was Toronto Maple Leafs goaltender Bernie Parent, who joined the Miami Screaming Eagles on February 22, 1972. Parent signed a five-year deal worth $750,000, with signing bonuses that included a house, a boat and a car.

The Miami club never did hit the ice, becoming the Philadelphia Blazers before having ever played a game, but the potential instability of the new loop wasn't a concern

for many of the NHLers who decided to sign up.

"Guys doubled and tripled their salaries in one day," Tom Webster said of the league's appeal.

Charlie Finley, owner of the NHL's California Golden Seals, laughed at his players' contract demands and told them to take the WHA money. He also told them they'd regret it.

So Bobby Sheehan, Paul Shmyr, Wayne Carleton, Norm Ferguson, Gary Kurt and Tom Webster all signed with the new league, and each made a splash with their WHA clubs. Sheehan, Shmyr, Carleton and Ferguson all hit career highs in single season points, and Webster even won a championship, something the Seals could only dream of.

Even the lure of repeating as Stanley Cup champions wasn't enough to keep Boston Bruins Gerry Cheevers, Derek Sanderson, Ted Green and John McKenzie from bolting to the rival league.

"[Entering the WHA] was the first time that players had a chance to bargain," explained Hull.

"The majority of hockey fans I talk to were upset when I went to Winnipeg," Hull said. "I don't feel that same way. I feel that we did a lot of great things in the WHA. We made room for a lot of great hockey players."

Consider a few of the innovations, now commonplace in the NHL, that were

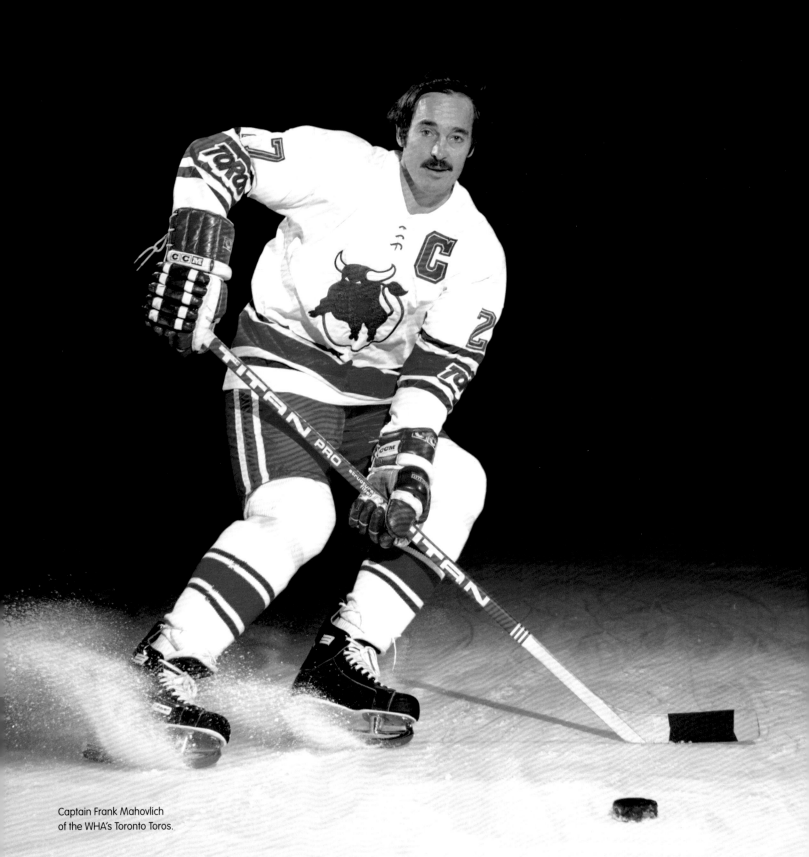

Captain Frank Mahovlich
of the WHA's Toronto Toros.

Chicago Cougars jersey worn by goalie Keith Le Livre in the WHA's inaugural season.

spawned by the WHA: regular-season overtime, the drafting of 18-year-olds and the influx of European stars into North American hockey.

It was also the WHA that brought Gordie Howe back to the ice in 1973, uniting him with sons Mark and Marty in Houston and giving another generation of fans the chance to watch the game's most legendary player.

The WHA also presented Wayne Gretzky with his first chance at the pro stage, at a time when some NHL people doubted whether the Great One could cut it in the big time.

Most WHA-watchers believe the 1977–78 Winnipeg Jets is the finest squad assembled in league history, led by its top forward line of Bobby Hull with Swedes Anders Hedberg and Ulf Nilsson.

Those 1978 Jets beat the Soviet national team, the same squad that had humbled the NHL All-Stars 6–0 in the deciding game of the 1979 Challenge Cup.

The WHA, with Hull driving the bus, lasted for seven years, ultimately forcing the NHL to usurp it. Four WHA teams — the Jets, Edmonton Oilers, Quebec Nordiques and Hartford Whalers — joined the NHL in 1979.

"After the first year of amalgamation [with the NHL], out of the top 20 scorers, 10 of them were from the WHA," Hull said. "I think that a lot of people overlook what we did for the game of hockey, what we did for the hockey players and what kind of talent and what kind of entertainment we had in the WHA."

"People didn't recognize that we had great talent in our league," WHA cofounder Dennis Murphy added. "I think we proved it to the rest of the hockey world when we merged with the NHL [in 1979] and Edmonton won four Stanley Cups in the first seven years."

1973

—

BORJE SALMING DEBUTS WITH LEAFS

After missing the Stanley Cup playoffs in 1972–73, the Toronto Maple Leafs underwent a major overhaul. There were nine new faces in the lineup when the Leafs opened the 1973–74 season, including two intriguing additions: defenseman Borje Salming and forward Inge Hammarstrom, for whom the Leafs had paid a reported $100,000 to acquire from the Swedish Ice Hockey Association.

Salming and Hammarstrom were not the first Europeans to land in the NHL. It was Ulf Sterner who broke the barrier when he appeared with the New York Rangers for four games in the 1964–65 season. Nearly a decade later, Thommie Bergman played the entire 1972–73 season on defense for the Detroit Red Wings. However, it was Salming who quickly established himself as a bona fide star. In Toronto they called Salming the King, and it was an appropriate handle because, on the ice, he was hockey royalty.

"He was a phenomenal player and a phenomenal athlete," former Leafs captain Darryl Sittler said. "When we watched him

practice, you knew he was the real deal."

Among the first Europeans to play regularly in the NHL, Salming was frequently put to the test. Opponents often spent the early years of Salming's career trying to crown the king.

"There was this mentality in the NHL, that Swedes coming into our league were tested mentally and physically more than North Americans were," Sittler said. "And Borje was an elastic band, just coming back, facing the challenges that were there and playing great hockey on top of it."

This was the era of the Philadelphia's Broad Street Bullies, and they were at the top of the list in dishing out crass treatment to Salming.

"It was tough because they really tried to kill you," Salming said of the Flyers. "If they did some of those things today, they would be suspended for life."

Salming persevered through the intimidation tactics and excelled, opening the NHL's doors to European players. He was named to the NHL's First or Second All-Star Teams six times and was twice runner-up in Norris Trophy voting.

Back home, he was opening the eyes of

Swedish youngsters who now believed that they, too, could play in the NHL.

"Borje Salming was my big hero growing up," said fellow Hockey Hall of Famer Nicklas Lidstrom, who won seven Norris Trophies with the Detroit Red Wings. "He was my [defense] partner in the Canada Cup in 1991. I had a chance to partner up with him, and that was a big thrill for me."

"Borje is a living legend in Canada and Toronto, but he's even bigger in Sweden," added former Leafs captain Mats Sundin.

Salming played 16 seasons with the Leafs and closed out his NHL career with the Red Wings in 1989–90. He holds the NHL record for most points by a defenseman (787) who wasn't selected in the NHL entry draft and is the Leafs' all-time leader in assists (620) and plus/minus (181). His 148 goals are the most ever scored by a Toronto defender.

He may not have been the first European to play in the NHL, but he was far and away the best. His ability to succeed forever changed the landscape of the league for the better.

Borje Salming competes against the Chicago Black Hawks early in his NHL career.

Philadelphia's Bobby Clarke screams encouragement from the bench in the 1970s.

1974

BROAD STREET BULLIES BATTLE WAY TO STANLEY CUP

The *Philadelphia Bulletin* came up with the handle following a 3–1 Flyers victory over the Flames: "Broad Street Bullies Muscle Atlanta," read the headline in the January 4, 1973, edition of the paper.

The genesis of the Bullies, however, had begun much earlier.

The Flyers finished first in the NHL's West Division during 1967–68, their inaugural season, but they were dispatched in the first round of the playoffs by the heavier, rougher St. Louis Blues. They were outmuscled again by the Blues the following spring, and owner Ed Snider and GM Keith Allen made team toughness a priority.

Don Saleski, Bob Kelly and Dave Schultz, who would set an NHL penalty-minute record with 472 in 1974–75, were added in the next two drafts. By the 1972–73 season, the Flyers were using intimidation as a strategy and cutting a swath through the rest of the NHL.

The Bullies would fight with anybody — opponents, fans, even game officials. You didn't just fight one Flyer, either. You fought them all. But to suggest they were nothing more than thugs and goons would be inaccurate.

"We've never been given proper credit," Flyers captain Bobby Clarke said. "We were not just a bunch of Broad Street bullies.

"We played good hockey."

Flyers coach Fred Shero intrinsically understood the capabilities of his players. He never asked any of them to do anything they couldn't handle.

Shero's philosophy was simple but effective, "There are four corners in a rink, and there are two pits, one in front of each net." He told *Sports Illustrated* in 1975. "To win a game, you've got to win the corners and the pits. You give punishment there, and you take it, which is why we have more fights than most teams."

Shero's game plan demanded that his players consistently outwork the other team. Following the example of their leader, Clarke — a diabetic blessed with a chip on his shoulder because hockey people never thought he'd be able to play in the NHL due to his illness — the Flyers developing a work ethic was never an issue.

They surrounded their toughness with skill in the form of Rick MacLeish and Bill Barber, and behind them they reinstalled the game's best goalie, Bernie Parent, an original Flyer who had returned to the NHL from the WHA. Parent allowed the Flyers to bend the rules in the corners and the pits because nothing kills penalties like great goaltending.

In the spring of 1973, the Flyers won the first playoff series in franchise history. The next spring they won the Stanley Cup, becoming the first of the 1967 expansion teams to do so, defeating the Boston Bruins in a six-game final series.

"We didn't beat Boston by fighting," Schultz proclaimed. "We beat Boston by good, honest hard work."

Just in case anyone didn't believe in the Flyers, they did it again the next season, beating the Buffalo Sabres to take their second straight Stanley Cup.

1975

———

A NEW YEAR'S EVE TO REMEMBER

Nobody was feigning objectivity on the CBC broadcast as Canada prepared to flip the calendar with a very special event. Speaking to viewers on New Year's Eve 1975, the always-enthusiastic Howie Meeker was extremely optimistic about the Montreal Canadiens' chances against the visiting Red Army. Meeker believed the Canadiens — playing for all of Canada on this night, just as the visiting club was representing the entire Soviet Union — held an advantage at every position, something the analyst felt should assuage any Canadian anxiety about how the game would go down.

"Canada," Meeker barked, "sit back, relax, enjoy yourself, have a ball, the Canadiens are going to win!"

Much of Meeker's analysis was spot on.

Montreal held a distinct advantage over the Red Army up front and on defense, and they carried the play for long stretches. But Meeker missed the mark when he declared Ken Dryden a superior goalie to Vladislav Tretiak.

Considering the magnitude of the game, Tretiak's 35-save performance in a 3–3 tie might be one of the signature goaltending performances in the history of hockey. And given the Canadiens' status as an emerging dynasty combined with the supremely talented skaters that dotted the Red Army lineup, it's no surprise the two teams produced 60 minutes of action that is still considered among the most enthralling hockey the world has seen.

The exhibition was part of Super Series '76 (played between December 1975 and

January 1976), which took advantage of the hysteria surrounding the USSR-Canadian clashes that began with the landmark Summit Series in 1972 and continued with the WHA's version of the same event in 1974. For the Super Series, two Soviet clubs — the Red Army and the Soviet Wings — played four games apiece against different NHL squads. With the Cold War still being waged and Canada's narrow hockey victory in 1972 (and humbling loss in 1974) still fresh in their minds, Canadians remained extremely defensive about their national passion.

Against that backdrop, Tretiak and the Red Army skated into the Montreal Forum, the same rink where the Soviets had shocked Canada 7–3 in the first contest of the '72 Series.

Like the opening game three and a half years earlier, the home team came out

AN
INTERNATIONAL
HOCKEY
EVENT

U.S.S.R. vs. NHL

The cover of the Super Series '76 tournament program showing the Soviet Wings logo (left) and the Red Army logo (right).

swarming. With the Forum already whipped into a frenzy, sniper Steve Shutt blasted a slapper past Tretiak to give Montreal a 1–0 lead before the game was four minutes old. Then, 7:25 into the frame, Yvon Lambert slid another puck home to give the Flying Frenchmen a 2–0 advantage.

Though the Canadiens — who were on the verge of a four-year run as Stanley Cup champions — continued to push in the second, the Russians struck back, narrowing the score to 2–1. By the halfway point, Montreal led 3–1 in a game that featured an almost melodic back and forth. Yes, more notes were being played in the Red Army zone, but the Russians were adept at cashing in on chances when they got them.

Aiding the visiting squad was Dryden's overactive mind (which also plagued him in the Summit Series). The goalie had a hard time simply trusting his instincts against the Soviets because they played their own unique brand of hockey, complete with different shooting and passing tendencies.

Montreal defenseman Larry Robinson, who considers Dryden the best goalie of the era, acknowledged that Dryden's stand-up style of play left him at a disadvantage when facing the Red Army's novel lateral attack: "He didn't have a great record against the Russians," Robinson concedes.

Valeri Kharlamov — who'd received a rousing ovation before the game from a Montreal crowd that recalled his artistry from the '72 Series — drew his team closer when he whipped a backhander past Dryden. When Boris Alexandrov buried on a two-on-one opportunity, the Red Army pulled even.

Though chances occurred at both ends of the ice, neither team was able to find the go-ahead goal. The game, which had a magical, frenetic feel the whole way through, ended in a draw. While Canada didn't get to celebrate the way Meeker had promised, it also didn't suffer the indignity of a loss to hockey's other superpower. It was a spectacular saw-off and a rare example of a sporting event both sides can reflect back on with pride.

VLAD THE GREAT

CANADIAN FANS (AND Canadiens fans, for that matter) had a complex relationship with Soviet stars in the 1970s. The confluence of feelings included wonder, fear, disdain and, in no small amount, respect. With apologies to speedster Valeri Kharlamov, no Russian player earned more admiration than goalie Vladislav Tretiak. Just 20 years old when the 1972 Summit Series occurred, Tretiak immediately stole the spotlight, grabbing the attention of the hockey world with his catlike reflexes and improbable saves.

As international events became more commonplace throughout the decade, rumors began to surface that Tretiak would relish the chance to play professionally in the NHL for the Montreal Canadiens. In a Cold War world, though, that just wasn't an option. When the Habs drafted Tretiak 138th overall in 1983, players like Slovakian Peter Stastny had begun to leave Eastern Europe for North America, but Russians had yet to make that leap.

After winning gold at the 1984 Olympics, Tretiak hung up his pads, and many say it was because the Soviet authorities wouldn't let him try his hand at hockey in the NHL.

His 12 years guarding the net for one of the world's most feared international hockey squads is what fans are left to judge. He never consistently faced the world's best players, but when he did, he had a tendency to shine brighter than anyone else on the ice.

Vladislav Tretiak makes a save during the
legendary Summit Series of 1972.

1976

—

SITTLER'S BIG NIGHT

It hadn't quite been 10 years, but for fans of the Toronto Maple Leafs, who had last seen a Stanley Cup parade in 1967, clinging to the small victories had become a way of life. So Darryl Sittler's unforgettable night against the Boston Bruins on February 7, 1976, was a chance to celebrate.

Sittler, arguably hockey's best player at the time, insists that the night started like any other: "There was nothing different," he says, "[though there was] a buzz in the city when an Original Six team was in town."

For too much of his career, Sittler suffered either from a lack of quality teammates or from being treated poorly by the very organization that employed him. But on the night

in question, the stars aligned as he posted six goals and four assists for a 10-point showing versus coach Don Cherry and his formidable Bruins. It's the rare offensive record that survived the assaults of Wayne Gretzky, Mario Lemieux and the wide-open 1980s, standing to this day as the all-time benchmark for points in a single outing.

"It's nice to have that record. But I never expected it to be still standing 40 years later." Sittler says.

Prior to the game against Boston, Sittler had endured criticism from outlandish Maple Leafs owner Harold Ballard, who'd said that the team was looking for a center to play between young wingers Lanny

Darryl Sittler sidesteps a check from Pittsburgh in the mid-1970s. At left is a ticket stub from Sittler's 10-point game in 1976.

Darryl Sittler watches the play behind Boston goalie Dave Reece during his record-breaking 10-point game in 1976.

McDonald and Errol Thompson. The person presently filling that role was Sittler, who has publicly stated many times that Ballard's comments prior to the game had little effect on him. Still, the timing of the NHL's biggest single-game offensive output was a counterpunch well received.

At the end of 20 minutes versus the Bruins, the Leafs led 2–1, with Sittler having collected an assist on both goals. In the middle frame, however, the Sittler show really began as he pumped home three goals and two assists for a total of seven points. During the intermission, Sittler was informed that the league record for points in a game was eight, established in 1944 by Maurice "Rocket" Richard of the Montreal Canadiens.

Just 44 seconds into the third, Sittler notched his fourth goal to equal Richard. Then, right before the period's halfway mark, Sittler scored for the fifth time, establishing the new points mark. He threw in one more goal for good measure — famously scoring on a shot from below the goal line that caromed off Bruins defenseman Brad Park and into the net — giving him six in the 11–4 victory to go along with four assists.

"That one was unreal." Sittler told *The Hockey News* of his final tally. "That kind of told the story. It was just one of those nights."

Nearly 39,000 games later, it is still a touchstone for results-starved Leafs fans and a record that seems as unlikely to be broken as it was to be set.

DAVE REECE'S LAST NHL GAME

EVEN BEFORE THE puck dropped on Darryl Sittler's historic 10-point night, the Leafs captain caught a bit of a break.

Though Stanley Cup–winning goalie Gerry Cheevers had just returned to the Boston Bruins from a long stint in the World Hockey Association, coach Don Cherry decided to start rookie Dave Reece, preferring to save the 35-year-old Cheevers' energy for a game the next night in Boston. The powerhouse Bruins also entered the night 20 points ahead of Toronto in the standings, so Cherry likely figured Reece wouldn't have to do too much to make a game of it.

As it turned out, Sittler's big night at Maple Leaf Gardens in front of a national audience was Reece's final taste of big-league action. Cheevers' return pushed Reece to the minors, and he never again played in the NHL. Despite the lopsided result of the February 7th tilt, Reece's brief stint was fairly successful; he went 7-5-2 with a 3.32 goals-against average.

"I wasn't bad," Reece told the *Toronto Star*. "I had five great games coming in [to the Toronto game]. But the sixth? Wow."

The following season, after having represented the United States at the 1977 World Championships, Reece hung up his pads for good.

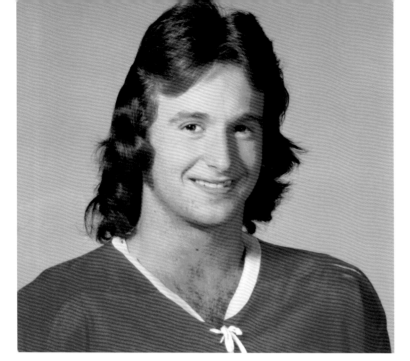

Ken Linseman as a member of the junior Kingston Canadians.

1977

KEN LINSEMAN TURNS THE DRAFT TABLES

THE ALL-TIME DRAFT

WHEN THE NHL lowered its age of draft eligibility to 18 in 1979, it was like telling teams they could suddenly mine gold in a previously undiscovered country. As such, the '79 draft is almost always cited as the best ever, with names like Mark Messier, Ray Bourque, Mike Gartner and Michel Goulet being called.

In all, 17 players from that draft appeared in at least 1,000 NHL games, and seven eclipsed the 1,000-point barrier. As the first draft with an eligibility age lower than 20, there were eight 18-year-olds selected and fifty-one 19-year-olds. Put another way, 47 percent of the 126 players chosen would have been ineligible for selection had the draft age stayed at 20.

The closest rival for the unofficial title of "Best Draft Ever" is the 2003 event, which saw the likes of Marc-Andre Fleury, Eric Staal, Jeff Carter, Ryan Getzlaf, Corey Perry and Patrice Bergeron selected.

Ken Linseman loved to push the envelope on the ice, which is how he got a nickname like "The Rat." Away from the rink, Linseman could be just as pushy, which wound up accelerating how young players jumped to professional hockey.

As a junior scoring star with his hometown Kingston Canadians in the late 1970s, Linseman, like many players before him, looked ready to play pro hockey even though he was a teenager. The problem, though, was that both the National Hockey League and World Hockey Association prevented players from being drafted until the year in which they turned 20. As such, Linseman wasn't eligible to be selected until 1978.

When the Birmingham Bulls ignored the rules and drafted Linseman in 1977 as a 19-year-old, the WHA ruled against the club's selection and maintained Linseman wasn't allowed to play in the league.

Having scored 53 goals and 127 points in 63 games for Kingston in 1976–77, Linseman was a dominant major junior player. Knowing the current rules would force him to return to Kingston for another season — where he made just $75 per week — Linseman was ready to fight for change. He launched a lawsuit against the WHA and agreed to a six-year, $500,000 contract with the Bulls, asserting there was no reason he shouldn't be able to earn the best living possible. The court agreed, and in the fall of 1977, Linseman was in the Birmingham lineup instead of back in Kingston kicking around teenage players.

"I was aware of the ramifications of what we were doing," Linseman later said of the lawsuit to *Sports Illustrated*. "For me, it made sense."

The next season, 1978–79, the Bulls (and a handful of other WHA clubs) were at it again. The WHA had been in negotiations to merge with the NHL, but those talks had slowed, so the Bulls began plucking the best 18-year-old talent from the junior ranks as a way to rankle the NHL and galvanize the merger talks.

The WHA folded at the conclusion of the 1978–79 season, and four teams merged into the NHL. Starting that spring, 18-year-olds were eligible to be selected in what was known as the NHL Entry Draft. One of the players with a 1961 birthday selected in 1979 was Mark Messier, taken 48th overall by the Edmonton Oilers. Messier had played a handful of games in the WHA as an underager, as had future Hall of Famers Michel Goulet and Mike Gartner.

Linseman, meanwhile, went on to play 860 NHL games during a career spent almost entirely with the Boston Bruins, Philadelphia Flyers and Edmonton. And despite the fact that he had some productive seasons with those clubs, there's little doubt his biggest impact on the sport occurred before he played a single professional game.

1977

—

MONTREAL'S UTTER DOMINANCE

In the spring of 1976, the Montreal Canadiens won a battle for hockey's soul. The following fall, the Habs set out to conquer everything that was left.

The Canadiens' Stanley Cup triumph in '76 came at the expense of the Philadelphia Flyers, who'd won the previous two championships with their rough-and-tumble style. Having wrested the silver mug away from the Broad Street Bullies with a dash of class, speed and unrelenting checking, Montreal's powerhouse team won one for the good guys and those who thought the Bullies had sullied the spirit of the game.

The next season, the recharged Canadiens found another gear. By almost any measure, Montreal's 1976–77 campaign is the most impressive season waged by an NHL team. While establishing records for both wins and points, the Canadiens dropped just a single game on home ice in 40 outings. Montreal's complete dominance of the league culminated with a satisfying sweep of the only squad that had managed to give it trouble.

For a team that ultimately put together hockey's all-time historic season, the Canadiens began 1976–77 in relatively modest fashion. They had finished first overall in each of the past two years, so expectations were high. While their 9-3-1 October record — which included the team's sole home loss, a 4–3 setback at the hands of the Boston Bruins — was nothing to complain about, it also wasn't a clear signal that this Montreal team was markedly better than other recent iterations.

As the months rolled by, however, the Canadiens pulled away from the league. On January 17, 1977, Montreal lost its seventh game overall and third of the season to the Bruins. At that point, the Canadiens had a 33-7-6 record (tie games ended after three periods, without an overtime) for an eye-popping .783 winning percentage. Then they got hot.

Montreal lost just one more time in its remaining 34 contests to establish a new NHL record for wins with 60, compared to just eight losses and 12 ties. (The 1995–96 Detroit Red Wings managed to best the mark by recording 62 wins in an 82-game schedule.) The Canadiens' winning percentage of .825 — also a record for any season

of 70-plus games — is an almost comical number, and their 132 points is an achievement that still stands.

"This isn't a complaint, but I didn't enjoy this last season very much," said Montreal's Ken Dryden during the playoffs following the historic season. "We had a great team and a great record, but there were an inordinate number of games which we won without even a reasonable amount of difficulty."

Dryden, the cerebral sort, continued, "There were moments when we'd win a game and you'd go into the dressing room and there would be a certain amount of emptiness … You become a little spoiled after a while, and maybe a little bored by the lack of challenges. There is a certain intensity missing."

It's no wonder he retired two seasons later.

Bored or not, Montreal's scorers continued to light the lamp. The club's goal differential of plus-216 was positively astounding, as the team led the league in both goals scored and fewest allowed. Leading the offensive charge was Guy Lafleur, who at age 25 had matured

BEST WINNING PERCENTAGE IN A 70-PLUS GAME SCHEDULE

1976–77	Montreal Canadiens	.825
1977–78	Montreal Canadiens	.806
1995–96	Detroit Red Wings	.799
1975–76	Montreal Canadiens	.794
1970–71	Boston Bruins	.763

Guy Lafleur holds both the Stanley Cup and the Conn Smyth Trophy after his Montreal Canadiens won the league championship following their record-setting season.

into the scoring star many had projected he would be when he was drafted in 1971. Lafleur registered a career-best 136 points en route to winning the scoring title and his first-ever Hart Trophy as league MVP. At the other end, goalies Dryden and Michel Larocque combined to record a 2.12 goals-against average.

As for the playoffs, the Canadiens were pushed in the semifinal by the New York Islanders, but they ultimately won the series in six games. That set up an odd final whereby a team that had set every record imaginable faced a foe who had actually gotten the better of it all year. Montreal went 2-3-0 versus Boston in the regular season, but they swept them in four games with the Cup on the line. The title-clinching goal came in overtime compliments of the hard-checking Jacques Lemaire, and the dominate Guy Lafleur was awarded the Conn Smythe Trophy as playoff MVP. It all provided a perfect exclamation point to conclude hockey's most impressive single-season showing.

1979

—

NHL-WHA MERGER

Though a couple seasons removed from their glory years of the late 1970s, the Montreal Canadiens were still a powerhouse team when the 1981 playoffs began. So when the Habs met the upstart Edmonton Oilers in a best-of-five first round series, nobody gave the Oilers — playing in just their second NHL season — much of a chance versus the league's longtime standard-bearers. But in a four-day blink of an eye, the youngsters from Edmonton blitzed Montreal, sweeping three straight games. It was the Oilers' first NHL postseason series win and an undeniable sign of change and validation in a fast-evolving league.

Edmonton's triumph shocked a hockey world that was already no stranger to unrest. Despite the fact that the NHL had grown from six to 14 teams between 1967 and 1972, WHA cofounders Gary Davidson and Dennis Murphy banked on there being more hockey talent to mine — and that some

existing stars would happily play on the moon if it meant meatier paychecks.

The new league began play in the 1972–73 campaign, and its biggest splash came when Bobby Hull — fresh off a 50-goal season with the Chicago Black Hawks — signed on to skate for the Winnipeg Jets, thanks in large part to a $1 million signing bonus. While that was far and away the most jolting shot across the bow, there was a lot of other roster raiding that angered the old guard in places like Toronto and especially Boston, who, after just winning the Stanley Cup, lost multiple players to higher salaries, including stars Gerry Cheevers and Derek Sanderson.

Cheevers, who made $45,000 in 1971–72 with the Bruins made more than 10 times that by signing with the Cleveland Crusaders.

"I'm leaving the best team in hockey," Cheevers told the *Akron Beacon Journal*. "The priorities came down to one thing — security for my family. I have some regrets about leaving Boston, but you have to sacrifice

some things if you want to be happy."

Further legitimizing the new circuit was Gordie Howe's decision to come out of retirement at 45 to play alongside sons Mark and Marty on the Houston Aeros for the WHA's second season. But even as the war for talent waged, some circles kicked around the notion of a settlement that would see hockey follow a larger trend in professional sports.

The National Football League and American Football League merged into one entity in the mid-60s, as did the National Basketball Association and American Basketball Association, also started by Davidson and Murphy, in the mid-70s. In both cases, getting all sides on the same page was a challenge, especially because of the natural power imbalance. Some people running teams in the established leagues wanted nothing to do with reconciliation, believing it would be akin to offering a helping hand to someone who had only recently declared war on you.

Vancouver's Gary Lupul charges toward Winnipeg's Bryan Hayward in 1983.

The potential for a deal became much more likely when John Ziegler replaced Clarence Campbell as president of the NHL in 1977. Campbell had run the league with an iron fist for decades and had derided the WHA at every turn: "The WHA isn't going to be with us very long," he told the *Cincinnati Enquirer* in 1974.

Removing Campbell from the equation allowed for a bit of a thaw in negotiations, and by the late-70s, a deal was inching closer and closer to completion, but the NHL's Canadian teams — Montreal, Toronto and Vancouver — weren't anxious to share the television revenues they received from *Hockey Night in Canada*, as would most certainly be the case if WHA cities like Edmonton, Winnipeg and Quebec City suddenly iced NHL teams.

When word leaked out that Canada's NHL clubs were against the deal and had voted down the proposed merger on March 8, 1979, fans in Canadian cities that also wanted a team boycotted Molson products. The tactic was geared specifically at hurting the Canadiens, who were owned by the Molson family, and it worked. Montreal and Vancouver changed their votes, and the merger was approved (with the pending sanction of the players' association).

"Our primary consideration in changing our vote was selling beer," said Canadiens president Jacques Courtois.

Not surprisingly, the conditions of the agreement benefited the larger league, and the move was treated more like an expansion than a merger. The four clubs making the transition — the Oilers, Jets, Quebec Nor-

diques and New England Whalers — all had to pay fees similar to those forked over by expansion teams that had joined the NHL in recent years.

And while previous newcomers were afforded picks at the top of the draft to jump-start the building process, the incoming WHA squads were placed in the bottom four slots of the 1979 draft board. They were allowed to protect up to two goalies and two skaters, but the rest of their roster was subject to being reclaimed by NHL outfits that had previously held the players' rights. As for NHLers made available in the expansion draft, most were either well past their prime or guys who struggled just to stay in the league. When the dust finally settled, Edmonton and Winnipeg joined the Smythe Division, Quebec became part of the Adams, and Hartford, which had

Quebec's Anton Stastny in action against the Montreal Canadiens at the Montreal Forum.

changed its name from New England, was folded into the Norris.

While none of the new clubs finished above .500 in their inaugural seasons, both Edmonton and Hartford made the playoffs under a format that saw 16 of 21 teams advance to the postseason. In addition, Edmonton's Wayne Gretzky, who had one WHA season on his résumé, tied Los Angeles Kings star Marcel Dionne for the league lead with 137 points, while Blaine Stoughton of the Whalers notched 56 goals, the same NHL-high total as Danny Gare of the Buffalo Sabres and the Kings' Charlie Simmer.

Though the quartet of fresh clubs was the most noticeable change to the NHL in 1979–80, there were also less-visible alterations tied to the WHA's legacy. While salaries had yet to explode, the competition introduced

by the WHA started a spike in player compensation and ultimately contributed to more frequent player movement via free agency. The idea of an organization holding a player's rights for the entirety of his career quickly became antiquated.

The search for skill also prompted the WHA to open its doors to Europeans. Some NHL clubs — like the Maple Leafs, who signed Swede Borje Salming — had broken down barriers, but the WHA was far more open to foreign players. Some of Hull's best years with the Jets came while skating beside Anders Hedberg and Ulf Nilsson, Swedes of positively sublime skill.

"No one I ever saw could handle the puck at high speed like [Hedberg] could," said Hull of his swift-skating Winnipeg linemate.

Players like Hedberg helped North Americans

understand hockey was a global game, and around the time of the merger, the NHL became a more viable option for European talent, prompting some Eastern Europeans, like Quebec's Peter Stastny, to take a huge gamble and defect from behind the Iron Curtain.

While the new clubs, predictably, had a hard time keeping up during their maiden voyages, things turned around quickly. Though Edmonton lost in the second round of the 1981 playoffs after defeating Montreal, the Oilers soon rose to the status of league power. By 1984, Edmonton was winning its first of five Stanley Cups in seven years. While no other club came close to matching what the Oilers achieved, the Nordiques, Jets and Whalers had all become competent outfits by the mid-80s.

Gordie Howe as a member of the Hartford Whalers in his final NHL season (1979–80).

In Hartford, players like Ron Francis, Ray Ferraro and Kevin Dineen carved out a respectable image for the team, while the Jets, behind stars Dale Hawerchuk, Paul MacLean and Thomas Steen, might have fared better had they not been competing in a stacked division with Edmonton and the Calgary Flames.

The Nordiques, meanwhile, offered a new and welcomed dimension to the league due to instant animosity with the Canadiens. Just as Montreal's rivalry with Toronto had begun to fade thanks to an unfavorable divisional alignment and the latter's inability to ice a true contender, a new, intense feud sprung up with its provincial foe. The Habs and Nords met four times in six playoff seasons between 1982 and 1987, and the visceral hate

witnessed in the stands and on the ice matched anything seen in the history of hockey.

Unfortunately, Quebec was also the first of the four WHA teams to experience real turbulence. The team faltered badly in the late-80s and, just as a string of high draft picks had it poised to rise, owner Marcel Aubut sold the club. In 1995–96, the Nordiques became the Colorado Avalanche and — most painfully for those francophone fans left behind — won the Stanley Cup during their first season in Denver.

One year later, the Jets were saying goodbye to Winnipeg, bound for a new life as the Coyotes in Arizona. And, finally, one year after that, the Whalers became the Carolina Hurricanes, where the franchise was able to reach the top of the mountain by beating

their old WHA cousins, the Oilers, in the 2006 Cup final.

While Edmonton is the only WHA team that hasn't moved since the merger, NHL hockey returned to Winnipeg in 2011, when the Jets were, in a sense, repatriated by the Atlanta Thrashers moving north. As for Quebec City, it remains a huge part of any conversation about additional expansion or relocation.

Regardless of whether NHL hockey returns to Quebec City, the WHA's reverberations can be felt more than 35 years after hockey's great splice. Much of the modifications that came about because of the smaller league would have been introduced eventually, but there's no doubt that the WHA's existence expedited all kinds of critical changes.

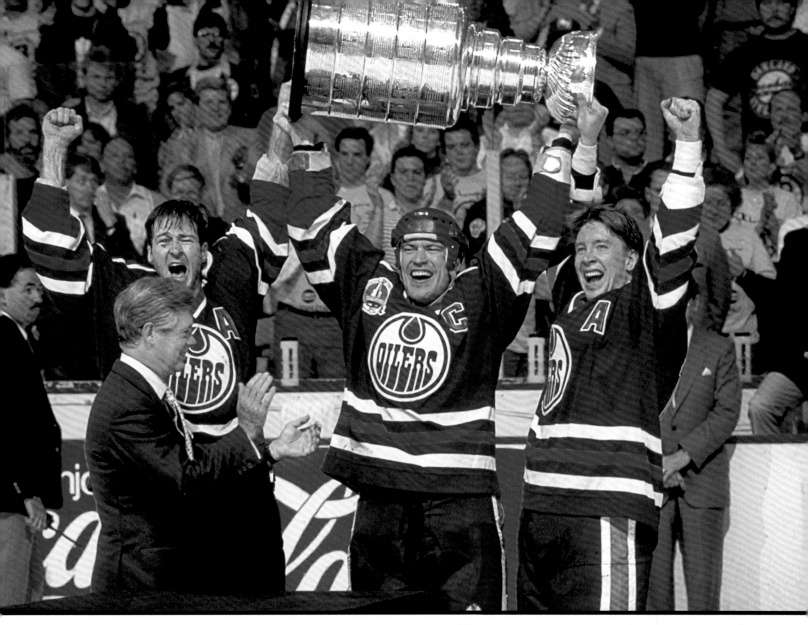

Left to right: Kevin Lowe, NHL president John Ziegler, captain Mark Messier and Jari Kurri hoist the Stanley Cup after Game 5 of the 1990 Stanley Cup final.

1979 DRAFT BONANZA

NOT MUCH ABOUT the conditions related to the NHL-WHA merger were favorable for the four teams entering the established league, but the Edmonton Oilers, Winnipeg Jets, Harford Whalers and Quebec Nordiques did catch one break.

Dovetailing with the new clubs' arrival was the decision to lower the age of eligibility for the annual draft from 20 to 18. While labor law was largely driving the move, it also made sense to have more players available in a year when the league was growing substantially. As such, a cornucopia of young talent was available when the teams gathered at the Queen Elizabeth hotel in Montreal.

Despite being placed at the bottom of the draft order, the Nordiques and Oilers — with the 20th and 21st picks — found first-round gems in

Michel Goulet (Quebec) and Kevin Lowe (Edmonton). The lowering of the draft age wound up being critical for Edmonton, which selected 18-year-old Mark Messier 48th overall after he had played 52 games for three WHA teams the preceding winter. Like Lowe and Glenn Anderson, drafted 69th overall that same year, Messier was an integral member of the Oilers dynasty and the last NHLer to have skated in the WHA when he retired in 2004.

As impressive as Edmonton's haul was, the real coup surrounded the team's ability to keep one of its existing players out of the draft. Like Messier, Wayne Gretzky was born in 1961, making him eligible for selection. However, Gretzky and the Oilers successfully leveraged a technicality to keep him away from other teams.

Because Gretzky was signed to a personal-services contract that tied him specifically to Edmonton owner Peter Pocklington, the franchise swung a deal whereby Gretzky remained an Oiler in exchange for the club being placed at the very bottom of the draft ladder.

Though none of the other three teams — particularly Hartford — had nearly as much success as the Oilers, some key decisions were made at that initial draft. After nabbing Goulet, the Nordiques also grabbed thorny Dale Hunter and slick Anton Stastny, two linchpins of their successful mid-80s teams. Winnipeg also continued its tradition of being a landing spot for Swedish players, choosing franchise stalwart Thomas Steen with the 103rd pick in the draft.

Bob Nystrom is mobbed by his
teammates after scoring the Stanley
Cup–winning goal in the 1980 final.

1980

ISLANDERS DYNASTY BEGINS

The New York Islanders won the Stanley Cup in an instant, but it took years of growth and pain for the club to finally become champions. The Islanders dynasty arrived in dramatic fashion, with Bob Nystrom tipping home a John Tonelli pass in overtime of Game 6 to win the 1980 final. Of course, the hockey world didn't know at the time that New York, led by the young core of captain Denis Potvin, gritty center Bryan Trottier and scoring right-winger Mike Bossy, was going to emerge as league champs in each of the next three years.

People did know, however, that the Isles had paid their dues and more before the long-term vision of GM Bill Torrey and coach Al Arbour finally came to fruition.

The Islanders began playing as an expansion franchise during the 1972–73 season and experienced predictable struggles. The team won just 31 of 156 games during its first two campaigns, but things started to turn around in their third year. By that point, Torrey, who had hired Arbour as coach in the club's second season, had already drafted Potvin, Trottier and a number of key support players like Nystrom and Clark Gillies.

In 1977, when Torrey stole Bossy with the 15th overall pick, the Islanders had already become a regular-season power but had failed to punch through in the playoffs. After being upset by their archrivals, the New York Rangers, in the 1979 semifinal, it was clear the Isles still lacked a certain something.

That missing piece came in the form of veteran two-way center Butch Goring, acquired by Torrey from the Los Angeles Kings before the 1980 trade deadline.

"In the past we didn't have what it took," said Torrey before the 1980 final began. "We analyzed our weaknesses and went out and did something about it."

With Goring the Isles had the grit needed to finally break through, beating a strong Philadelphia Flyers team for their first Stanley Cup. And they were just getting started.

In the following seasons, the Islanders established themselves as one of the most durable dynasties sports has ever known. They were a perfect blend of strength and skill, backstopped by clutch goaltender Billy Smith. In 1983, after beating the upstart Minnesota North Stars and Vancouver Canucks in the previous two finals, New York downed the Edmonton Oilers to win its fourth consecutive championship.

It wasn't until the following spring that Wayne Gretzky and his teammates were finally able to topple the grizzled champs. Still, in the course of winning four straight titles and then advancing to one more final, the Isles set a North American pro sports record that will likely never be broken by claiming 19 consecutive playoff series. So while the winning took a little time to come, the legacy of what they ultimately accomplished will last for generations.

JOY AND PAIN

FOR A WHILE, it seemed like the party might never end on Long Island. But when it finally did, the hangover was awful. For as great as the New York Islanders were in the early 1980s — and you could easily argue no club ever did it better — the team's fans have endured more than their share of hardship since the glory days.

While the Isles remained a competitive squad in the back half of the '80s, things turned ugly, and downright farcical, at times during the '90s and early 2000s. Terrible trades and ownership instability plagued the once-proud franchise. In 2015–16, they began playing in Brooklyn after years of unsuccessful attempts to get a state-of-the-art arena built on Long Island.

The new chapter kicked off with the franchise still in search of its first playoff series victory since a miracle run to the 1993 conference final. After all the misery that's swirled around the team during the past couple of decades, there's finally legitimate hope as captain John Tavares and his increasingly strong support have restored the club's credibility, ridding themselves of the 23-year playoff stalemate by dispatching the Florida Panthers on home ice in Game 6 of Round 1 in 2016.

1980

—

PETER STASTNY DEFECTS

Peter Stastny is one of the precious few who can say that they were among the top two or three players in the game for an entire decade. But that would not have been possible had he not been a member of another small group of players, ones who risked everything to play in the NHL.

The world first got a look at Stastny when, on the eve of his 20th birthday, he suited up for Czechoslovakia at the 1976 Canada Cup. Living in a country that fell under Soviet rule meant Stastny's playing options were limited. It also meant that on international trips, he was under surveillance by government agencies.

"He was the youngest player at the 1976 Canada Cup and I had seen him play a lot in the 1980 Olympics," Gilles Léger, director of player personnel for the NHL's Quebec Nordiques, said of scouting Stastny. "I tried to talk to him in Lake Placid but we felt he was being followed, so I had my own people, inside, talking to him."

That prompted Stastny to take a huge risk, choosing to defect with his brother Anton from Czechoslovakia to Canada before the 1980–81 season.

Léger knew getting the brothers to Canada was risky but that it could be done. He was the man responsible for hockey's first defection, having helped spring Czech star Vaclav Nedomansky, "Big Ned," from the Soviet-controlled country in 1974 to join the WHA's Toronto Toros. Big Ned, however, was a veteran star, whereas Peter and Anton were entering their prime.

In Innsbruck, Austria, in August of 1980

for a series of games against Finland and the USSR, Stastny made his way undetected to a post office to call Léger and tell him of his desire to defect. The next day Léger and Nords owner Marcel Aubut were in Austria and conducting cloak-and-dagger meetings with the brothers to arrange a contract and a plan.

As the brothers were whisked by car to Vienna (with a driver sometimes described as a Canadian spy), the Canadian embassy was alerted of the plan. Czech authorities caught up to the Stastnys, however, though they ultimately failed to keep them — along with Peter's pregnant wife, Darina — off the plane to Montreal.

A year later, after suffering many sanctions to his hockey and home life, their older brother, Marian, also took the leap.

When Peter and Anton joined Quebec,

Sitting, from left to right, are Marion, Peter and Anton Stastny.

Peter Stastny skates against the Philadelphia Flyers in the mid-1980s.

the franchise was entering its second season in the NHL following the merger with the World Hockey Association. With the foreign arrivals and team both attempting to gain some traction, Peter led all rookies with 109 points in 77 games to win the Calder Trophy. In his second season, Stastny took things to another level, finishing with 46 goals and 139 points in 80 games. That spring, the Nords were one of the biggest stories of the 1982 playoffs. Not only did they gain their first-ever NHL postseason series victory by upsetting the Montreal Canadiens, they also scored a win in Round 2, advancing all the way to the Wales Conference final before being ousted by the powerhouse New York Islanders. Stastny netted a team-leading 18 points in just 12 playoff contests.

As the decade wore on, the Nords continued to be a very competitive club. In the 1985 playoffs, Stastny had, perhaps, his signature on-ice moment when he scored in overtime of Game 7 to eliminate the hated Habs in the Adams Division final. Once again within spitting distance of playing for the Cup, the Nordiques fought the Philadelphia Flyers hard in the conference final but ultimately succumbed in six games.

When play resumed the next fall, Stastny was Quebec's captain. Though Swede Lars-Erik Sjoberg wore the C for the Winnipeg Jets during their inaugural NHL campaign, Stastny's more daring journey to North America and the fact that he was one of the best players of his generation combined to make his appointment more of a watershed moment. By the late '80s, Czechoslovakians were becoming more common in the NHL, and there's little doubt Stastny, who finished the decade with more points than everybody except Wayne Gretzky, played a huge role in making the dream of pro hockey seem like a possibility for players behind the Iron Curtain.

"Europeans playing in the National Hockey League today should never forget the major role Peter Stastny played in opening the doors," said former NHL coach Jacques Demers.

Stastny's final NHL days were spent with the St. Louis Blues, the team his son, Paul, now plays for. The junior Stastny has carved out his own reputation as a quality NHLer competing in a league that, thanks to people like his dad, is populated with fantastic players from all over the planet.

STASTNY'S COLORFUL INTERNATIONAL CAREER

LIKE MANY GREAT NHLers, Peter Stastny also had notable performances on the international stage. What sets him apart, though, is the number of countries he represented at various tournaments. After suiting up for Czechoslovakia during the 1976 Canada Cup, Stastny then represented Canada at the same event in 1984. Following the fall of communism and the splintering of Czechoslovakia, Stastny had the honor of skating for his homeland, Slovakia, at the 1994 Olympics. Despite being 38 years old, Stastny had a fantastic tournament, potting five goals and nine points in eight games while wearing the C for his country.

BOSSY NETS SECOND-EVER 50 IN 50

Mike Bossy scored his record-tying 50th goal on this shot in 1981.

Mike Bossy knew how to play hardball. He also possessed, as his signature season proved, a flair for the dramatic.

Bossy was already an established sniper with the New York Islanders when, in 1980–81, he joined Montreal Canadiens legend Maurice Richard as the only player to score 50 goals in his team's first 50 games. Reaching that elite standard required some late-game heroics, but — as most opposing teams learned the hard way — when it came to burying the puck, it was best never to doubt Bossy's abilities.

Before he hit the NHL big-time, even people who had a vested interest in Bossy's success expressed hesitation over what exactly he could do. A scoring sensation in the Quebec Major Junior League, Bossy was drafted 15th overall by the Islanders just as the team was turning into a league power in 1977. Bossy reportedly dug into his first contract negotiations the way he might plant his feet in the slot, telling Islanders GM Bill Torrey his offer wasn't appropriate for somebody who was going to score 50 goals. Torrey agreed, with the caveat that Bossy, as an

NHL rookie, didn't fit that description and would do well to net 25 or 30. As it turned out, the precocious player's assessment — not the experienced hockey man's — was bang on the money.

After establishing a new league record with 53 goals as a freshman in 1977–78, Bossy took things to another level in his second year, netting an NHL-best 69 goals. By his fourth season, Bossy was the premier goal-scorer in the NHL, and the Islanders were embarking on a dynastic run.

But Bossy had his own fireworks planned. Before the start of the season he confided to friends that he thought he could match the Rocket's record. Through 49 contests in the 1980–81 season, Bossy hit the back of the net 48 times. The Isles' 50th contest, on January 24, 1981, was at home versus the Quebec Nordiques. With fewer than five minutes remaining in the game, Bossy still hadn't found the range. In fact, he hadn't even registered a shot on goalie Ron Grahame through two periods.

"I was a little sorry in the third period," Bossy said after the game. "I thought, 'If I don't get it maybe I talked once too much.' "

But just minutes from seeing his chance at history evaporate, Bossy managed to slip a backhander past Grahame for goal No. 49. Then, lurking on his off wing just below the face-off dot, Bossy one-timed a pass from Bryan Trottier to reach the magical benchmark.

"When that 50th one went in, it was one of the happiest moments of my life," Bossy said. "I was really hurting inside before that. I didn't want to disappoint myself or anyone I told I would do it."

And Bossy didn't stop scoring.

Bossy's 50-in-50 season was the fourth consecutive year since entering the league that he'd managed to hit the 50-goal mark. Just as the Islanders continued winning Cups — four straight from 1980 to 1983 — notching 50 goals became routine for Bossy, who reached that total in a record-setting nine straight seasons. Only in his 10th campaign, felled by a back injury that forced his premature retirement, did Bossy fall short of 50 goals.

By that point, the conversation had long shifted from how many goals he could score at the NHL level to whether anybody in the history of the game did it better.

Mike Bossy celebrates tying Maurice Richard's 50-game goal record.

BEST GOAL-SCORERS IN THE MODERN ERA

PLAYER	CAREER GOALS PER GAME	GAMES PLAYED
Mike Bossy	0.76	752
Mario Lemieux	0.75	915
Pavel Bure	0.62	702
Alex Ovechkin*	0.61	921*
Wayne Greztky	0.60	1,487
Brett Hull	0.58	1,269
Bobby Hull	0.57	1,063
Tim Kerr	0.57	655
Rick Martin	0.56	685
Phil Esposito	0.56	1,282
Maurice Richard	0.56	978

Player is still active.

1981

—

GRETZKY DESTROYS 50-GAME GOAL RECORD

Through 37 games, Wayne Gretzky resembled your average, unbelievable superstar. Then, for two games, he started playing like he was from another planet.

Gretzky started the 1981–82 season, his third in the NHL, with 41 goals in 37 games. That put him on pace to join Montreal Canadiens legend Maurice Richard and Gretzky's contemporary, New York Islanders sniper Mike Bossy, as the only players in the history of hockey to reach 50 goals in their team's first 50 contests.

But Gretzky being Gretzky, he wasn't happy merely setting a record. Instead, he absolutely smashed the precedent. Both Richard and Bossy required the full 50 games, and each waited until late in the third period to get their 50th goals. Gretzky did the unthinkable, hitting the half-century mark in his 39th outing.

The Oilers' 38th date of the season came at home versus the Los Angeles Kings. Gretzky opened the scoring less than two minutes into the contest and added another tally before the first period concluded. Gretzky's next two goals were of the shorthanded variety, as Edmonton stomped the Kings 10–3.

One night before the calendar flipped to 1982, the Oilers hosted the Philadelphia Flyers. Gretzky — now with 45 goals for the season — once again went to work early, parking himself at the right side of the Flyers crease, where he was in perfect position to gather a point shot that slammed off the backboards and deposit it in the cage. The next three goals Gretzky put past Philly puckstopper Pete Peeters served to illustrate an often-overlooked aspect of his repertoire: he could really shoot the puck. On goal number two, the Great One cut hard to the middle, cocked his signature red-and-white Titan and blasted a laser past Peeters' glove and just under the crossbar.

After a couple more slappers, Gretzky sat one goal from 50. His team, though, was up 6–3 on the Flyers with fewer than 15 minutes to play in the third. Had the score stayed that way, or had somebody else on Edmonton netted a goal, the NHL may have missed out on a magical night. However, Philadelphia tallies that occurred just 17 seconds apart set the stage for an empty-net scenario late in the game.

With Peeters on the bench in favor of a sixth attacker, Gretzky picked up the puck near his own blue line and burst through the neutral zone. Once at the Flyers line, Gretzky slid home goal number five of the game and 50 during a season that hadn't yet reached its halfway point.

"Any superlatives that I might suggest would be inadequate after a performance like that," Philadelphia coach Pat Quinn told the Associated Press.

Just a few days earlier, the notion anybody — even Gretzky — would require fewer than 40 games to score 50 times was unthinkable. Now, the only thing that's hard to believe is that any player, in any era, will ever even approach Gretzky's standard.

FASTEST TO REACH 50

Player	Number of Games	Season
Wayne Gretzky	39	1981-82
Wayne Gretzky	42	1983-84
Mario Lemieux	46	1988-89
Wayne Gretzky	49	1984-85
Maurice Richard	50	1944-45
Mike Bossy	50	1980-81
Brett Hull	50	1990-91
Brett Hull	50	1991-92

Wayne Gretzky, with his signature
red-and-white Titan stick,
in the early 1980s.

1982

ILITCH FAMILY
SAVES WINGS

The once-mighty Detroit Red Wings had been floundering for nearly two decades when pizza-baron Mike Ilitch rode to the rescue.

When Ilitch purchased the team from Bruce Norris for $8 million on June 7, 1982, the Wings had won only one playoff series since 1966. They'd missed postseason play in 14 of the previous 16 seasons.

Turning around this sinking ship wouldn't be easy. Everyone in the Ilitch family rolled up their sleeves and got to work. Co-owner Marian Ilitch remembered when she and her husband first broke the news of the purchase to their children.

"They said, 'is this ever glamorous,'" she recalled. "And I said, 'I'll show you how glamorous it is.'"

She took her kids to Joe Louis Arena and told them to work the phones and sell season tickets.

Mike Ilitch (who died on February 10, 2017) used the wealth from his Little Caesars Pizza chain to acquire top coaches, players and management. By 1987 the Wings were in the Western Conference final, and a decade later they were Stanley Cup champions for the first time since 1955.

"We worked our way out of the quicksand and back on the road," Mike Ilitch said. "Then we saw how good it felt to put the top down and cruise along."

Today, the Wings are considered the model NHL franchise.

"It's most gratifying to have had a little part in taking a franchise that was one of the worst in the NHL, setting out without a real game plan or anything and turning it into a successful franchise," Mike Ilitch said.

1984

OILERS END ONE DYNASTY AND START ANOTHER

Having just lost the 1983 Stanley Cup final in four games to the New York Islanders, Wayne Gretzky and a few of his young Edmonton Oilers teammates had to endure a little more ignominy before they could leave the Nassau County Coliseum.

In order to exit the Islanders' home rink, the Oilers had to pass by the New York dressing room, where they expected to see the players who'd just swept them living it up. As Gretzky and his teammates tried to slide by, they couldn't help but notice that it was the people wearing suits who were driving the jubilation. Everyone who'd been on the ice was still half dressed in hockey equipment, wearily savoring a well-earned beer. That revealing snapshot may have served as the final piece of Edmonton's own championship puzzle.

Gretzky has cited the Islanders' celebration numerous times when he's talked about realizing what it would take for his team to get on top. Edmonton had fast emerged as a league power in the early 1980s, but it wasn't until seeing how depleted the New York club — which in '83 had won its fourth-consecutive championship — was after the victory that the high-flying Alberta boys precisely understood the premium each player must pay to win it all.

Losing to the Isles wasn't the first hard lesson for Gretzky and company, however. In 1982, Edmonton had played a second-round series versus a Los Angeles Kings team it had outstripped in the regular season by 48 points. In Game 3, the Oilers gagged on a 5–0 third-period lead, losing to the Kings in overtime. Los Angeles went on to claim the best-of-five series in the fifth game, injecting a serious dose of humility into the cocky Oilers.

By 1984, though, it was going to take something truly special to thwart the Oilers.

As it turned out, there was something unique on the line as New York once again made the final and was attempting to become just the second team ever to win five straight titles. The Oilers squeaked out a 1–0 win in Game 1, but before leaving Long Island, the home side clobbered Edmonton 6–1 in Game 2 to square the proceedings.

Any doubts about where the series was headed, however, were quickly erased once it moved north. Playing under the 2-3-2 series format, the Oilers had the benefit of three consecutive home games and won them by a combined score of 19–6 to secure their first title.

"I've been fearing this club for three years," Islanders coach Al Arbour told the Associated Press following the Islanders' first playoff series loss after 19 straight series wins.

With 13 goals and 35 points in 19 games, Gretzky led the league in playoff scoring, while two-way force Mark Messier won the Conn Smythe as postseason MVP. All both men cared about, though, was finally getting their hands on the Cup that had for so long eluded their grasp.

1985

KURRI, NOT GRETZKY, TIES PLAYOFF GOAL RECORD

Jari Kurri looks up ice in the mid-1980s.

When the 1985 playoffs rolled around, it was Jari Kurri's time to shine.

Having won their first Stanley Cup the previous season by dethroning the New York Islanders, the Edmonton Oilers were clear favorites to claim the mug again in 1985. But the way Edmonton tore through the postseason — registering a 15–3 mark — let everybody know the hotshot kids from out west were for real.

Leading the way from a goal-scoring standpoint was Kurri, who tied a record previously set by Reggie "The Rifle" Leach with 19 playoff goals. To be fair, Leach notched his 19 tallies in just 16 games while leading the Philadelphia Flyers to a Cup final appearance in 1976. Kurri may have needed a couple more contests to reach his total, but it was a staggering feat nonetheless. Of the 19 times Kurri bent the twine during Edmonton's romp to the Cup, 16 goals came at even strength, with one occurring on the power play and another two coming shorthanded.

Kurri's goal-scoring feat also included a remarkable performance in the conference final. In the six-game win over the Chicago Black Hawks, Kurri scored 12 times, setting the single series record for goals. Even more spectacular: he had three separate hat tricks in the series, breaking the record of two, first set in 1944.

In addition to being deadly around the net, Kurri was also a whiz defensively, making him one of coach Glen Sather's most trusted — and sometimes lethal — penalty-killers.

Unlike Leach, Kurri did not win playoff MVP honors in his big postseason, thanks to the fact that his center, Wayne Gretzky, posted an incredible 47 points in 18 contests to claim the Conn Smythe. What Kurri did do — along with his outrageously talented linemate — was end any shred of doubt about whether he and the Oilers were a force to be reckoned with.

1985

GRETZKY QUIETLY SETS NEW SCORING MARK

Ask any hockey fan about Wayne Gretzky's finest achievements, and you'll soon hear talk of 50 goals in 39 games or earning points in 51 straight contests to start a season. What may not immediately come up are his exploits during the 1985–86 campaign. That's because, incredible as it seems, Gretzky's most productive season in the NHL sometimes gets a little lost in the shuffle.

Gretzky is linked to more all-time NHL moments than any other player because he holds essentially all of the high-profile records, but also because he set more than a few of them in dramatic fashion.

The Great One scored five goals in one game to get to 50 goals in 39 games during the 1981–82 season. He equaled then broke Gordie Howe's all-time scoring record as a member of the Los Angeles Kings playing in Edmonton against his old team, the Oilers. But Gretzky's 215-point campaign was, relatively speaking, put together without a signature moment.

By the fall of 1985, Gretzky had six NHL seasons under his belt, and if he had decided to retire from the game at age 24, he would have likely gone straight into the Hall of Fame. Gretzky had won MVP honors every year since entering the league, hadn't scored fewer than 71 goals in each of the past four seasons and had three 200-point campaigns on his résumé.

"His points are out of touch," Marcel Dionne noted in 1985. "The old guys who complain about him couldn't carry his jockstrap."

While many were spellbound by his artistry, there may have been a little Gretzky fatigue by the mid-1980s. In some ways,

Wayne Gretzky watches the action from the bench in the early 1980s.

Wayne Gretzky celebrates during the 1984 Stanley Cup final.

he was a victim of his own unimaginable success, having made the ridiculous realistic with his video-gamelike dominance.

But while the 1985–86 season may not always get its due in the pantheon of Gretzky's great moments, it could be argued no stretch of play more accurately reflects what the Great One was all about: playmaking. The year prior, Gretzky had set a new league mark with 135 helpers. In 1985–86, Edmonton's captain bettered that mark by almost 30 assists, finishing the year with 163. The biggest beneficiary of Gretzky's largesse was Jari Kurri, who'd netted a career-best 71 goals in 1984–85 then led the league with 68 in 1985–86. In doing so, Kurri became the first person not named Wayne Gretzky to lead the Oilers in goals since the latter had entered the league.

Another event that may have taken some of the spotlight away from Gretzky was teammate Paul Coffey's pursuit of Bobby Orr's record for goals by a defenseman. The fleet-footed Coffey managed to eclipse Orr's mark of 46 tallies by netting 48, narrowly missing out on a 50-goal season from the blue line.

When the dust settled, Edmonton finished with a .744 winning percentage, equaling the franchise-best mark set in 1983–84. That year, the Oilers went on to win their first championship, and nobody in the league thought Edmonton would do anything other than claim its third consecutive title in 1986. However, in one of the most galling defeats in the history of hockey, the Oilers lost Game 7 of the Smythe Division final on home ice to the Calgary Flames. The visitors went ahead in the third period when Edmonton defenseman Steve Smith inadvertently banked a clearing pass off the skate of goalie Grant Fuhr and into his own net.

When the season ended, people tended to talk more about the spectacular manner in which Edmonton's dynasty was derailed rather than what may have felt like just another otherworldly season from Gretzky. As it turned out, he never again reached 200 points, so there's all the more reason to appreciate how special his final trip there was.

GRETZKY'S PRIME

ANY WAY YOU view Wayne Gretzky's numbers, it's an eye-popping experience. But when you zoom in on his prime, No. 99's stat line is almost too much to take in. Gretzky's best seasons came between 1981–82 and 1986–87. During those six campaigns, Gretzky netted 1,219 points in 473 games for an average of 2.6 per contest. The Great One very nearly registered a goal per game in that stretch, scoring 437 times for a 0.92 nightly output. By comparison, the second-most prolific scorer in those six years was Mike Bossy of the New York Islanders. Bossy recorded 698 points in that time — barely half of what Gretzky put up.

1987

HEXTALL SCORES

Ron Hextall displays the shooting ability that made him famous in 1987.

The question was probably never going to be asked, but Ron Hextall already had the answer.

Speaking to reporters in Philadelphia after becoming the first goalie to shoot on net and score, Hextall — a player more often associated with anger than humor — quipped, "Before you guys say anything, I was aiming for that corner."

In addition to learning about Hextall's lighter side that night, the hockey world also, for the first time, saw that it was possible for goalies to get their offense on. Yes, other puckstoppers had been credited with goals

before, but that was based on being the last player to touch the puck before something went horribly wrong for the team that was scored on.

This was entirely different.

Hextall was a second-year NHLer on the December 1987 night when he scored against the Boston Bruins. During a sensational rookie season in which he had won both the Vezina and Conn Smythe Trophies — and also carved out a reputation for chopping down people with his goal stick — the Flyers goalie showed a willingness to leave his net and play the puck beyond anything that had

been seen before. It was only a matter of time before he scored.

With Bruins goalie Reggie Lemelin on the bench in favor of a sixth attacker, Hextall fielded a dump-in that bounced just to his left. After quickly settling the puck, the 6-foot-3 masked man fired the puck toward the gaping net, landing a roughly 185-foot shot just inside the right post.

The home fans went crazy, the Flyers mobbed their unlikely sniper, and hockey officially had a new type of scoring play.

EDMONTON STARTS A STANLEY CUP TRADITION

The Edmonton Oilers had barely beaten the Boston Bruins in the 1988 Stanley Cup final when Wayne Gretzky started riding his teammates. Hard. And it wasn't just the players he was after. Coaches, management, equipment staff, everybody was being urged by Gretzky to gather together at center ice for an impromptu photo.

Given Gretzky's off-the-charts hockey sense, it's possible he knew change was in the air when he implored everybody associated with the Oilers to come together after Edmonton's fourth championship in five years.

A few months later, Gretzky was traded to the Los Angeles Kings in the biggest deal in hockey history. But while Gretzky's time in Edmonton was coming to an end, the on-ice photo he had arranged instantly became a cherished tradition.

Because Oilers owner Peter Pocklington was known to be in financial trouble, whispers were already swirling during the 1988 final about what kind of mega-move might

happen in the summer. Edmonton, stocked with players who had grown up together and who were still largely in their mid to late 20s, was an extremely tight group. Today, there's almost a bittersweet element to the celebratory photo.

The ecstatic, youthful faces convey a sense of pure joy, but one feels an undeniable pang of sadness when looking at No. 99 alongside his talented teammates and wondering what might have been had they all stayed together.

As for the other 25-plus similar photos that adorn rec room walls around the world, the feelings associated with them are pretty pure. The on-ice photo, when the players are still sweating from their hard-earned victory, captures people in a moment that represents the realization of a childhood dream.

Regardless of what happens next, though, there's always evidence of everything being right that night. Rings may shine, but the smiles in those photos tell the real story of what it's like to win the Cup.

GRETZKY'S BEST PASS

WAYNE GRETZKY MADE a lot of great passes in his NHL career, but his most meaningful one may have come with his gloves off and his stick laying flat on the ice.

In 1987 — one year before Gretzky started the championship photo trend — the Edmonton Oilers were celebrating their third title in four years. That win may have represented the team's fourth straight Stanley Cup had rookie Steve Smith not banked a clearing pass off goalie Grant Fuhr for the winning goal in Game 7 versus the Calgary Flames in the 1986 Smythe Division final. Knowing full well how that moment had tormented Smith, Gretzky — right after taking the cup from NHL president John Ziegler in '87 — found the steady Oilers defenseman and handed him the silver mug. Every player who touches the Cup for the first time is thrilled, but in the case of Smith, it's hard to imagine there's ever been a happier person on the planet.

Gretzky is all smiles as he is announced as a member of the Los Angeles Kings.

1988

THE TRADE

The corks had barely popped on the Edmonton Oilers' 1988 Stanley Cup celebration when Wayne Gretzky heard some sobering news.

The day after Edmonton won its fourth championship in five years, Gretzky received a phone call informing him he could soon be on the move. That was the start of a summer-long saga — mostly played out behind closed doors — until the day Gretzky, while dabbing away tears, told a city and country the whispers were true: the best player ever to pick up a stick was leaving Canada's heartland for the Hollywood Hills.

The fallout from the Gretzky trade was fierce and lasting. But in the moment, what Edmontonians felt — along with many other Canadians — was a sense of loss and betrayal. While the Oilers painted the move as a hockey transaction, everybody understood cold, hard dollars were the driving force behind the deal.

Regardless, the hockey landscape underwent a monumental shift on August 9, 1988, one with reverberations so great they can still be felt today.

The phone call Gretzky got in the immediate aftermath of Edmonton's triumph came from Nelson Skalbania, the businessman who'd originally signed Gretzky to play in the WHL. He indicated he was on the verge of buying the Vancouver Canucks and claimed Oilers owner Peter Pocklington was willing to sell Gretzky to address money problems. While nothing came of Gretzky moving to Vancouver, a new, forceful contender for Gretzky's services emerged in the form of Los Angeles Kings owner Bruce McNall. The big move from McNall came at the NHL Awards, when after a few weeks of prodding Pocklington, the former told the latter he'd pony up $15 million, plus players and draft picks, for Gretzky's services.

For his part, Gretzky had married American actress Janet Jones that summer, with all the pomp and circumstance of a royal wedding. The notion of playing for the Kings, once unthinkable, was beginning to hold more appeal, especially as the whole process prompted Gretzky to start viewing Pocklington in a different light.

With the deal all but done and ready to be presented to the public, Pocklington and Oilers GM Glen Sather — who at one point was willing to resign over the whole ordeal — pulled Gretzky aside and said if he really didn't want to go through with it, the trade could still be killed. The horse, though, was out of the barn, and Gretzky went in front of a room full of cameras at Molson House in Edmonton to say good-bye to the city and fans he'd delighted for nine seasons.

Northern Alberta's loss, however, wasn't just Los Angeles' gain. Hockey itself obtained a huge foothold in a previously untapped territory the moment Gretzky made the game cool in California. Nearly 30 years after the trade, the state is home to three quality NHL clubs — to say nothing of the "Sunbelt expansion" in other parts of the U.S. — and an ever-growing number of youngsters who've played the sport all their lives.

It's quite a legacy for Gretzky, even if a small, nagging pain still lingers in Edmonton.

1988

—

MARIO GOES FIVE WAYS

It's been said of many great players that they can beat you any way they want, but the only one to actually prove it in a single game is Mario Lemieux.

By the late 1980s, Lemieux was wresting the mantle of "World's Greatest Player" from Wayne Gretzky. In 1987–88, Lemieux broke Gretzky's streak of eight consecutive Hart Trophies when he was named league MVP.

The next season, he pushed the 200-point barrier while emerging as the most dominant force in hockey.

Right from his first NHL shift, Lemieux exuded greatness. Playing in the Boston Garden, Lemieux blocked a Ray Bourque shot, streaked in alone on Pete Peeters and juked to his backhand before burying the puck. Lemieux went on to record 43 goals and 100

points as an NHL rookie in 1984–85, living up to his billing as the best first overall draft pick since Guy Lafleur in 1971. The Penguins, however, were terrible. It wasn't until the 1988–89 campaign that Pittsburgh truly became relevant, and Lemieux's brilliance made Penguins hockey appointment viewing.

Exhibit A came on December 31, 1988, when Lemieux put on a New Year's Eve

show for the ages. Playing the New Jersey Devils, Le Magnifique posted eight points, including five goals scored in five distinct ways: even strength, shorthanded, power play, penalty shot and empty net. On his first goal, Lemieux's centering pass deflected off a Devils defenseman past Devils goalie Bob Sauvé. The next goal, however, was all skill. With his team down a man, Lemieux made a beautiful inside-out deke on forward Aaron Broten then slipped a backhander past Sauvé.

New Jersey's Kirk Muller, who had tied the game 2–2 before 10 minutes had elapsed in the first period, was in the box when Lemieux netted his third goal. The Penguins' 5-on-3 advantage allowed Lemieux all kinds of room to operate at the left circle, where power play quarterback Paul Coffey set him up with a dish he hammered home to complete a first-period hat trick.

Before the second period was 60 seconds old, Lemieux sent a pass to Rob Brown that the winger easily converted. That assist gave Lemieux 100 points in just the 38th game of the season. Later in the frame, Lemieux was awarded a penalty shot after it was determined that Devils goalie Chris Terreri — who'd replaced Sauvé — threw his stick. With the Penguins fans standing and roaring, No. 66 swooped in on Terreri, made a quick move to his forehand and whipped the puck between the goalie's pads.

Having racked up four goals just past the game's midway point, it suddenly seemed possible that Lemieux could take a run at the modern NHL record of six tallies in a game. While that didn't materialize, Lemieux was still able to put a bow on things, getting an empty-netter in the dying seconds to secure an 8–6 victory and his place in the history

books as the only player ever to score five goals in a game in five different ways.

When the calendar flipped to 1989, Lemieux kept pouring on the points, winding up with 199 in 76 games. And while Lemieux did get to experience his first NHL playoff action that spring, he was snubbed when it came to the year-end hardware.

After not winning the Hart in 1988, Gretzky — who finished with 168 points — once again skated away with MVP honors after leading the Los Angeles Kings to the postseason during his first year in California. It was an undeniable slight against Lemieux, still an outsider of sorts who had yet to earn NHL-wide affection the way the affable Gretzky had. But even if people wanted to believe Gretzky had the better personality, there was no denying Lemieux had firmly made his bid as the league's best player.

Captain Mario Lemieux stalks the puck during the 1992 Stanley Cup final.

MARIO GETS ONE WAYNE DIDN'T

THERE WASN'T MUCH that Mario Lemieux could do that Wayne Gretzky hadn't already done. He did get a few all-time marks, but breaking The Great One's records, while tantalizing, was never *truly* expected of Le Magnifique. Still, the debate raged. Who was the better player?

"As much as the Universal Gretzky Admiration Society does not want to admit it, the time has come when Lemieux perhaps should no longer be held in comparison to Gretzky," sportswriter Jeff Jacobs wrote in 1988. "At this point, Gretzky probably should be compared to Lemieux."

The volume of the debate turned up whenever the two played against each other — 25 times, with Gretzky's teams taking the unofficial series 17-7-1 — but turned down on those rare occasions when Gretzky and Lemieux played together. It first happened at the international All-Star series Rendez-vous '87, where Lemieux was voted in a fan ballot ahead of Gretzky as the NHL's starting center against the visiting Soviets.

Then came the 1987 Canada Cup. The tournament-clinching goal scored by Lemieux — who had a tournament best 11 goals — on a feed from Gretzky stands as one of the most memorable goals for a generation of Canadian fans not old enough to recall the 1972 Summit Series or the 1976 Canada Cup.

Lemieux's performance catapulted him into the spotlight. Much of his success thereafter he attributed to Gretzky.

"It turned my career around playing with Wayne in the Canada Cup," Lemieux told Ken Rappoport prior to the 1997 All-Star Game, the last time the pair would play together. "In 1987, I know he raised my game to another level."

But, given Lemieux's health problems and the long gaps between professional-level international competitions, the world didn't really get another chance to see the two players stand side by side in a game that mattered.

Lemieux wasn't done, though. Despite retiring in 1997 and missing the 1998 Nagano Olympics — the first to feature NHL players, one of whom was Gretzky — Lemieux came out of retirement in time for the Salt Lake Olympics in 2002.

After Canada failed to medal in '98, the pressure was on the Red and White to perform. Gretzky was the front office architect of the team, and Lemieux was its captain. Le Magnifique notched five points in six games and had, perhaps, the most prescient play of the tournament to help Canada tie the gold-medal game early against the United States. Instead of redirecting a perfect pass in the slot from Chris Pronger, Lemieux faked his shot and let the pass slide through his legs to Paul Kariya, who had a better angle of attack. Kariya deposited the puck past a surprised Mike Richter.

"He's sneaky," Richter said.

Canada went on to win 5–2, and Mario got the one award Gretzky hadn't.

The pucks Wayne Gretzky deposited on his march to become the NHL's all-time leader in points. Counting up, right to left and starting at the bottom row are pucks 1,843 to 1,851.

1989

―――――

GRETZKY PASSES MR. HOCKEY

I t was a confluence of events so perfect that if it had been pitched as a Hollywood script, it would have been turned down for being impossible. But much of what Wayne Gretzky accomplished in his incredible career seemed similarly implausible — so why not this record?

The record — the 1,850 NHL points set by his boyhood idol Gordie Howe — was once thought unassailable. But as Gretzky raced through the scoring charts while rewriting the record books for the Edmonton Oilers, even the most hardened fan knew Howe's mark was bound to fall to the Great One.

However, that the stars would align with such kismet was unexpected. With 1,669

points already on his résumé after nine years with the Oilers, Gretzky was traded to the L.A. Kings in the summer of 1988. He added 168 more points in his first season in Southern California, for 1,837, and he scored 12 points through the Kings' first five outings in 1989–90 to sit one point behind Gordie Howe's career mark.

That the Kings' first road trip of the year had them visiting Edmonton with the record all but ready to fall seemed too perfect, even for Gretzky.

"If it does happen in Edmonton," Gretzky told the Associated Press, "maybe its fate..."

On October 15, 1989, with Edmonton fans still wrapping their heads around the fact

that Gretzky could set this mark while playing his old teammates, the Great One set up Bernie Nicholls for the game's opening goal to pull even with Howe.

At that point, it seemed like a forgone conclusion that Gretzky would eclipse the record, but as the contest wore on, Edmonton wrested control and built a 4–3 lead. With time winding down in the third, Kings coach Tom Webster pulled goalie Mario Gosselin for a sixth attacker. On a face-off deep in the Edmonton zone, Gretzky lined up wide to the left on the blocker side of Oilers goalie Bill Ranford. Edmonton defenseman Kevin Lowe nearly cleared the puck off the glass and out of the zone, but Kings blue-liner

Wayne Gretzky is in his "office" behind the net, as a member of the L.A. Kings.

Steve Duchesne did well to keep the play onside and rolled it back toward a tangle of bodies near the crease.

Ever the elusive one, Gretzky drifted, uncovered, to Ranford's right, as opposed to behind the net, where he usually situated himself. When the puck kicked out of the scrum, it went right to Gretzky, who swept it in with a quick backhand.

Just 53 seconds remained on the clock as the arena exploded in jubilant celebration, the home crowd abandoning any pretense about rooting for the Oilers. The record was one more chance to cheer the player who'd meant so much to them, and the ovation was a fitting response on a night when the game wasn't really about team allegiances so much as two men who'd lifted the entire sport with their achievements and graciousness.

The game was suspended so, among others, Mr. Hockey himself could come out and pay tribute to hockey's new scoring king.

"In all honesty," Howe told the crowd, "I've been looking forward to today. It's really nice for me to be part of this."

When play finally resumed, Gretzky went back to his natural habitat, picking up a puck behind the net and executing a perfect wraparound on Ranford to win the game in overtime, adding a fitting exclamation point to an already unbelievable evening.

By the time he retired, Gretzky had tacked on another 1,000 points to end with 2,857. And even in the unlikely event somebody breaks that barrier one day, it's impossible to believe it will match the incredible theater that unfolded on that perfect night in Alberta.

The gloves, stick and helmet, as well as the puck, Wayne Gretzky scored with, and the net he scored in, to become the NHL's all-time leader in goals.

GRETZKY GETS THE GOAL MARK

WAYNE GRETZKY WAS on the giving side of more beautiful passes than any player in league history. But when No. 99 finally broke the NHL's all-time goal-scoring mark of 801 goals, also held by Howe, he was on the receiving end of a wonderful dish.

Hosting the Vancouver Canucks on March 23, 1994, Gretzky cruised down the left wing during an odd-man rush on a Los Angeles Kings power play. When defenseman Marty McSorley spotted him from the opposite wing, he sent a crisp, cross-ice pass right on the tape. Gretzky one-timed the offering behind bewildered Canucks goalie Kirk McLean for the 802nd goal of his career.

Igor Larionov with the San Jose Sharks in the mid-1990s, where he established himself as a point-per-game player.

1989

THE RUSSIANS ARRIVE

Despite the success of European players like Borje Salming and Anders Hedberg in the late 1970s, as well as the inclusion of a handful of Czechoslovakian stars who had defected to North America in the early 1980s, the NHL was still not a truly global league. That's because, despite some solid efforts from NHL general managers, the league had yet to include any Soviet stars.

It was common place by the late 1970s for Russian names to be called in the late rounds of the NHL draft, with teams taking a chance that they may get permission from the Soviet government to let the player join the NHL. Montreal attempted to nab Vicheslav "Slava" Fetisov in 1978 and Vladislav Tretiak in 1983, the same year Calgary tried to pry sniper Sergei Makarov from the communist state and New Jersey selected Fetisov, who was again "draft eligible."

But it wasn't until the political landscape shifted — under Mikhail Gorbachev and his glasnost (or openness) policy — that Soviet players had any opportunity to play in the NHL.

However, even then it wasn't easy. Leading the way were Soviet stars Igor Larionov and Fetisov, both of whom risked their careers — and in Fetisov's case the chance of a military posting in Siberia — to get the freedom to play in the NHL.

In the fall of 1988, Larionov wrote a 7,000-word missive to a Moscow newspaper decrying the heavy-handedness of the Soviet hockey system. He was almost immediately removed from the national team, but a players' revolt, led by Fetisov, led to his reinstatement.

For his part, while Fetisov was touring with his club team, CSKA Moscow, as part of an exhibition series with NHL squads early in 1989, he publicly announced that he was ready to play in the NHL. His decision to

speak out prompted the Soviet brain trust to leave him off the 1989 World Championship roster later that spring, but when his teammates threatened to boycott if he wasn't reinstated, Fetisov was quickly back on the ice.

That summer, Fetisov, Larionov and fellow veterans Sergei Makarov, Helmut Balderis, Sergei Mylinkov, Sergei Starikov and Vladimir Krutov were granted permission to join NHL clubs for the 1989–90 season (Sergei Pryakhin had been given the same permission in time to join the Calgary Flames at the tail end of the 1988–89 season, thus making him the first Russian-born-and-trained star to skate in the NHL). The caveat for all of the veterans was that they had to return to play for the national team.

That same freedom, however, was not granted to any of Russia's younger stars, and in the spring of 1989, just as the veterans were negotiating their permissions, 20-year-old

Sergei Makarov looks to redirect a pass behind Grant Fuhr in the late 1980s, just before he came to play in the NHL.

Alexander Mogilny defected to the U.S. after the Soviets won gold at the World Championships in Sweden. The bold move rocked the establishment and set the scene for others to follow. Sergei Fedorov defected the year after, and by 1991 the Soviet Union had dissolved, essentially opening the NHL's doors to Russian players.

Despite already having many hard miles on their bodies, both Fetisov and Larionov carved out impressive North American careers, eventually joining forces with the Detroit Red Wings, where they both captured the Stanley Cup. Mogilny, meanwhile, was soon followed by fellow young stud countrymen Pavel Bure, who won the Calder in 1992, and Fedorov, who became the first European-born-and-trained MVP in league history (1994). Fedorov's last NHL stop was with the Washington Capitals in 2008–09, a team led by Russian Alex Ovechkin.

"Ovie" was likely just beginning to skate when the first Soviets realized their goal of playing NHL hockey. Once they did, the North American game finally reached its full potential.

Sergei Fedorov

TOP-10 RUSSIAN NHL SCORERS

1. SERGEI FEDOROV	1,179
2. ALEX OVECHKIN*	1,035
3. ALEXANDER MOGILNY	1,032
4. ALEXEI KOVALEV	1,029
5. PAVEL DATSYUK	918
6. SLAVA KOZLOV	853
7. EVGENI MALKIN*	832
8. ILYA KOVALCHUK	816
9. SERGEI GONCHAR	811
10. ALEXEI YASHIN	781

*Player is still active.

1991

NHL INSTALLS VIDEO REVIEW

When fans watching at home became better equipped to make calls than NHL referees, something had to change.

Hockey has always been a swift-moving game, and officials often have to work to keep up. But beginning in the 1991–92 season, after years of internal pressure, the men in stripes got some assistance. The NHL began using instant replay as part of its process for taking a second look at crucial moments.

"We can at least … provide assistance to those people, who, under great pressure and at very difficult times, have to make these difficult decisions," NHL president John Ziegler told the Associated Press.

Replays had long been part of the broadcasts on TV, giving fans a closer, slower view of plays than the officials ever got. The replays that officials could choose to view were originally limited to situations when extra help was needed to determine if the puck had crossed the goal line fairly and completely. And even with a replay, the call wasn't always black and white. Still, having a better chance to get the call right was an improvement.

Over the years, video review has expanded to cover more than mysteries about whether a puck crossed the line or not — and that has gotten better too, with cameras now imbedded in the posts and crossbar, providing a variety of angles. Officials can also use reviews to determine whether or not an offside occurred during a play that produced a goal. Coaches can even request a review if they feel their goaltender was interfered with on a scoring play.

Manon Rhéaume in her first exhibition with the NHL's expansion Tampa Bay Lightning.

1992

THE NHL'S FIRST WOMAN

In 1992, team founder Phil Esposito tried to drum up some publicity for his fledgling Tampa Bay Lightning by offering Manon Rhéaume the first professional hockey contract ever tendered to a female. The 20-year-old appeared in one period during a preseason game versus the St. Louis Blues, surrendering two goals on nine shots. Rhéaume was given a minor league contract and invited back the following year, once again appearing in a single frame during the exhibition schedule.

While Rhéaume's presence in camp was about trying to get some attention for an NHL team playing in a non-traditional market, it still shone a light on females in the game. Rhéaume, who also broke a barrier when she became the first female to play professionally in a regular season game with the International Hockey League's Atlanta Knights, instantly became an identifiable face in the hockey world. Her profile helped drive awareness around the women's game as it emerged on the international scene during the 1990s.

"What she is doing will help women in the future," said NCAA goalie Jenny Hanley. "More women are going to emulate her…. She is a role model."

Rhéaume was part of Canadian teams that won gold medals at early versions of the Women's World Championship, and she was also on the 1998 Olympic squad that lost to the U.S. in the gold medal final, as women's hockey made its first Olympic appearance, in Nagano, Japan. Women's hockey now has two major North American leagues as well as a vibrant international presence.

Since leaving the ice, Rhéaume has become an outspoken advocate for female participation in the sport and for the empowerment of young girls in general. Now based in Michigan, where she lives with her family, much of her work is done through the Manon Rhéaume Foundation, which aims to help young women "win at the game of life."

For a person with a 40-minute NHL career, Rhéaume has made large, lasting contributions to hockey.

HOCKEY'S HALL WELCOMES WOMEN

WHILE THE DECISION to let women into the Hockey Hall of Fame may have taken longer than it should have, the call on who to let in first was easy.

Angela James and Cammi Granato — both members of the International Ice Hockey Federation Hall of Fame — blazed one more trail when they became the first female players inducted into the Hockey Hall of Fame in 2010.

James, the early face of her sport in hockey-mad Canada, scored 11 goals in five games for the Canadian team that won gold at the inaugural Women's World Championship, in 1990.

Granato was captain of the U.S. squad that took top spot at the 1998 Olympics, scoring a huge upset victory over Canada at the first Games to feature women's hockey.

The Hall has welcomed two more female members since James and Granto were added, opening its doors to Canadian Geraldine Heaney in 2013 and American Angela Ruggierrio in 2015.

BETTMAN NAMED COMMISSIONER

As the 1993 playoffs unfolded, Gary Bettman — a little more than three months's into his time as the NHL's first commissioner — was already defending what many saw as his American, business-centric focus:

"It's just not true," he said to the *Washington Post* when it was suggested the league would rather see a Stanley Cup final between the New York Islanders and Los Angeles Kings than the all-Canadian dream matchup of Montreal and Toronto. "You want the two best teams in there, period. That's all you can ask for."

It wound up being an L.A.–Montreal final, with the Canadiens claiming the Cup — the last Canadian team to do so.

When you couple Canada's 20-plus-year Cup drought with the perception of Bettman as an outsider brought in to fix a game he didn't innately understand, the casting of the commissioner as a villain is easy to understand. That notion gets even more attractive when you consider that, under Bettman's stewardship, the league has endured three labor stoppages.

His mandate from Day 1 was to grow the game in the United States to ensure the league could secure national television coverage — an essential tool for survival and relevance that the NHL was missing in the early 1990s. Bettman accomplished that nearly right out of the gate, signing a deal with Fox to televise hockey in the fall of 1994 while also rapidly expanding the league into the southern United States.

His first state of the union also outlined his desire to establish a good working relationship with the players' association, which was quickly becoming militant under new director Bob Goodenow. Bettman's wish was a collective bargaining agreement and the end to the bitter labor relations that had spiked in the early 1990s.

Bettman got his collective agreement, but it came at a cost. Three labor stoppages, including the cancelation of an *entire season*, and the imposition of a salary cap galvanized claims that Bettman was only in the game for the owners and didn't care about the fans or the players.

Shortly after the resolution of the league lockout in 2012, an unrest that claimed 34 games, Chicago Blackhawks captain Jonathan Toews summed up his perception of Bettman: "[Lockouts seem] to be our commissioner's bread-and-butter; it's almost like he is excited to take away hockey from the fans and the players just because he can."

But juggling Canada's national pride along with players' expectations and owners' expectations while also growing the league takes physical and fiscal gumption, and Bettman has both in spades. His ability to steer the league along his desired path has, it could be argued, done more good for the game than the efforts of all five league presidents before him.

Under his stewardship, the NHL has grown from 24 to 31 teams, expanding into non-traditional markets and growing the league's fan base. His Canadian-currency assistance program helped save fragile franchises in the late 1990s. His deal with the International Ice Hockey Federation saw NHLers play in the Olympics, improving the game's global reach. The salary cap he introduced helps keep the league competitive, and he has also negotiated risky but ultimately rewarding television rights deals and ushered in a new era of hockey as must-see TV with the league's slate of outdoor regular-season games.

As a result, the NHL's revenue has more than quintupled under his watch, from $735 million to nearly $4 billion.

"The league has never been more competitive. I think we have the most competitive balance in all of sports and it's fun to see," Bettman said in 2015.

With a contract that will extend his tenure until 2022 — nearly 30 years after his arrival — Bettman has put his stamp on the league in a way no other chief has, making the villain argument increasingly hard to swallow.

1993

MONTREAL WINS HISTORIC CUP

The Montreal Forum was usually a rollicking joint during Stanley Cup finals, but late in Game 2 of the 1993 showcase series, a critical stick measurement had the fans in hockey's signature cathedral as quiet as church parishioners.

Down 2–1 and having already dropped Game 1 on home ice, the desperate Montreal Canadiens told referee Kerry Fraser that they wanted to see if Los Angeles Kings defenseman Marty McSorley was using an illegal curve. And like everything else that magical spring, the call went the Habs' way.

Already the proud owners of 23 championship banners, the Canadiens celebrated the 100th anniversary of the Stanley Cup by claiming their 24th title in unlikely fashion. Montreal set a stunning record with 10 consecutive overtime victories in the 1993 playoffs, including three against McSorley, Wayne Gretzky and the rest of the Kings in the final. That timely scoring — combined with the stellar goaltending of Patrick Roy — made it easy to believe the Forum ghosts were calling in some favors to make sure the silver mug made its way "home" on its centennial birthday.

While the Canadiens would come to own overtime in the spring of '93, the first

Patrick Roy during Montreal's 1992–93 Stanley Cup–winning season.

MONTREAL'S OT GOAL-SCORERS

VINCENT DAMPHOUSSE
Game 3 vs Quebec Nordiques

KIRK MULLER
Game 5 at Quebec Nordiques

GUY CARBONNEAU
Game 2 vs Buffalo Sabres

GILBERT DIONNE
Game 3 at Buffalo Sabres

KIRK MULLER
Game 4 at Buffalo Sabres

STÉPHAN LEBEAU
Game 2 vs New York Islanders (2OT)

GUY CARBONNEAU
Game 3 at New York Islanders

ERIC DESJARDINS
Game 2 vs Los Angeles Kings

JOHN LECLAIR
Game 3 at Los Angeles Kings

JOHN LECLAIR
Game 4 at Los Angeles Kings

postseason game they played that year was actually a fourth-period loss to the Quebec Nordiques. After dropping Game 2 of that first-round series, Montreal was in a serious hole. But a Game 3 win sparked a string of 11 consecutive victories for the Canadiens as they blasted their way to the final.

The Kings proved to be a formidable foe, with their 4–1 win in the series opener. Los Angeles was perfectly positioned to steal two games on the road, but then the call came to check McSorley's twig late in Game 2.

"I took the stick from him and I remember visually, just visually, it was so far beyond the acceptable curve — which was a quarter-inch at the time," Fraser told Sportsnet in 2013. "I said, 'Marty what are you thinking? I don't even have to measure this thing.' He never said anything, but he just kind of sagged."

The Canadiens, meanwhile, surged. With Roy on the bench to provide a six-on-four advantage, defenseman Eric Desjardins — who had Montreal's lone goal to that point — scored again to tie the game with 73 seconds remaining in regulation. Then, in the blink of an eye, Desjardins tallied again in the extra frame, becoming the only blue-liner in league history to score a hat trick in the final.

After more OT magic from John LeClair, who scored the winners in Games 3 and 4 on the road, Montreal returned home and vanquished the Kings with a 4–1 Cup-clinching victory in Game 5. It wasn't the domination Montreal clubs had exhibited in the past, but it was certainly an entertaining way to win a championship that somehow always seemed destined to belong to the Habs.

1994

EAGLESON EXPOSED AS FRAUD

Alan Eagleson and Canadian Prime Minister Pierre Trudeau present the 1981 Canada Cup to the Soviet champions.

In 2012, members of the original Team Canada — the professional squad that first played under that name while facing the Soviet Union in 1972 — gathered to celebrate the 40th anniversary of the ground-breaking Summit Series. Most of the men who had played central roles in Canada's victory, from Game 8 hero Paul Henderson to inspirational leader Phil Esposito, were in attendance. However, the person one could argue had the most to do with the series' creation, Alan Eagleson, was nowhere to be found. He was still paying the price for the decades during which he had abused his power.

For close to 30 years, few people held a more prominent role in hockey than Eagleson. During most of that time, it appeared Eagleson was improving the state of the game for all involved, especially the men who played it. But as whispers of wrongdoing developed into legal charges in 1994, Eagleson experienced one of the most precipitous and disgraceful falls in NHL history.

After earning his law degree, in the early 1960s Eagleson essentially became hockey's first player agent. He was also a driving force behind the creation of the National Hockey League Players' Association in 1967. Negotiating contracts for the likes of Toronto Maple Leafs defenseman Carl Brewer and young Boston Bruins phenom Bobby Orr, Eagleson quickly rose to prominence in the hockey world.

His reputation grew on an international level when he helped execute the 1972 Summit Series. On the strength of that exhibition, Eagleson became a key figure behind the Canada Cup tournaments that began in 1976.

But while Eagleson appeared to be doing work on the players' behalf, accusations he was doing something entirely different started growing louder and louder. In the early 1990s, Massachusetts-based journalist Russ Conway began following up on some players' complaints.

That was the start of a process that ultimately led to Eagleson — who for years had misled players about their finances while lining his own pockets — being hit with a variety of charges. On March 3, 1994, the United States Department of Justice leveled a 32-count federal indictment against Eagleson in Boston, charging him with racketeering, embezzlement and fraud, including stealing funds from the Canada Cup tournaments that had been earmarked for players' pensions.

Canada later followed suit with more criminal charges, and after extradition to Canada, Eagleson pled guilty to lesser charges in 1998 and spent six months of an 18-month sentence in a medium-security prison in Mimico, Ontario.

In 1998 he also resigned from the Hall of Fame following the protests of many players, including Bobby Orr, Ted Lindsay and Brad Park.

As Park told reporters, "I challenge today the Hall of Fame to remove Alan Eagleson. If they do not, I will request that I be removed. I will not be on that wall with that man."

Eagleson, via letter, resigned from the shrine days before the board of directors was to vote on his expulsion.

Some 14 years later, feelings hadn't changed much for Park, Esposito and a few others celebrating the Summit Series anniversary.

"I didn't like him then and I don't like him now," Esposito told the *Globe and Mail*.

Many of the players from Canada's famous 1972 squad actually wanted Eagleson to be included in the 40th anniversary celebrations, believing he'd paid the price for his misdeeds. But the small faction that still wanted nothing to do him threatened to pull out of any events he attended. It was a hard line to take, but it was indicative of the damage inflicted by one of hockey's most controversial figures.

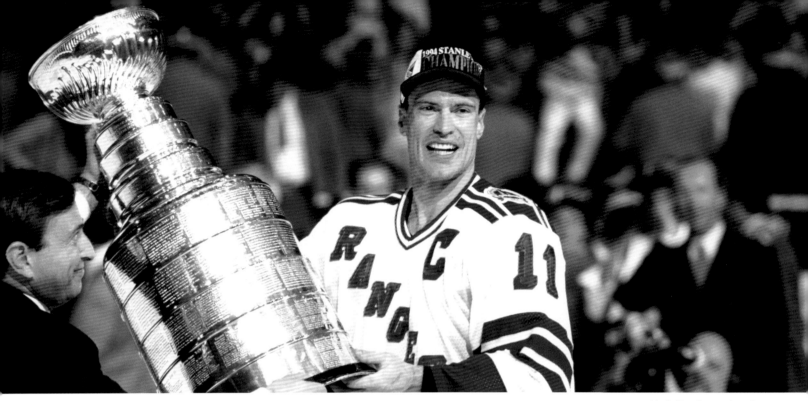

Mark Messier receives the Stanley Cup from commissioner Gary Bettman in 1994.

1994

RANGERS SNAP LONGEST CUP DROUGHT

Before the party could officially start, Gary Bettman made one last reference to the pain, but this wasn't going to hurt anyone: "Well New York," the NHL commissioner said while standing next to the Stanley Cup, "after 54 years, your long wait is over."

The world's most famous arena, Madison Square Garden, has been home to some memorable nights over the years. From a hockey perspective, nothing approaches June 14, 1994, when the Rangers ended what, at the time, was the NHL's longest championship drought by defeating the Vancouver Canucks in a thrilling Game 7 showdown.

Even if you discount the tension brought on by the Rangers trying to end their dubious streak, New York's run to the Cup — especially the final two legs — would still be among the most compelling runs in hockey history. With a star-studded team led by captain Mark Messier, defenseman Brian Leetch

and goalie Mike Richter, the Rangers soared through the regular season, finishing first overall with 112 points.

The Rangers then drew the New Jersey Devils in the Eastern Conference final and fell behind their rivals 3–2 in the series. After captain Mark Messier delivered a third-period hat trick on the heels of publically guaranteeing his team would win Game 6, the Rangers returned home to host the decisive Game 7. Holding a 1–0 lead with under 10 seconds to play, New York coughed up the equalizer to Valeri Zelepukin and, in an instant, all of MSG felt ill.

But Stéphane Matteau saved the Rangers in double overtime with his now-famous wraparound attempt that just squeezed under Devils rookie goalie Martin Brodeur.

In the final, New York jumped out to a 3–1 series lead versus Trevor Linden and the Canucks only to watch Vancouver claw back and square things 3–3. Messier put the Rangers

ahead 3–1 in the second period of the final game, but Linden's second tally of the game closed the gap to one goal with more than 15 minutes remaining in the third. This time, though, New York was able to hang on, surviving a struck post by Vancouver forward Nathan Lafayette before securing the 3–2 victory.

"Mark [Messier] told me it would be the toughest game to win that I'd ever been a part of," Leetch told the Associated Press following the decisive game. "He underestimated it."

Leetch, with a playoff-best 34 points in 23 games, became the first American to win the Conn Smythe Trophy as playoff MVP. And with the win, supporters of the New York Islanders could no longer gleefully shout "1940!" at their hated adversaries.

But all anybody in Manhattan really cared about was seeing Messier take that Cup from Bettman and delighting in the knowledge that any talk of curses or droughts had finally been banished from Broadway.

Joe Mullen, late in his career with the Pittsburgh Penguins.

1997

THE FIRST AMERICAN TO 500 GOALS

Joe Mullen's pro career began as a long shot and ended with a milestone.

The New York City native was never drafted, spending four years with the Boston College Screaming Eagles as an undersized scorer before the St. Louis Blues decided to offer him a contract in the summer of 1979. Nearly 20 years and three Stanley Cups later, Mullen set an important benchmark for his hockey-playing countrymen, becoming the first American-born player to register 500 goals over his NHL career.

The Blues' decision to sign Mullen paid off almost immediately, as the 5-foot-9 right-winger found the range 25 times during a 45-game debut season in 1981–82. In his third year, Mullen posted the first of six consecutive 40-goal seasons, establishing himself as one of the most dependable goal-scorers in the NHL.

Traded on the first day of February 1986, Mullen was sent to the Calgary Flames, a club desperate to knock off its Alberta rivals, the two-time defending Stanley Cup–champion Edmonton Oilers. And they did just that

with Mullen, and they also knocked off Mullen's former club on their way to the Stanley Cup final. The championship series ended in defeat, but Mullen paced all goal-scorers that spring with 12 tallies in 21 playoff outings.

Mullen again led the postseason with 16 goals in 21 contests in 1989 as the Flames avenged their loss to Montreal, sending the Canadiens packing in six games for Calgary's first Stanley Cup. Mullen was a force that entire season for Calgary, notching 51 goals — his only 50-goal season — and 110 points in 79 games while claiming his second Lady Byng Trophy.

Contributing meaningful playoff minutes became his calling card, and the Pittsburgh Penguins brought in Mullen for his playoff pedigree. He won back-to-back Cups with the Penguins in 1991 and 1992, and he was a significant contributor for the first, scoring 17 points in 22 games in the 1990–91 playoffs.

Mullen entered the 1996–97 season — the last of his career — with 495 goals and

admitted that hitting 500 "was a big part of me coming back." In January of that season, the 40-year-old sniper buried his milestone marker. It was a footnote in an otherwise forgettable Pittsburgh loss to the defending-champion Colorado Avalanche, but his teammates knew how much it meant.

"His career's been phenomenal," said teammate Ron Francis on the eve of Mullen's retirement. "Everything he's accomplished is well deserved. He's going to be in the Hall of Fame one day."

Sure enough, on November 13, 2000, Joe Mullen was inducted into the Hockey Hall of Fame.

AMERICAN-BORN 500-GOAL CLUB

MIKE MODANO	561
KEITH TKACHUK	538
JEREMY ROENICK	513
JOE MULLEN	502

1997

HASEK WINS HART

Hockey has had its share of hits and misses when it comes to nicknames. One of the best — and certainly most appropriate — is "The Dominator."

In the summer of 1993, Dominik Hasek was a 28-year-old goalie with 53 unremarkable NHL games on his résumé. By the end of the 1993–94 season, however, Hasek had launched into an eight-year stretch during which he arguably played his position better than anybody in the history of the game.

Not only did nobody see this coming, nobody was quite sure how Hasek was doing it while it was actually going on. While other goalies of his generation adopted a distinct style, namely the butterfly style perfected by Patrick Roy, Hasek flung his body all over the crease in a way that looked utterly arbitrary if not for the fact that he always seemed to stop the puck.

Shooters seemed to have no idea what Hasek was doing, and this only helped to grow the myth of the Gumby-like goalie who, out of nowhere, came to haunt the dreams of even the best NHL snipers.

"You kind of think that you don't have a chance against him," New York Rangers center Peter Nedved told Bloomberg News in 1998.

Boston's Joe Thornton echoed those remarks to the *Detroit Free Press* during the 1998–99 Eastern Conference semifinals: "He's the best goaltender in the world. If you're not thinking about him, I think you're a little bit crazy."

The zenith of Hasek's powers came when he won back-to-back Hart Trophies in 1997 and 1998. His first win marked the first time a goalie had been named league MVP since the Montreal Canadiens' Jacques Plante won the award in 1962.

Beginning in the 1993–94 campaign, Hasek posted the league's best save percentage in six consecutive seasons and claimed the Vezina Trophy in six of eight years. That kind of dominance was rarely seen outside of the Original Six era, with the exception of Ken Dryden's time with the powerhouse Montreal Canadiens in the 1970s.

But unlike Dryden, who benefitted from a stellar defense on one of the top-scoring teams in the league, Hasek set his marks and won his MVP nods while guarding the cage for the goal-starved Buffalo Sabres. Hasek's miracle work nearly included a Stanley Cup for the franchise, which was instead awarded to the Dallas Stars after a disputed goal by Dallas' Brett Hull ended the series in overtime of the sixth game.

With Hasek in the net, no one was going to write off the low-scoring Sabres in that 1999 Cup final, especially since he had snagged an Olympic gold medal the year before by backstopping the low-scoring Czech Republic to an upset victory. In the first Olympics to feature NHL talent, Hasek posted some of the most shocking numbers in the history of goaltending, registering a 0.98 goals-against average and .963 save percentage in the six games it took to deliver the stunning victory.

Hasek finally got his name on the Cup when he backstopped the Detroit Red Wings to the 2002 championship. That team was stacked with future Hall of Famers, meaning Hasek had to mind the store rather than steer the entire ship.

The memory of that title might be something Hasek cherishes forever, but for hockey observers, nothing will ever equal his back-to-back Hart wins and his uncanny ability to almost single-handedly bring mediocre teams to the summit.

Buffalo's Dominik Hasek during the 1994–95 season, the second of his six straight years with the league's best save percentage.

Slava Fetisov makes history, along with Detroit teammates Igor Larionov and Slava Kozlov, by bringing the Stanley Cup to Russia in 1997.

1997

—

THE CUP TRAVELS TO THE KREMLIN

It wasn't until the Stanley Cup's centennial celebration in 1993 that the champions — in this case the Montreal Canadiens — got to spend any quality time with the famous trophy.

Before then, the players who won the NHL championship saw the Cup on the ice, in the dressing room and at a few team events. Otherwise, for the first half of its life it stayed in Montreal, where the NHL's head office was located and where the engraver who etched the names had his practice. When the Hockey Hall of Fame opened in Toronto in 1961, the Cup moved there — and there it mostly stayed.

With the success of the centennial celebration and the popularity of the 1994 champions, the New York Rangers, the winning players' privilege to have a day with the Cup became formalized in 1995. And with that, the Cup's travel itinerary became something to envy. As Europeans like Jaromir Jagr, Sergei Fedorov and Peter Forsberg became dominant NHL stars, it was only a matter of time before those players began winning championships and taking the Cup to their homelands.

Of all the trips the Cup made across the Atlantic, its most notable may have come in 1997, when members of the Detroit Red Wings took it to Moscow. While Russians were well established in the league at that point, never had a group of former Soviets made such an impact on their team's championship. Defensemen Viacheslav Fetisov and Vladimir Konstantinov, along with forwards Sergei Fedorov, Igor Larionov and Viacheslav Kozlov — dubbed the Russian 5 — controlled the play with their smarts and skill.

In the days immediately following Detroit's victory, Fetisov and Konstantinov were involved in a car accident that left Konstantinov paralyzed. While that cast a pall over the entire celebration, there was a small bright spot when Fetisov, Larionov and Kozlov took the trophy to the Kremlin. As one of the keepers of the Cup, Phil Pritchard had a close-up look:

"It was a rainy, dreary day, but there were thousands of people there to see the Stanley Cup," said Pritchard. "Fetisov walked the Cup over to the chain link fence, and people stuck their fingers through it to touch the Cup."

That enthusiasm was on display across the continent as another Cup keeper, Bill Wellman, noted: "To see the way people react to the Stanley Cup in countries that seldom see NHL hockey was mindboggling," he told HHOF.com. "It made me appreciate even more the impact this trophy has on people."

1998

THE NHL GOES TO THE OLYMPICS

I t was a long time coming and, for most of the participants, a long way to go. But from the second NHL players landed in Nagano, Japan, for the Olympics, the excitement was palpable.

Following the lead of the National Basketball Association, the NHL decided to make its professional players available for the first time at the 1998 Games. While the hockey universe had long been treated to great best-on-best tournaments at the Canada and World Cups, the majesty of Olympic participation was something else entirely.

"Oh, man, that would be sweet," American Keith Tkachuk told *The Arizona Republic* of the possibility of medaling at the Olympics. "The World Cup was … a great experience. But playing in the Olympics is the big one … a lot of pride comes into it."

Heading into the tournament, Canada and Tkachuk's American side were firmly established as co-favorites, the United States having claimed the 1996 World Cup of Hockey while Canada had earned top spot at the three previous Canada Cups, in 1984, 1987 and 1991. There was an extra-special vibe around Team Canada because Wayne Gretzky, at age 36, was almost certainly wearing his country's colors at a big international event for the final time.

Canada lived up to its pre-tournament hype in the round robin, earning wins over both the U.S. and Sweden to claim the top spot in its group. The Americans, meanwhile, struggled in the group stage and were ousted in the quarterfinals by the Czech Republic.

Nobody had paid much attention to the Czechs before the tournament, but that was

quickly changing thanks to the goaltending of Dominik Hasek. The NHL's reigning MVP was an absolute brick wall at the competition, one Canada ran into headlong in the semifinals.

While Trevor Linden scored with just over a minute to play in regulation time to tie the game 1–1, Hasek stopped all five Canadians he faced in the shoot-out — coach Marc Crawford famously chose not to send Gretzky — providing the Czechs with a berth in the final.

Hasek's brilliance continued in the gold-medal game, where the Czechs downed Russia 1–0 to win it all.

It may not have been the result anyone anticipated, but it still marked a memorable entry into a new era of international hockey.

Jaromir Jagr wore this jersey during the 1998 Nagano Olympics. His Czech Republic squad took home the gold medal.

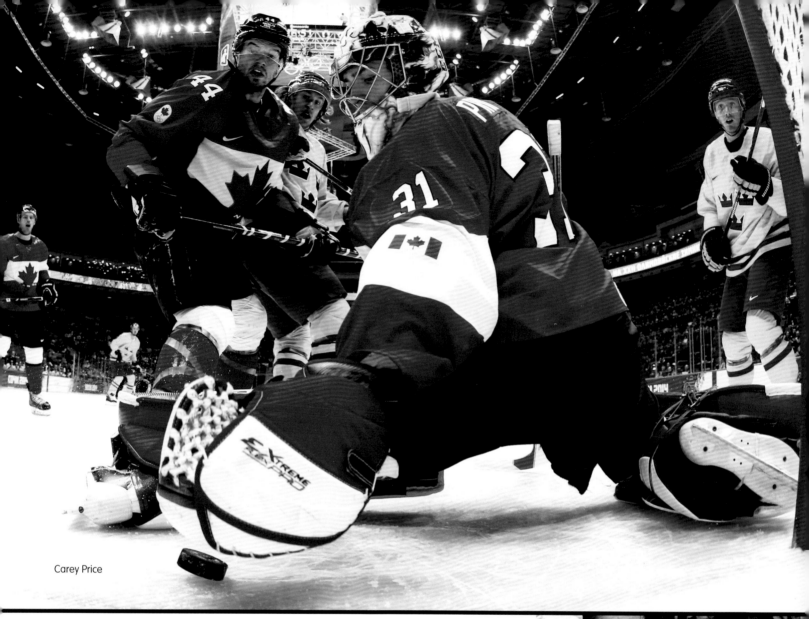
Carey Price

BEST-ON-BEST INTERNATIONAL GOALIE LEADERS*

GOALIE	YEAR	TOURNAMENT	GAMES	GAA	SV%	TEAM RESULT
Carey Price	2014	Olympics	5	0.59	0.972	1st
Dominik Hasek	1998	Olympics	6	0.98	0.963	1st
Martin Brodeur	2004	World Cup	5	1.00	0.961	1st
Carey Price	2016	World Cup	5	1.40	0.957	1st
Antero Niittymäki	2006	Olympics	6	1.34	0.951	2nd
Vladislav Tretiak	1981	Canada Cup	6	1.33	0.947	1st
Ryan Miller	2010	Olympics	6	1.35	0.946	2nd
Henrik Lundqvist	2014	Olympics	6	1.50	0.943	2nd
Rogie Vachon	1976	Canada Cup	7	1.39	0.941	1st
Evgeni Nabokov	2006	Olympics	7	1.34	0.940	4th
Miikka Kiprusoff	2004	World Cup	6	1.48	0.939	2nd
Bill Ranford	1991	Canada Cup	8	1.75	0.939	1st
Patrick Roy	1998	Olympics	6	1.46	0.935	4th
Martin Brodeur	2002	Olympics	5	1.80	0.917	1st

Minimum five games played.

Dominik Hasek

1999

CREASE CONTROVERSY FOR THE CUP

"All I want is a review." That was the refrain of frustrated Buffalo head coach Lindy Ruff following the conclusion of the 1999 Stanley Cup final. The close of the league's marquee event turned into a nightmare scenario for the NHL, one that continues to haunt an infamous hard-luck sports town.

The Buffalo Sabres, who advanced to the 1999 Stanley Cup final largely on the strength of a plucky roster and otherworldly goaltending by Dominik Hasek, landed on the wrong side of a controversial non-call that handed the championship to the high-powered Dallas Stars on a now-infamous goal by Brett Hull.

Entering the 1998–99 campaign, the NHL instituted a policy whereby it would disallow any goal scored while an attacking player occupied any part of the crease. The rule's intent was to provide goalies with the room required to do their job and protect them from players crashing the net. The unintended

result, however, was a bunch of negated goals because skaters who were in no way inhibiting the goalie had half a skate in the blue paint.

It didn't take long for the hockey world to realize that the rule was flawed. It wasn't until near the end of the year that the NHL quietly circulated a memo stating that a player could enter the crease if he had clear possession of the puck. The memo was ill enforced and vague, and the NHL should have issued a formal statement to clarify the rule. So, against that backdrop, the Sabres and Stars waged an extremely tight-checking series that Dallas led 3–2 heading into Game 6 in Buffalo.

A contest tied 1–1 at the end of regulation chugged through two extra periods and most of a third before Hull slid a puck past Hasek from the lip of the crease. Actually, Hull's left foot was ever so slightly inside the crease when he deposited the puck. And there's the rub.

"The man was in the crease and the puck was out," Ruff said in the aftermath of the

goal. "You can't explain [why the goal should count] to me. They've tried, and they cannot explain that."

Hull didn't come close to interfering with Hasek on the goal, but by the letter of the law, it seemed the goal should have been disallowed. The NHL's explanation was direct from the memo: Hull was always in possession of the puck during the goalmouth scramble (playing a rebound still constituted possession according to NHL rules), so he was entitled to that small piece of real estate. That reasoning, however, felt a bit flat to anybody who'd seen similar scoring plays waved off during the year.

"That was the worst-case scenario; an overtime game, pandemonium sets in and they can't take it back," Ruff complained.

The league's stance certainly didn't do anything to appease the stung Sabres. During a rally held for the team that summer, Ruff was still hot under the collar and left the crowd with the two words that still come up in bars around the city today: "No goal."

Colorado's Patrick Roy guards the Avalanche net during the club's 2000–01 Stanley Cup–championship season. Right: Roy receiving the Conn Smythe Trophy in 2001.

2001

ROY'S CONN JOB

Patrick Roy was not the player on everybody's mind when the Colorado Avalanche clinched the 2001 Stanley Cup with a Game 7 victory. The man of the moment was undeniably Ray Bourque, who, after spending two decades as one of the best defensemen in the NHL, finally got to celebrate his first championship.

All the attention on Bourque, though, distracted from the fact that Roy had just staked his claim as the best clutch player in the history of the game.

In defeating Martin Brodeur and the New Jersey Devils, Roy was named playoff MVP for the third time in his career. His hat trick of Conn Smythe Trophies elevated him to rarified air — since the award was first handed to Jean Béliveau in 1965, no player has claimed it more than twice.

Roy's spectacular MVP performances spanned 15 years. The Quebec City native burst onto the scene as an unheralded rookie in 1985–86. Widely credited with popularizing the butterfly technique that eventually became ubiquitous, the 20-year-old Roy clearly established his ability to play in the league during the regular season, but nobody saw his spring coming. Playing for a Canadiens team that was no powerhouse, Roy posted a stellar 1.92 goals-against average through 20 postseason contests and helped Montreal to a five-game victory over the Calgary Flames in the final.

By the time Roy won his second Cup with the Canadiens in 1993, he was firmly established as one of the best goalies in the world. But nothing will grow your legend quite like 10 consecutive overtime wins, which Roy and the Habs put together en route to another surprise title. Roy's excellence in all that extra time cemented his status as one of the greatest high-pressure puckstoppers ever to strap on the pads.

But a messy divorce with the Habs in 1995 ended an era in Montreal and gave a jolt to a new era in Colorado. When Roy arrived in Denver, the recently relocated Avalanche were a young team loaded with talent that had never been able to get over the hump during its days as the Quebec Nordiques. Roy joined the team during the organization's first year there, and six months after his arrival, Colorado claimed the Cup. And while Roy did not win the Conn Smythe in 1996, he was a vital, swaggering presence for a club still learning to believe in itself.

By 2000–01, Roy was a 35-year-old goalie with three Vezina Trophies on his shelf and absolutely nothing left to prove. However, as one of the fiercest competitors the sport has ever known, an internal fire continued to push him. Statistically speaking, Roy had the best postseason of his career in 2001, posting a playoff-leading .934 save percentage and 1.70 goals-against average.

His signature performance came on the road in Game 6 of the final, when he blanked New Jersey to save Colorado's season and force a decisive seventh game in Denver. After the Devils scored just a single goal in that contest, Bourque got his Cup, and Roy's case for being the all-time playoff performer became just about bulletproof.

2001

—

BOURQUE GOES OUT A CHAMPION

ockey prides itself on being a team game, but the Stanley Cup playoffs may never have been more about one person than the night Ray Bourque finally got to hoist the mug.

Win or lose, Game 7 of the 2001 championship was going to be the final act of Bourque's Hall of Fame career. The only question was whether, after 1,826 NHL games (214 of them in the playoffs), he'd find the hockey happiness he so richly deserved or taste a final bitter disappointment.

Just 12 months prior, Bourque had endured one of his most agonizing ends to

a season when his Avalanche advanced to within a single victory of the Cup final only to lose Game 7 of the Western Conference final 3–2 to the Dallas Stars. That represented Bourque's first postseason with Colorado after the powerhouse Avalanche had acquired him from the Boston Bruins — the only NHL home he'd previously known.

In 20-plus seasons with Boston, Bourque stocked his shelf with a Calder Trophy as rookie of the year in 1979–80 and five Norris Trophies, given each year to the league's top defenseman. He'd also played 180 playoff games, including two trips to the final. But

the Stanley Cup remained an elusive prize.

That's why, when Bourque opted to come back for one more crack at the Cup in the 2000–01 campaign, there was a groundswell of support around him. For years, Bourque had been one of the very best players at his position in both the offensive and defensive zones while always playing a clean, hard game. That continued right through his final season with Colorado, when Bourque — who turned 40 halfway through the year — averaged over 26 minutes of ice time per night and registered seven goals and 59 points in 80 games, which was more points

Ray Bourque wore this jersey during the second period of Game 7 in the 2001 Stanley Cup final.

Ray Bourque checks Patrik Elias during Game 3 of the 2001 Stanley Cup final.

than all but two blue-liners.

Bourque's strong play continued in the playoffs, and by the time the Avs faced off against New Jersey in the final, Devils fans were the only people left who weren't saying, "Win it for Ray."

A 3–1 victory in the decisive contest allowed Colorado to do just that, and after posing for a picture beside commissioner Gary Bettman, Avalanche captain Joe Sakic called Bourque over to be the first player to hoist the Cup.

Bourque put it simply: "What a feeling."

Teammate Alex Tanguay summed up the reaction from where he stood: "It brought a tear to the eye of everyone in the hockey world," he told the *Washington Post*.

MOST CAREER REGULAR-SEASON GAMES BY A PLAYER WHO HAS NOT WON A STANLEY CUP

1. JAROME IGINLA*......................1,554
2. SHANE DOAN* 1,540
3. PHIL HOUSLEY.......................1,495
4. PATRICK MARLEAU*.................1,493
5. JOE THORNTON* 1,446
6. MIKE GARTNER......................1,432
7. SCOTT MELLANBY..................1,431
8. LUKE RICHARDSON 1,417
9. HARRY HOWELL 1,411
10. NORM ULLMAN......................1,410

Player is still active.

Phil Housley

2002

SCOTTY BOWMAN COACHES RECORD NINTH CUP WINNER

Confetti fell like rain onto the Joe Louis Arena ice surface. Red carpets rolled into celebratory position. In the midst of the pandemonium, Scotty Bowman held firm to the decision he'd made so many months ago. Bowman sought out Detroit Red Wings GM Ken Holland, and the coach of the newly crowned Stanley Cup champions calmly delivered a message to his boss: "I just coached my last game," Bowman told Holland.

Hello Stanley. Goodbye Scotty.

Bowman passed the same information along to Wings owners Mike and Marian Ilitch. "Let's think about this," Mrs. Ilitch told him.

He had.

"I made up my mind in February," Bowman recalled of his plan to step down. "I knew it was time."

Bowman was ready to go — and what a way to go, with more Stanley Cups to brag about than any coach in the history of the game.

He doffed his jacket and donned his skates to carry the Cup — just as he'd done five years ago, the first time he had brought Lord Stanley's mug to Detroit. Then he hung his skates up for good.

A 3–1 Wings victory over the Carolina Hurricanes brought the Stanley Cup back to Hockeytown and gave the hockey legend behind the Detroit bench his record ninth Stanley Cup.

Legendary Montreal Canadiens coach Toe Blake, the man who had shared coffee and his vast hockey knowledge with a young Bowman, no longer shared the coaching record for Stanley Cup championships with his protégé.

Scotty Bowman, then-director of player development, hoists the Stanley Cup following the Pittsburgh Penguins 1991 championship. He would coach Pittsburgh to the Cup the following year.

Bowman coached more games (2,141) and posted more wins (1,244) than any coach in NHL history. Montreal (23), Toronto (13) and Detroit (11) are the only franchises with more Cups in the NHL than Bowman. But more than victories, Bowman's legacy is measured by his ability to adjust to changing times and to get the best out of his players.

"There are very few times in sports that you can watch something unfold and say, 'We're never going to see that happen again,'" Carolina coach Paul Maurice said of Bowman's career.

As it ended, Bowman tipped his cap to the legend of Blake: "I think he was far and away the best coach that's ever coached in the league," he said.

The last time they met in a game that mattered, Blake had guided the Canadiens past rookie coach Bowman's St. Louis Blues for the 1968 Stanley Cup. It was Blake's eighth and final Cup and Bowman's first crack.

When the end came for Bowman, he showed he'd absorbed another lesson from his teacher: when it comes time to go, go out on top.

MOST STANLEY CUPS WON BY A COACH

COACH	TOTAL WINS
Scotty Bowman	9
Montreal Canadiens (5), Pittsburgh Penguins (1), Detroit Red Wings (3)	
Toe Blake	8
Montreal Canadiens	
Hap Day	5
Toronto Maple Leafs	
Al Arbour	4
New York Islanders	
Punch Imlach	4
Toronto Maple Leafs	
Glen Sather	4
Edmonton Oilers	
Dick Irvin	4
Toronto Maple Leafs (1), Montreal Canadiens (3)	
Jack Adams	3
Detroit Red Wings	
Pete Green	3
Ottawa Senators	
Tommy Ivan	3
Detroit Red Wings	
Joel Quenneville	3
Chicago Blackhawks	

2003

—

HOCKEY GOES (BACK) OUTSIDE

The day before the NHL's first regular-season outdoor game, Montreal Canadiens goalie José Théodore was chatting with his brother about the tuques on display when the Habs and Edmonton Oilers alumni hit the ice for a practice session.

"[My brother] told me it would be real cool if I put it on top of my helmet," Théodore told NHL.com. "So I kind of kept it in mind."

Sure enough, when Théodore led the Habs onto the ice at Edmonton's Commonwealth Stadium, the tuque — complete with pom-pom — adorned his mask. And what started as a fun idea instantly grew into something larger, a perfect symbol of the spirit behind the festivities.

The inaugural Heritage Classic will be remembered for many things, but neither the score nor the frigid temperatures, which approached –22ºF (–30ºC) when you account

for the wind, tend to be front and center in people's memories. More likely to be recalled of the November 22, 2003, afternoon are things like the 55,000 fans who braved the cold, Théodore's fashion statement and seeing legends of the game shovel snow during an alumni contest that featured the likes of Wayne Gretzky and Guy Lafleur.

The idea, of course, tapped into the notion that, even at the NHL level, hockey is a game played by grown-up kids who first learned to love it in a very different setting. The lure of playing outside prompted Mark Messier — still an active NHLer with the New York Rangers at the time — to return to Edmonton for the alumni game. Even No. 99 himself couldn't resist, despite his stance on skating after your best days are done.

"I'm not a big believer in old-timer games," he told NHL.com. "I think that people don't want to see us play when we're

slow and old. They like to remember when you could actually play … [Still,] it was one of the great days of my life."

The Oilers alumni posted a snowy 2-0 win over the all-time Canadiens, before Théodore and his NHL teammates—with two points on the line—snuck out a 4-3 victory over the home side for the regular-season tilt.

The whole experience was an instant hit and triggered one of the league's most cherished traditions. Starting in 2008, the NHL has made outdoor games a part of its fabric. Each one holds its own special appeal, especially for the people taking part for the first time.

"It was the best hockey experience of my life," Montreal's Max Pacioretty told the *Montreal Gazette* of the 2016 Winter Classic. "Everything was so perfect about it. The ice was perfect, the weather, the fans, the accommodations. It was just so perfect."

HISTORY OF NHL REGULAR-SEASON OUTDOOR GAMES

Commonwealth Stadium, November 22, 2003
Montreal Canadiens 4 at Edmonton Oilers 3

Ralph Wilson Stadium, January 1, 2008
Pittsburgh Penguins 2 at Buffalo Sabres 1 (SO)

Wrigley Field, January 1, 2009
Detroit Red Wings 6 at Chicago Blackhawks 4

Fenway Park, January 1, 2010
Philadelphia Flyers 1 at Boston Bruins 2 (OT)

Heinz Field, January 1, 2011
Washington Capitals 3 at Pittsburgh Penguins 1

McMahon Stadium, February 20, 2011
Montreal Canadiens 0 at Calgary Flames 4

Citizens Bank Park, January 2, 2012
New York Rangers 3 at Philadelphia Flyers 2

Michigan Stadium, January 1, 2014
Toronto Maple Leafs 3 at Detroit Red Wings 2 (SO)

Dodger Stadium, January 25, 2014
Anaheim Ducks 3 at Los Angeles Kings 0

Yankee Stadium, January 26, 2014
New York Rangers 7 at New Jersey Devils 3

Yankee Stadium, January 29, 2014
New York Rangers 2 at New York Islanders 1

Soldier Field, March 1, 2014
Pittsburgh Penguins 1 at Chicago Blackhawks 5

B.C. Place, March 2, 2014
Ottawa Senators 4 at Vancouver Canucks 2

Nationals Park, January 1, 2015
Chicago Blackhawks 2 at Washington Capitals 3

Levi's Stadium, February 21, 2015
Los Angeles Kings 2 at San Jose Sharks 1

Gillette Stadium, January 1, 2016
Montreal Canadiens 5 at Boston Bruins 1

TCF Bank Stadium, February 21, 2016
Chicago Blackhawks 1 at Minnesota Wild 6

Coors Field, February 27, 2016
Detroit Red Wings 5 at Colorado Avalanche 3

Investors Group Field, October 23, 2016
Edmonton Oilers 3 at Winnipeg Jets 0

BMO Field, January 1, 2017
Detroit Red Wings 4 at Toronto Maple Leafs 5 (OT)

Busch Stadium, January 2, 2017
Chicago Blackhawks 1 at St. Louis Blues 4

Heinz Field, February 25, 2017
Philadelphia Flyers 2 at Pittsburgh Penguins 4

The New York Rangers and Philadelphia Flyers contest the 2012 Winter Classic; the visiting Rangers won 3–2.

2004

STEVE MOORE'S CAREER DERAILED

While anarchy reigned around him, Steve Moore lay motionless. The Colorado Avalanche rookie was at the bottom of a pile of bodies just moments after he'd been struck from behind by Vancouver Canucks winger Todd Bertuzzi.

In the frantic first minutes of the ensuing brawl, nobody on the ice or in the stands suspected anything truly awful had happened. But as the melee calmed and the players started to separate, the fact that Moore wasn't moving became a concern. He eventually left the ice on a stretcher and never again set foot on an NHL playing surface.

The fallout from Bertuzzi's blind-side attack on Moore was protracted and extreme. A league that was never too far removed from questions about the violent aspects of its sport was, perhaps more than ever, asked to account for how such a thing could happen.

Following the incident, former player Rick Wamsley, then-director of the International Centre for Olympic Studies at the University of Western Ontario, told the *Pittsburgh-Post Gazette*: "The league has been marketing violence explicitly since the 1970s ... Until the NHL takes a good hard look at itself, this violent subculture is going to continue … fighting's got to go."

Bertuzzi faced discipline not just from the NHL but also the courts. Most affected, though, was Moore, whose dream, which he'd worked tirelessly to achieve, was snatched away in the name of reckless retribution.

Everybody associated with the March 8, 2004 game in Vancouver knew trouble was brewing. Less than a month earlier in Denver, Moore had laid a hit on Canucks captain Markus Naslund that had knocked him out of a couple games.

Everybody in Vancouver — including coach Marc Crawford — seemed to take exception to Moore's actions. When the Avs and Canucks hooked up again in B.C., many players on the home side tried goading Moore into a fight. A four-year college player at Harvard who had logged two-plus seasons in the AHL before becoming a full-time NHLer, Moore played the game hard but was nobody's idea of a pugilist. As such, he did his best to avoid the proposed confrontations.

But as the score got out of hand — Colorado wound up winning the game 9–2 — the Canucks grew angrier and refused to drop the beef. Finally, Bertuzzi trailed Moore through the neutral zone and threw a punch to the back of his head. Moore crumpled headfirst onto the ice as Bertuzzi fell on top of him and a number of other bodies crashed onto the pile. The result was a concussion and three broken vertebrae, which ended Moore's days as a pro hockey player.

Bertuzzi was given a 20-game suspension by the league and didn't play again during the regular season or playoffs that year. He pled guilty to assault charges and was sentenced to probation and community service. Moore also launched a $38-million

Steve Moore, who is just visible at the bottom of the fray, had his spine broken in this attack by Todd Bertuzzi on March 8, 2004. Below: Moore makes a statement to the media on December 23, 2004, as his brothers Marc and Dominic stand by in support.

lawsuit against Bertuzzi and the Canucks. Bertuzzi in turn filed a third-party suit against Crawford, claiming the coach had instructed Vancouver's players to go after Moore. That case was eventually dropped.

In subsequent years, critics of the NHL's violence grew, and those voices began to break down the barriers guarded by "the culture of hockey." While fighting has not been legislated out of the game, the number of incidences continues to decline. In 2003–04, when Bertuzzi assaulted Moore, there were 789 fights in 1,230 games, which equals a fight in more than 40 percent of all NHL games played. At the conclusion of the 2015–16 season, fighting had dropped nearly 50 percent, to 344 fights in the same number of games.

Bertuzzi's career continued. His suspension was lifted in time to play the 2005–06 season (after all players sat out the cancelled 2004–05 season), but his chance at becoming a league star had passed. Twice a top-ten finisher in points before the incident, his play dipped, though he was good enough to find consistent work in the NHL until he was 39.

For Moore, recovery and retribution were a slower and more agonizing process.

"The injuries I sustained in my rookie year, the years I spent trying to return to my NHL career, and dealing with the loss of my career and the ensuing legal case, have been long and trying experiences," said Moore in a story that appeared in the *New York Times* following the settlement of his suit against Bertuzzi in 2014. "While nothing replaces the loss of one's dream, I am happy my family will no longer be burdened by an unresolved legal case, and I am grateful to be able to move forward."

With that, Moore turned the page on one of the ugliest incidents the league has ever known.

2004

THE LOST SEASON

The members of Team Canada were all smiles as they gathered around a new trophy. The Canadians had just won the World Cup of Hockey, held late in the summer of 2004. What those grins belied, however, was a sense of pending doom in the hockey world.

The NHL season was scheduled to start in just a few weeks, but nobody expected that to happen. For years, there had been talk of labor strife impacting the 2004–05 campaign as the National Hockey League Players' Association and the NHL owners attempted to agree on a new collective bargaining agreement.

Everybody was expecting a battle; what they got was complete devastation.

On February 16, 2005, NHL commissioner Gary Bettman announced the cancellation of the 2004–05 season. It marked the first time any of the four major North American sports leagues had lost an entire regular season and playoffs to a labor disruption. The main issue was a belief on the owners' part that player salaries had become too high and had to be managed by a salary cap. The players, led by NHLPA executive director Bob Goodenow, swore they'd never accept a limit on their earning power.

Both sides clung staunchly to their position as the owners' lockout began costing everybody NHL hockey games on October 13, 2004. In December, players offered to roll back their salaries by 24 percent, but they still refused to include a cap. The owners gladly took the rollback but said they still wanted a cap.

With no agreement on the horizon through mid-January, NHLPA president Trevor Linden tried to kick-start negotiations without either Goodenow or Bettman involved. Faced with the prospect of losing a whole season's worth of paychecks, the players finally capitulated and proposed a salary cap of $52 million. That still wasn't good enough for the owners, whose take-it-or-leave-it counter was a cap of $42.5 million. The players passed, and, one day later, Bettman stood in front of a microphone and told the world there would be no NHL hockey that year.

Only in the summer were the players and owners finally able to come together on a new CBA, which included a salary cap of $39 million. At the time, it was a resounding victory for the owners, but it came at an incredible cost for those who love the game.

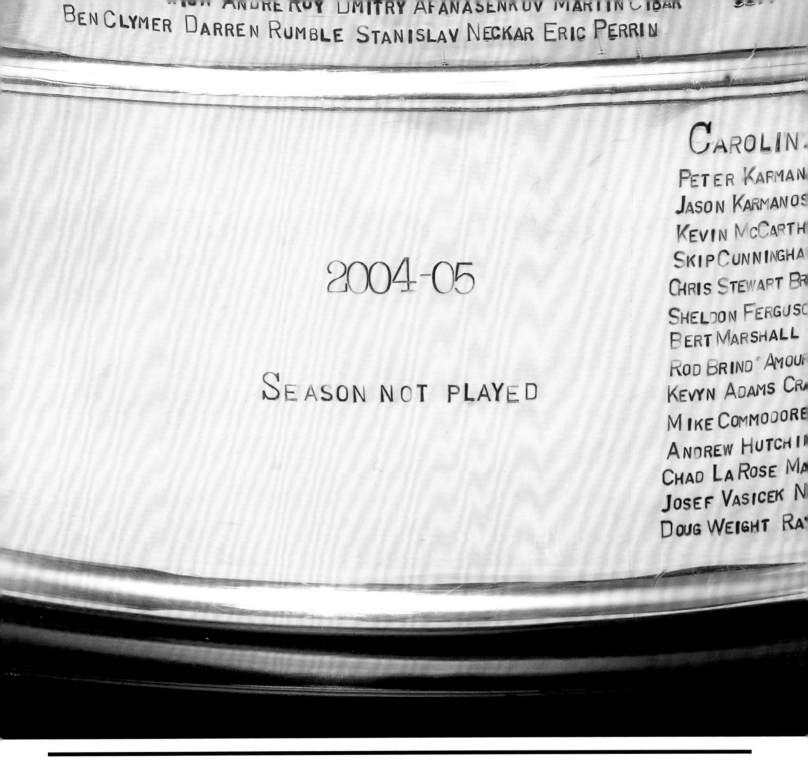

BEN CLYMER DARREN RUMBLE STANISLAV NECKAR ERIC PERRIN

ANDRE ROY DMITRY AFANASENKOV MARTIN CIBAK

2004-05

SEASON NOT PLAYED

CAROLIN

PETER KARMAN
JASON KARMANOS
KEVIN McCARTH
SKIP CUNNINGHA
CHRIS STEWART BR
SHELDON FERGUSC
BERT MARSHALL
ROD BRIND' AMOUR
KEVYN ADAMS CRA
MIKE COMMODORE
ANDREW HUTCHI
CHAD LA ROSE MA
JOSEF VASICEK N
DOUG WEIGHT RA

GROWING PAINS

AS THE NHL moved from, essentially, being a mom-and-pop league in the late 1980s to a major business in the 1990s, a few side effects were inevitable. One such consequence was serious labor strife for a circuit that had previously experienced almost none.

In April 1992, new National Hockey League Players' Association executive director Bob Goodenow led his union on a 10-day strike just before the playoffs. A little more than two years later, the NHL owners, now represented by commissioner Gary Bettman, initiated a lockout that very nearly wiped out the entire 1994–95 campaign.

That work stoppage, to an extent, contributed to the next one because some owners felt they ultimately capitulated to the players' demands in 1995 and were determined not to let that happen again. That's why the NHL became the first of the big four North American pro sports leagues to lose an entire season and playoff to a labor dispute, in 2004–05.

Less than 10 years later, the owners once again locked the players out, this time demanding a cap on the length of contracts. The union and league worked out a deal just in time to salvage a 48-game season in 2012–13.

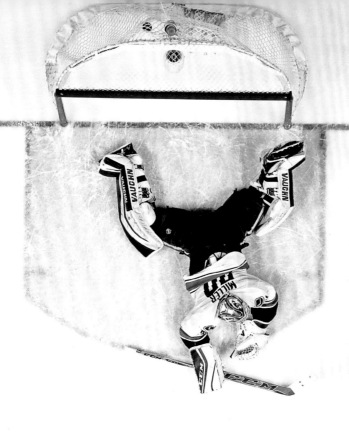

The Nashville Predators' Craig Smith scores a shoot-out goal past Vancouver's Ryan Miller in 2016.

2005
NHL 2.0

In the spring of 2005, Sidney Crosby was being hacked, whacked and held. Playing for the Rimouski Oceanic at the major-junior Memorial Cup, Crosby was mauled by opposing teams desperate to stifle his offensive ability. Not long after, he was selected first overall in a makeshift NHL entry draft following the National Hockey League Players' Association's new collective bargaining agreement with NHL owners.

By the time he suited up for the Pittsburgh Penguins the following October, rule changes and enforcement — some of which had been flirted with previously but never seriously considered — provided the freedom skilled offensive stars needed to shine while also ensuring no NHL game would end in a deadlock. Unlike his frustrating experience at the Memorial Cup, Crosby's time in the NHL would be marked by relative freedom.

Clutching, grabbing and impeding players had plagued NHL hockey for at least a decade before the 2005–06 season. And once the NHL and its players reached an agreement to come back to the ice, the league did a good job seizing the opportunity to "fix" parts of the game.

The alterations ushered in excitement, but players, coaches and fans all required an adjustment period to calibrate themselves to the new reality. Suddenly, the neutral zone was smaller, making each offensive zone larger. Obstruction of any kind was a big no-no: the second you put a free hand on an opponent or impeded his path to a loose puck, you were sent to the penalty box; same if your stick was parallel with the ice and against an opponent's body. And if a game was tied after regulation and the new four-on-four overtime, a shoot-out settled the affair.

In addition to the death of ties, the NHL also abolished the two-line pass. Now teammates could connect on long bombs that traveled two-thirds of the ice surface.

Further emphasizing the need to create offensive opportunities, the NHL pushed back against puckhandling goalies like Martin Brodeur of the New Jersey Devils. New rules limited the space where a goalie could play the puck below the goal line, preventing keepers from fielding corner dump-ins.

In the same spirit was the rule change for teams that iced the puck. The perpetrating team was no longer permitted a line change, meaning a collection of five potentially fatigued skaters would have to remain on the ice for a defensive-zone face-off, which often caused coaches to burn their time-out earlier in the game than preferred.

It all added up to a more wide-open brand of hockey. In 2003–04, the last year of the so-called "Dead Puck" era, the Detroit Red Wings were the only team in the NHL to average more than three goals per game. In the first season after the rule changes, 16 clubs — more than half the league — averaged better than three tallies per contest.

"I think it's a more exciting game," super scorer Jaromir Jagr concluded in early November of the pilot season. "It's more skating, up-and-down hockey. For offensive players, you can get more scoring chances and shots."

While scoring has become a bit scarcer in the decade since the big shift, there's no doubt hockey changed for the better after it emerged from the darkness of the lockout.

Pittsburgh's Sidney Crosby smiles during a team training skate in Moncton, New Brunswick, before an NHL exhibition game in 2006.

2006
—

SID THE KID HITS 100

Not since Eric Lindros was destroying junior competition as a hulking teenager in the early 1990s did a future star create buzz in the same fashion as Sidney Crosby. Adding to the excitement was a unique set of draft circumstances created by the fact that Crosby's final season of major junior ended as the NHL was set to resume its schedule after a year lost to a lockout.

Technically, every team had a chance to win the lottery that would determine where Crosby played. And when the Pittsburgh Penguins did just that, Crosby immediately began turning around a lost franchise by becoming the youngest player ever to record 100 points in a season.

The fall of 2005 was a unique time for hockey in Pittsburgh. Not only had a new, brilliant ray of hope arrived in the form of Crosby, but the original franchise savior, Mario Lemieux, was still skating for the team at age 40. At 6-foot-4 and with an effortless stride and otherworldly puck skills, Lemieux,

perhaps more than anyone in the history of hockey, could make the game look easy.

Crosby, however, entered the game as a different brand of superstar. While he certainly had all kinds of natural ability, he also attacked the puck with the ferocity of a fourth-liner trying to keep his job.

"At the World Juniors, I saw a Swiss defenseman try to decapitate Crosby with a cross-check to the neck," San Jose Sharks scout Tim Burke told *ESPN The Magazine*. "He didn't miss a shift, and later he knocked

Sidney Crosby celebrates with teammates after scoring the overtime winner in Game 2 of the 2016 Eastern Conference final.

the guy flying. That's one of the things that sets Crosby apart. He won't need anyone else to fight his own battles. He can take it and he can give it back."

That spirit combined with his sublime hockey sense meant Crosby dominated from the start. After notching two helpers in his first two games, the young star — just two months past his 17th birthday — found the net for the first time during the Penguins home opener. A few weeks later, after Crosby scored a beautiful backhand shoot-out goal to down the Montreal Canadiens, his boy-hood favorite, TSN play-by-play man Gord Miller proclaimed: "Welcome to the Crosby show, Canada!"

Though the season was not an easy one for Pittsburgh — the team didn't win often and, in early December, dealt with the unexpected retirement of Lemieux due to heart issues — Crosby just kept on producing.

From March 31 to April 13, Crosby netted 17 points in seven outings to put himself within reach of 100. After a scoreless showing against the New York Islanders in his third-to-last game of the season, No. 87 notched points 98, 99 and 100 in a return match with the Isles on home ice. That enabled Crosby — at 18 years and 253 days old — to edge former Winnipeg Jets star Dale Hawerchuk as the youngest player ever to hit the century mark.

Just for good measure, Crosby tacked on two more points in his final game, leaving him with 102. That enabled the Nova Scotia boy to pass Lemieux as the highest-scoring rookie in Penguins history, though he couldn't quite reach Hawerchuk's record of 103 points in the same year he was drafted.

Still, all the hype around Crosby was justified, as Sid proved to be the best kid the NHL had ever seen.

POINTS-PER-GAME IN FIRST FIVE SEASONS OF CAREER

1. WAYNE GRETZKY 2.33
2. MARIO LEMIEUX 1.94
3. PETER STASTNY 1.53
4. MIKE BOSSY 1.49
5. ERIC LINDROS 1.47
6. JARI KURRI 1.41
7. SIDNEY CROSBY 1.36
7. BRYAN TROTTIER 1.36
9. ALEX OVECHKIN 1.34
9. TEEMU SELANNE 1.34

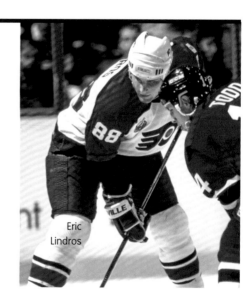

Eric Lindros

Detroit's Nicklas Lidstrom of Sweden holds the Stanley Cup in 2008, as the first European-born-and-trained player to captain a team to the Cup championship.

2008

NICKLAS LIDSTROM ACCEPTS STANLEY

When the Detroit Red Wings won the Stanley Cup in 2002, Nicklas Lidstrom made history as the first European-born-and-trained player to win the Conn Smythe Trophy. Six years later, the Wings would win another Cup, and their Sweet Swede would add to his legacy:

Lidstrom became the first European-born-and-trained captain to lift Lord Stanley's mug.

"It's a great honor," Lidstrom said. "But it doesn't compare to the team accomplishment."

Others stepped up to sing Lidstrom's praises.

"You can pick any given night on how he leads," Detroit forward Kirk Maltby said.

"Nick just kind of goes about his business day in, day out.

"You'd just kind of wonder if he's even human at times, just the way he was never hurt. Out on the ice, he wasn't flashy, but yet at the end of the night, you looked at his stats and it's like, it's unbelievable."

Even the man considered hockey's greatest

Nicklas Lidstrom with the Detroit Red Wings during the 1999–2000 season.

leader bowed in acknowledgment of Lidstrom's leadership qualities.

"He was the prototypical leader by example," Mark Messier said of Lidstrom. "If you talk about a consistent leader, he was the same guy game in and game out, he was consistent in his personality so that when the guys looked at him, he was always going to be the same guy."

The quietly efficient Lidstrom didn't fit the popular image of a captain. Those fascinated by the role of the on-ice leader think it's all about fire-and-brimstone speeches. Those who have worn the C insist this is a vast misconception.

According to former Wings captain Ted Lindsay, "Being captain, it's a recognition of leadership. A quality that you have to hold your team together, make them perform as a unit.

"I think this is where lots of mistakes are

made by people who think a guy gets in the dressing room and he makes a big show. That's not true leadership. You do it by leading by example."

The way Lidstrom did.

Former Detroit coach Mike Babcock said of Lidstrom, "I'd never coached anybody that good, never coached anybody as consistent, as intuitive, who had a great understanding of the game and was tuned into what's going on. He was such a professional, when you talked to him as a coach, it was an unbelievable experience for you. He was comfortable to share his thoughts with you."

The rest followed his lead down the path toward glory.

"You'd see the way Nick played at such a high level," former Detroit center Kris Draper said. "You wanted to be there right with him. It was just great to be playing with such a great leader, such a great captain."

DETROIT STEALS THE DRAFT

THE 1989 NHL Entry Draft began solidly for the Detroit Red Wings, and then it grew to epic proportions. Detroit's first two picks, center Mike Sillinger (11th overall) and defenseman Bob Boughner (32nd) would enjoy stellar NHL careers, but the best was yet to come.

"I don't think there's been a better draft [for a franchise] in the history of the game, but there was also some luck involved," said Jim Devellano, Detroit's GM at the time.

The Wings rolled the dice on relatively unknown Swedish defenseman Nicklas Lidstrom with the 53rd pick. Lidstrom would be a seven-time Norris Trophy winner.

They gambled correctly that they could get Russian center Sergei Fedorov, the 74th pick, from behind the Iron Curtain. Fedorov was the 1993–94 Hart Trophy winner. Both Lidstrom and Fedorov were inducted into the Hockey Hall of Fame in 2015.

They grabbed Dallas Drake, a solid role player on Detroit's 2007–08 Cup winner, with the 116th overall pick and Russian defenseman Vladimir Konstantinov at 221st overall.

Konstantinov was emerging as an All-Star and Norris contender and was considered among the toughest players in the league to play against when his career was cut short after he suffered head injuries in a limousine accident.

As great a draft as it was, it could have been even better. The Wings wanted to select another future Hall of Famer, Russian forward Pavel Bure, but were incorrectly informed by the NHL that Bure was ineligible for the draft. He wound up making history in Vancouver and later became a member of the Hall of Fame.

2009

MARTY SETS THE MARK

Martin Brodeur is honored with a sterling silver goalie stick for his record-setting 552nd win from New Jersey Devils co-owner Mike Gilfillan, left, and chairman Jeff Vanderbeek, center.

Martin Brodeur managed to be a goalie unlike any other by being parts of all of them — and the results were positively mind-boggling.

With a hybrid style and an easy smile, Brodeur carved out a career for the ages. From the moment he debuted with the New Jersey Devils, Brodeur brought a calming presence to the crease. Off the ice, he turned the brooding goalie stereotype on its ear

with his easy manner. His consistency, desire to be the best and the fact that he played on some championship-caliber clubs combined to help Brodeur pass all-time marks set by Patrick Roy and Terry Sawchuk while making his case as the best player ever to man the game's most important position.

Brodeur was different — and a difference maker — right from the get-go. He backed the Devils to Game 7 of the Eastern Conference final as a 21-year-old rookie. Stéphane

Matteau and the archrival New York Rangers squeezed by for their trip to the final, but the following year, Brodeur and his team claimed the 1995 Stanley Cup thanks largely to his .927 save percentage and 1.67 goals-against average in 20 postseason contests. In an age when Roy's butterfly was the principal style used by goaltenders worldwide, Brodeur stayed on his feet far more than the average stopper, sometimes making very difficult saves seem routine.

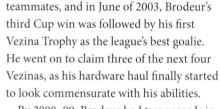

New Jersey's Martin Brodeur
in the late 1990s.

teammates, and in June of 2003, Brodeur's third Cup win was followed by his first Vezina Trophy as the league's best goalie. He went on to claim three of the next four Vezinas, as his hardware haul finally started to look commensurate with his abilities.

By 2008–09, Brodeur had two records in his sights. The first was Roy's all-time wins mark of 551, and the second was Sawchuk's total of 103 career shutouts. An elbow injury may have pushed back his timeline, but there was no stopping No. 30 in the long run. On March 17, 2009, the Montreal native beat the Chicago Blackhawks for victory No. 552. Then, on December 21 of the same year, Brodeur blanked the Pittsburgh Penguins with 35 saves to pass Sawchuk with 104 whitewashes. By the time he was done, Brodeur had racked up an unbelievable 691 wins and 125 shutouts while establishing the all-time mark for games played by a goaltender with 1,266.

"I have played on some very, very good hockey teams that have won Stanley Cups," Devils coach Brent Sutter told ESPN after Brodeur passed Roy. "As far as a goaltender is concerned, being around Marty … you can understand why he's accomplished what he's accomplished, and also understand why the organization's accomplished what they've accomplished. It goes hand in hand."

That realization was a long time coming for some, but Brodeur eventually made it impossible to arrive at any other conclusion.

The spiritual capital of the NHL's "Dead Puck Era" was New Jersey, where coach Jacques Lemaire implemented a stifling defensive "trap" system that suffocated opponents. Even after a second Cup in 2000, Brodeur didn't always get his due respect. Rarely pelted with pucks, his success was often chalked up to his surroundings, so he consistently watched the Vezina Trophy go to other goalies.

If there was a turning point in the way Brodeur was viewed, it occurred during the Salt Lake City Olympics, in 2002. Originally expected to play the role of backup for team Canada, Brodeur spelled the struggling Curtis Joseph and immediately steadied the ship, his play improving with every game, culminating with a solid performance versus the U.S. in a gold medal game won by Canada.

Brodeur's reputation was transformed, resembling that of Hall of Famer Ken Dryden's, who was also denounced for playing on strong teams. Brodeur, like Dryden, always seemed to find a way to make the big save when called upon, even if he had been inactive for long stretches of time. Following the Olympics, that great concentration was finally appreciated by more than just his

2010

CHICAGO STARTS A MODERN DYNASTY

The term dynasty is applied liberally in the NHL these days, but not since the Edmonton Oilers' five Cups in seven years, ending in 1990, has the league had a true dynasty. With 30 teams vying for the championship in a salary-capped league, winning Cups in bunches is extremely difficult.

"There are more teams and totally different rules," NHL executive Brian Burke said of the difference between the modern game and the last great dynasties of the 1980s. "The feat of winning three of four [championships] in a hard cap [league] would be comparable to winning four straight in the old system."

In 2010, the Chicago Blackhawks snapped their 49-year Stanley Cup drought — which dated back to the glory days of Bobby Hull, Stan Mikita and Glenn Hall in 1961 — for their first of three Cups in six years.

That drought-busting championship came courtesy of a seeing-eye shot from sniper Patrick Kane in overtime of Game 6 against the Philadelphia Flyers. Kane (who finished third in playoff points) and captain Jonathan Toews (who finished second) were Chicago's pulse that 2010 postseason; Toews won the Conn Smythe Trophy.

The duo had been tabbed for greatness since they had broken into the league together in 2007–08. Before their emergence, Chicago had been in free fall: for nine

Jonathan Toews (left) and Patrick Kane (right) hoist the Stanley Cup for the third time in their careers following the Blackhawks' 2016 championship.

Patrick Kane celebrates with goalie Antti Niemi and Patrick Sharp after he scored in overtime to deliver Chicago its first Stanley Cup in 49 years.

seasons, from 1997–98 to the pair's second season in the Windy City, the club had made the playoffs only once. The terrible results meant the franchise also picked up a few other key pieces through the draft, namely lights-out defenders Duncan Keith, Brent Seabrook and Niklas Hjalmarsson, as well as goalie Corey Crawford.

Nearing the end of Kane and Toews' rookie season, the pieces started to fit together. The club still missed the playoffs — albeit by 3 points — but the youth movement had rejuvenated Chicago. Staring in 2008–09, the Hawks made the conference finals in five of the next seven years, two more than any other team.

The keys to Chicago's winning ways were different from those of previous dynasties. Under a salary cap, teams can only afford to keep so many marquee players. Whereas the Edmonton Oilers' 1984 championship club

had 22 returning roster members when they repeated in 1985 and 20 returning members in their back-to-back run in 1987 and 1988, the Blackhawks had no such luxury. Eleven of the 23 Blackhawks on the 2010 roster were on the team when they won again in 2013; 16 Cup winners from 2013 were on the team in 2015.

Salary parity has meant, more than ever, that franchises need to be shrewd judges of talent. That means acquiring young depth players and leaning on scouting and a farm system that replenishes its resources responsibly. It also means getting star players to buy in to the team's system, which often means trading individual glory and reward for team success.

Some people call it the Detroit model, after the Red Wings clubs that won four Cups in 11 years (1996–97 to 2007–08), along with 25 straight postseason births (1990–91 to

2015–16), setting the NHL's benchmark for how to run a modern franchise.

"You need a core," Detroit GM Ken Holland told the *Globe and Mail* in 2013. "In order to be a good team year in and year out you need a core group of four to six players who really drive your team."

For Chicago, that core is made up of their draft darlings — Kane, Toews, Seabrooke, Keith and Crawford — along with savvy veteran Marian Hossa. It helps that the club has a good prospect pipeline and veterans willing to mentor the younger players, but the core is key.

"Those players were the ones who really made this thing go," said Stan Bowman, Blackhawks general manager. "When you get a group like that together, young players who show they can win, that's what you need in this day and age."

2011

HOCKEY'S HIDDEN COST

Few nicknames in the history of hockey have captured the ethos of a player quite like the "Boogeyman." Derek Boogaard was a 6-foot-7, 265-pound menace; a man even the toughest in the NHL feared to face in a fight. But for all the obsession around the pain he could inflict, the toll Boogaard's occupation took on his own body was tragically overlooked.

The summer of 2011 was a horrific time for hockey, as three young men lost their lives far too soon. And while the circumstances of each tragedy varied, they were linked by one common thread: all three NHLers were in the league because of their ability to fight. Boogaard was certainly the most prominent pugilist among them,

carrying the unofficial title as the league's heavyweight champion. His death, from an accidental overdose of painkillers on a night he'd consumed significant amounts of alcohol, caused the type of reverberations you'd expect when a man of his size falls.

"It's awful," forward Jamal Mayers told writer Chris Kuc. "You think about the fact they all had families. It certainly raises a lot of questions as to the why."

Those questions — the ones about the long- and short-term effects of trading punches with people — were getting asked a lot more often. The realization that even the hardest guys in the league could be in pain was also becoming clear. As John Scott, notable tough guy and friend of Boogaard,

told Kuc, "There's always stress being a tough guy in the league. Every day you're worried about fighting, keeping your job, getting in the lineup. It weighs on you."

From the time Boogaard made the jump to major junior hockey, there was little doubt that, if he was to crack an NHL roster, it would be to fill the role of enforcer. Though the league had moved a long way from the goon-filled days of the 1970s and '80s, fighting still held a major place in the game when Boogaard — a Prairie-hardened Saskatchewan boy — turned pro in the 2002–03 season.

During two years with the American Hockey League's Houston Aeros, Boogaard dropped his gloves an astonishing 47 times according to the website hockeyfights.com.

New York's Derek Boogaard squares off against Philadelphia tough guy Jody Shelley in 2010.

By 2005–06, Boogaard had carved himself out a roster spot on the Minnesota Wild, the team that had drafted him 202nd overall in 2001. He wore No. 24, in honor of the legendary fighter he modeled himself after, Bob Probert.

Boogaard quickly took his place in the pantheon of the NHL's all-time most-feared pugilists. He fought 16 times during his debut season and combined 20 fights in 82 games over the next two campaigns. Just as

with Probert when he wore the championship belt, fighting Boogaard became a proving ground for up-and-coming tough guys; a date with the Boogeyman could make or break a young fighter's career.

With the next challenger always just around the corner, Boogaard's brain and body started buckling under the weight of his profession. In addition to chronic shoulder and hand problems, the big man also had to deal with the effects of concussions. It wasn't

long before Boogaard was relying too heavily on strong painkillers to get by.

In 2009, Boogaard spent time in a California rehabilitation facility before rejoining the Wild for another season of policing the ice. The following summer he joined the New York Rangers for what turned out to be his final NHL campaign. After another visit to rehab in the spring of 2011, Boogaard was found dead in the Minneapolis apartment he shared with his brother, Aaron, on May 13, 2011.

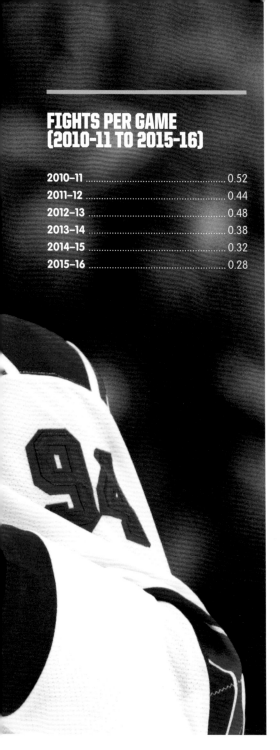

FIGHTS PER GAME (2010-11 TO 2015-16)

2010–11	0.52
2011–12	0.44
2012–13	0.48
2013–14	0.38
2014–15	0.32
2015–16	0.28

Florida's Wade Belak gets cracked by Minnesota's Derek Boogaard in 2008.

About three months after Boogaard's death, Rick Rypien of the Vancouver Canucks took his own life on August 15th. Suicide was also the suspected cause of death when, just a couple of weeks later, Wade Belak was found hanging in a downtown Toronto hotel room.

What role being an enforcer played in each man's death is impossible to know. Rypien suffered from mental health issues, but the lighthearted Belak was never known to complain about his vocation.

Whatever the situation, the Boogaard family filed a wrongful death suit against the NHL two years after Derek's death. A posthumous examination of Boogaard's brain revealed evidence of chronic traumatic encephalopathy, a degenerative condition with side effects similar to Alzheimer's that can be brought on by repeated blows to the head. The family also claimed the teams Boogaard played for over-prescribed the painkillers he took.

"He was there protecting his teammates at all costs, but who was there to protect him?" Joanne Boogaard, Derek's mom, said in a statement at the time.

The death of Boogaard — not to mention that of his hero, Probert, who died suddenly in 2010 at age 45 — sparked wide-ranging conversations about the role of fighting in hockey.

Addressing Boogaard's death, former Pittsburgh Penguin Mike Rupp told the *Pittsburgh Post-Gazette,* "If it is linked to fighting, it could change the face of hockey. I think the league would have to look to go down that road [to ban fighting]."

But the league and many of its players steadfastly maintain that the game polices itself. That phrase, when used in sports parlance, suggests players will take care of things when something gets out of hand, as Boogaard's former teammate Brandon Prust surmised for writer Rick Carpiniello: "I'm a pro-fighter, so I believe it should be in our game…. That's what makes our game unique, is that we can have the ability to police our own game."

But off the ice and in boardrooms, the game looks to be policing itself in other ways.

With the implementation of the salary cap in 2005, management teams are more often deciding a roster spot occupied by an enforcer is a wasted salary.

The number of players populating the league purely for their pugilistic prowess is in decline, and it appears less likely than ever that dedicated enforcers will be part of the game in 10 years — a fact that could mean less pain for everyone.

2015

—

PRICE'S HISTORIC HAUL

It was the culmination of a season's worth of brilliance, and it created a new benchmark for goaltenders league wide. Carey Price's 2014–15 season was one of the most dominant performances ever staged by an NHL netminder. His 44 wins, 1.96 goals-against average and .933 save percentage for the Montreal Canadiens made him the first goalie since Ed Belfour in 1990–91 to capture the unofficial Triple Crown. His 44 wins also set a record for the fabled franchise.

But most impressive was Price's showing at the NHL awards. There he became the first goalie to ever receive four awards, putting him in the company of skaters Bobby Orr, Guy Lafleur, Wayne Gretzky and Mario Lemieux.

Price's haul started with the Jennings Trophy, awarded to the goaltender(s) on the team with the fewest goals allowed (which Price shared with Chicago's Corey Crawford), and he was then voted the winner of three other prizes by three different voting parties.

The league's general managers, who vote for the league's best goalie, awarded Price the Vezina; the league's players, who vote for their MVP, awarded him the Ted Lindsay

Award; and the Professional Hockey Writers' Association, who vote for the league MVP, awarded him the Hart Trophy.

Price became the third goalie in the past 50 years to win the Hart Trophy as league MVP and just the third ever to claim the Ted Lindsay Award, first handed out in 1971 as the Lester Pearson Award.

While Price's big frame and wonderful athleticism provided him the building blocks of an NHL career, his journey from hotshot prospect to the unquestioned number-one goalie in the game wasn't necessarily an easy one.

Drafted fifth overall by the Canadiens in

Montreal's Carey Price
eyes the puck in 2015.

Carey Price holds the Hart Trophy while his other awards sit before him at the 2015 NHL Awards.

2005, Price arrived with much fanfare after having sparkled at the 2007 World Junior Championship for Canada and then leading the Hamilton Bulldogs to an unexpected AHL championship.

Though his on-ice performances were rarely subpar, it was difficult to live up to such enormous expectations as a 20-year-old in a hockey-mad city. Then, a few years into his career, Price was supplanted as the Habs' number-one starter when Jaroslav Halak backstopped the team to the 2010 Eastern Conference final. That off-season, the Canadiens elected to keep Price and trade Halak, a move that put the 6-foot-3 stopper back in the spotlight. Price responded with a fantastic 2010–11 campaign, and his status as one of the best in the game grew from there.

Price went on to backstop Canada to a gold medal at the 2014 Olympics and rolled his excellent performance into the conclusion of

the 2013–14 season and his record-setting 2014–15 campaign.

While accepting his awards, the subdued Price seemed genuinely touched and made sure to thank not only the people in his NHL home but also those in his tiny hometown of Anahim Lake, British Columbia:

"I would like to take a moment to encourage First Nations youth," said Price, whose mother, Lynda, is the former chief of the Ulkatcho First Nation. "A lot of people would say it's very improbable that I would make it to this point in my life. And I made it here because I wasn't discouraged…. I worked hard to get here, took advantage of every opportunity that I had, and I'd really like to encourage First Nations youth to be leaders in their community. Be proud of your heritage and don't be discouraged."

Important words from an athlete whose value obviously extends well beyond the field of play.

GOALIES TO WIN THE HART TROPHY

1929	Roy Worters, New York Americans
1950	Chuck Rayner, New York Rangers
1954	Al Rollins, Chicago Black Hawks
1962	Jacques Plante, Montreal Canadiens
1997	Dominik Hasek, Buffalo Sabres
1998	Dominik Hasek, Buffalo Sabres
2002	José Théodore, Montreal Canadiens
2015	Carey Price, Montreal Canadiens

GOALIES TO WIN THE TED LINDSAY AWARD

1981	Mike Liut, St. Louis Blues
1997	Dominik Hasek, Buffalo Sabres
1998	Dominik Hasek, Buffalo Sabres
2015	Carey Price, Montreal Canadiens

Washington Capitals goalie Braden Holtby warms up for a game with his stick wrapped in Pride Tape.

2016

—

BRINGING PRIDE INTO THE GAME

Nothing turns a mundane elevator ride into a joyous activity like seeing the most important idea of your professional career spring to life. That was the case for Jeff McLean of Calder Bateman Communications as he headed up a few floors from the basement of Rexall Place after speaking to media members about Pride Tape, a product designed to send a message of inclusiveness from the hockey world to members of the LGBTQ community.

The Edmonton Oilers were holding their annual skills competition on that January 2016 day, and the people behind Pride Tape hoped one or two players would use the tape to make their sticks look like the rainbow flag that is the universal symbol for LGBTQ love and acceptance. Then, with McLean watching on a TV monitor mounted inside the elevator, Oiler after Oiler hit the ice, each with his blade wrapped in those six wonderful colors. "There was a camera man really low to the ground as the skaters were coming on the ice, and we could see all the colored sticks at full speed, and I just got goosebumps," McLean said. "I just couldn't believe it."

Pride Tape may have been the brainchild of McLean — the idea popped into his head while he was driving to work one day — but many people across a wide spectrum had a hand in its existence. Kris Wells, faculty director of the Institute for Sexual Minority Studies and Services at the University of Alberta, had been working with the social marketing firm Calder Bateman on ways to spread the message of inclusiveness throughout the hockey community. The two parties had previously worked together to create nohomophobes.com, a site that tracked the casual use of gay slurs on Twitter. When McLean communicated his idea for Pride Tape, everyone believed it was a winner.

"[It's] a really easy way for hockey players to show they're supportive allies without even having to say any words; just tape your stick up," Wells said.

Producing Pride Tape, however, proved more difficult than initially expected. For one thing, tape manufacturers aren't in the business of producing just a handful of rolls here and there; the order had to be for a minimum of 10,000 rolls at a cost of $56,000. There was also the issue of getting six different colors on a single roll. Initially, McLean didn't want to tip his hand to the manufacturer, so he told them he wanted his team's colors on the roll. The manufacturer said it simply wasn't possible, but when McLean called back the next day and came clean about the cause, the manufacturer found a way to make it happen.

The money for that first tape order was raised via a Kickstarter campaign that attracted contributions from all over the world. The donation that put Pride Tape over the top came from Brian Burke and his family. The Calgary Flames president of hockey operations had lost his son Brendan, who was gay, to a car accident in 2010. To honor Brendan, the Burkes launched the You Can Play program aimed at making hockey a welcoming spot for LGBTQ athletes.

After the tape made its debut with the Oilers, buzz immediately spread. McLean would be in meetings working on other projects and his boss would quietly slip into the room and slide him a napkin with a message on it.

"It would just say, 'The Florida Panthers are in,'" McLean said. "And then another one: 'The Detroit Red Wings are in.'"

Just about everyone is on board now, from kids playing street hockey games right on up to the sport's highest levels. Although NHL regulations for equipment are such that we may never see Pride Tape in an actual game, many players use the tape on their sticks in pregame warm-ups, and each team should have it on display at some point in 2017–18, likely during the various Pride Nights held around the league. Of course, seeing the tape — and, really, how can you miss it? — is only the start.

"It's about the kinds of conversations that follow afterward, because that's really where the change is going to happen," Wells said.

2016

VEGAS, BABY!

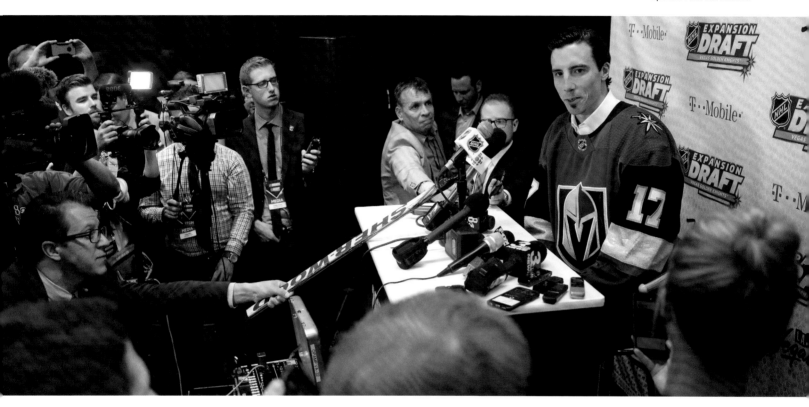

In some ways, it was a race to Las Vegas. And now that the NHL has won, we all get to see what the Las Vegas Golden Knights can do.

For years, rumors swirled around the professional sports scene that a major North American League would like to place a team in the gambling capital of the world. And while the NFL's Raiders — who currently call Oakland home and have also played out of Los Angeles — will also soon be in Sin City, the Golden Knights will always have the distinction of being the club that broke the barrier.

As the NHL's first expansion team since the Columbus Blue Jackets and Minnesota Wild joined in 2000, the Golden Knights are expected to struggle out of the gate, as is customary for most startups of any kind. But that doesn't mean the squad hasn't generated intrigue. In fact, the 31st franchise in the NHL was the main focal point of the league in June 2017 when they selected their roster. The rules were such that each of the other 30 NHL franchises could protect either seven forwards, three defensemen and one goaltender from exposure or eight skaters and a goalie, and the Golden Knights were allowed one player from each roster — to fill their roster with a minimum of 14 forwards, nine defensemen and three 'tenders — and many organizations fretted over whom the Knights' selections might be.

Vegas GM George McPhee played hardball with many teams, promising not to touch unprotected veteran stars in exchange for deals that landed the new club promising minor-league prospects and draft picks. In all, Vegas made 10 trades and accrued 11 draft picks.

When it finally came time for McPhee to announce the roster, it was understood that many of the players he took would be Golden Knights for only a matter of days, weeks or months as the franchise continued to flip players and play the long game to build a strong club.

"We want to put a competitive team on the ice right now, but we have to look forward, too," McPhee said. "It takes certain players that are going to be able to help us three years from now, four years from now, because we want to start at a certain level and keep going. I think it's a pretty good team."

In the coming years, we'll find out if McPhee's plan worked — and if pro sports in Vegas is, indeed, a winning idea.

2016

———

AUSTON MATTHEWS TANGLES WITH THE HISTORY BOOKS

No matter what the record book says, it was one heck of a start. The date was October 12, 2016 — the first night of the NHL's 100th season — and Toronto's Auston Matthews was already living up to the hype. Matthews, drafted first overall that summer, was supposed to be the "can't miss" prospect the Maple Leafs desperately needed to revive their storied franchise. After he scored two goals in the first period against provincial rival Ottawa, fans were ecstatic. When he added two more in the second, it seemed that something truly special had happened.

"What a luminescent night for Auston Matthews," gushed play-by-play man Paul Romanuk, who added a few seconds later: "You are looking at the first player ever to score four goals in an NHL debut."

Except we weren't, and he wasn't.

On December 19, 1917, the day the NHL debuted as a league, both Joe Malone of the Montreal Canadiens and Harry Hyland of the Montreal Wanderers scored five goals. These stats weren't hidden: both Malone and Hyland are listed in the NHL's Official Guide and Record Book atop the category "Most Goals by a Player in His First NHL Game." As television and newspapers got it wrong in declaring Matthews to be the new record holder, many were taking to Twitter and online chat groups to set the record straight.

Seldom, however, are things like this black and white. Malone and Hyland, two future Hall of Famers, weren't really rookies in that debut NHL game in the way that Matthews was in his debut.

Joe Malone was 27 years old in 1917 and had spent the previous seven seasons playing in the National Hockey Association, forerunner of the NHL. Harry Hyland was just shy of his 29th birthday and had also spent seven seasons in the NHA, as well as a year in the rival Pacific Coast Hockey Association. However, true rookies or not, there's no denying that Malone and Hyland did score five goals in their NHL debuts . . . because there had not been an NHL before that night! So within a short time, qualifiers such as "modern day" and "modern record" were being attached to Matthews' feat, which, even if it hadn't officially set a new NHL record, had at least moved him past Alex Smart (1943), Real Cloutier (1979), Fabian Brunnstrom (2008) and Derek Stepan (2010), who had all scored three goals in their first NHL games.

But, with all the attention to Matthews' feat and its place in history, something else that had been long forgotten came to light.

That was the opening night performance in 1917 of second-year professional hockey star, Reg Noble of the Toronto Arenas. Noble is recorded as having scored four goals in his — and the NHL's — debut. But knowledge

of Noble's achievement had been lost with time — and not even recorded in the Official Guide and Record Book (although that will be corrected).

It is unfortunate that the original NHL score sheets from the 1917–18 season have disappeared. Instead of consulting those, researchers have had to use the inconsistent newspaper accounts of the time to reconstruct the statistics from that first season. While most newspaper summaries on December 20, 1917, show Noble with four goals, some show Noble scoring only three times. Others credit him with just two goals. Although it's impossible to know for certain what the official scorer actually recorded for the Toronto center that night, the NHL does credit him with four goals for that game. So, not only was Matthews not the first player in NHL history to score four goals in his NHL debut, he wasn't even the first Toronto player to do so.

For hockey fans in general, Matthews' four-goal start was a stellar beginning to the NHL's 100th season. For hockey nerds, his near-historic debut gave reason to comb through the history books and discover something new about the game. And for Maple Leafs fans in particular, Matthews' entire debut season in 2016–17 was one of the biggest stories of the NHL's centennial celebration — and that is something to cheer about.

MOST GOALS IN FIRST NHL GAME

PLAYER	GOALS	YEAR
Joe Malone	5	1917
Harry Hyland	5	1917
Reg Noble	4	1917
Auston Matthews	4	2016
Alex Smart	3	1943
Real Cloutier	3	1979
Fabian Brunnstrom	3	2008
Derek Stepan	3	2010

Jaromir Jagr looks to score during the 2016 playoffs. Right: Jagr shows off his flowing locks in his early NHL days with the Pittsburgh Penguins.

2016

JAROMIR JAGR IS MAKING HISTORY

When a man plays NHL hockey into his mid-40s, it's fair to assume his relationship with the game is a touch different than other people's.

When he plays meaningful minutes and continues to be a difference maker, it means that as the game has changed and the demands on players have shifted, so too has the player. The NHL's current ageless wonder, Jaromir

Jagr, always finds a way to stay relevant.

He knew very early on that hockey was his ticket to a better life. Now he's trying to punch his ticket as the NHL's longest-serving member.

When Jagr first joined the Pittsburgh

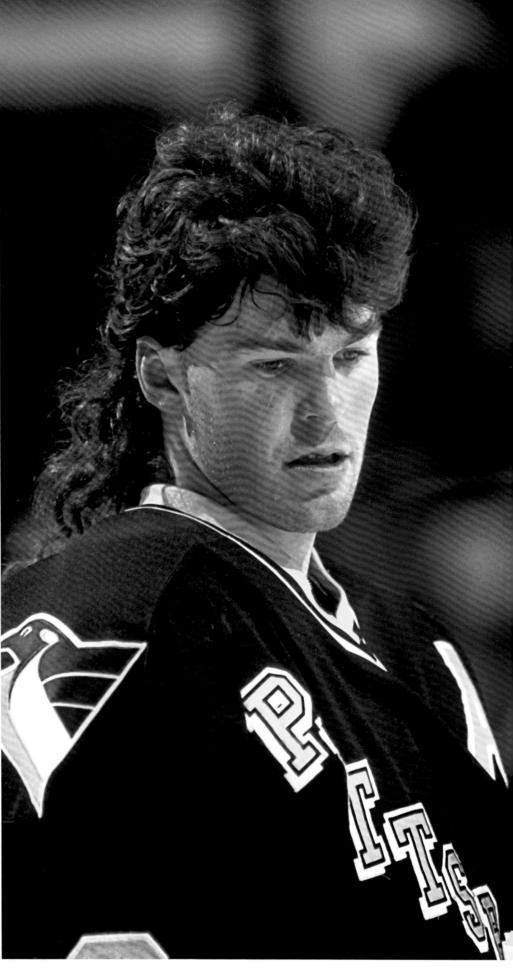

Penguins in 1990, as a teenager who spoke little English and had lots of hair, people weren't sure what to make of him. Cultural stereotypes still ran rampant, and many mused aloud about how devoted Jagr was to his craft. Those questions couldn't have been more off the mark.

More than 25 years after making his NHL debut, Jagr's unmatched work ethic has ensured he is still an offensive force in the world's best league. As the top-scoring European of all time, Jagr has carved out quite a legacy. And had he not returned to his home continent for a three-season hiatus, the affable Czech would be in even more exclusive scoring company.

As a youngster growing up under Soviet rule in Czechoslovakia, Jagr understood

Jaromir Jagr looks to cycle the puck against the New York Islanders during the 2016 playoffs.

that his options for an enjoyable existence were limited:

"That's the way it was, you had a better life if you were a sportsman or a singer in our country during the communist years," Jagr told *Sportsnet* magazine. "So I had only one chance — to be a sportsman. My parents decided — well, my dad decided — this was the only way we could have a better life."

Blessed with size and ability, Jagr's singular focus carried him the rest of the way. If he wasn't jogging beside his dad while the elder Jagr rode a bicycle, young Jaromir would likely be found molding his thighs, which eventually became like tree trunks.

"When I was seven years old, I started doing squats," Jagr told *Sportsnet*. "I did 1,000 a day, every day. And when you do that daily — now people work out, but back then nobody really did it — I just skyrocketed. For three to four years, I played with my age group, and two years later I was playing with

[guys] four years older than me and I was still better than them."

All of that work paid off when the Pittsburgh Penguins drafted Jagr fifth overall in 1990. Though Jagr earned Stanley Cup rings in each of his first two seasons, his personal point totals didn't really take off until his third year, when he registered 94 in 81 games. Two years later, Jagr earned the first of his five career scoring titles, all won with the Penguins.

By 2005–06, Jagr was having what seemed like a late-career renaissance with the New York Rangers. Despite his success on Broadway, Jagr opted to sign with the KHL before the 2008–09 season, and he played in Russia for three years. Similar to Gordie Howe's time spent in the WHA, Jagr's time in the KHL affected his NHL numbers. Had he stayed in the NHL, he would have certainly enhanced his already incredible stat line, likely becoming the only player

other than Wayne Gretzky to record 2,000 career points.

Still, when Jagr returned to the NHL in 2011, he continued to produce. As a member of the Florida Panthers, he passed Gordie Howe for third place on the all-time scoring list in 2015–16, and in 2016–17 he moved past Mark Messier to become the most prolific scorer in the game not named Gretzky.

At 45, he's still got hockey-playing plans. As he told *Sportsnet* in 2016: "The time between when I quit hockey and I die, I want it to be the shortest. It's not going to be as exciting, that time. So as long as I can play, that's what I'm doing. If I can play 'til I die, that's what I will do."

If Jagr plays just 57 more regular-season games, he'll eclipse Howe's all-time mark of 1,767 games played. If he scores 37 more goals, he'll join Wayne Gretzky as the only players in history to pass Howe's 801 tallies.

Don't bet against him.

2017

―

CONNOR MCDAVID'S CORONATION

It was only a short walk, but it sure felt like the coronation of Connor McDavid.

Just before it happened, the nominees for the Hart Trophy were read by the man who won an NHL-record nine league MVPs, Wayne Gretzky. Also up for the award were Columbus Blue Jackets goalie Sergei Bobrovsky and, fresh off a second straight Stanley Cup win, Pittsburgh Penguins superstar Sidney Crosby. When "The Great One" announced McDavid as the winner, the 20-year-old rose, hugged his family, and then shook the hands of his GM, Peter Chiarelli, and coach, Todd McLellan. As he descended the steps toward the stage, McDavid quickly turned to acknowledge congrats from Crosby, a two-time winner of the award himself. After accepting a replica Hart from Gretzky, McDavid got a couple of backslaps from No. 99. "It's amazing to receive this [award] from Wayne, the greatest player of all time," the youngster said.

McDavid may not be in the historical

Edmonton's Connor McDavid poses with the Art Ross Trophy, the Hart Memorial Trophy and the Ted Lindsay Award in June 2017.

"best ever" conversation yet, but increasingly, it's hard to argue the Oilers' current wunderkind is anything other than the greatest show on skates. And the league's players thought so too, sending him home with the peer-voted Ted Lindsay Award for most outstanding player.

On that June Las Vegas night, McDavid also got to collect the hardware he'd earned on the last day of the regular season. With two assists against the Vancouver Canucks, McDavid hit the elusive 100-point mark to claim the Art Ross Trophy for having the most points in the league. McDavid's being the only player in the league to notch 100 points, and to do it in the last game of the NHL's centennial season — that feels a little magical.

Had McDavid not missed almost half his rookie season of 2015–16, he may have been a league scoring champ right off the hop. His 48 points in 45 outings marked the third-best points-per-game mark (1.07) behind only Patrick Kane (1.29) of the Chicago Blackhawks and the Dallas Stars' Jamie Benn (1.09). McDavid — who became the youngest

captain in NHL history when the Oilers gave him the C following his first year in the league — telegraphed his intentions for the 2016–17 campaign right away, netting six points in his first two contests. He went on to notch three-point nights on nine other occasions, including his first career hat trick on November 19, 2016, in Dallas versus the Stars. For much of the year, McDavid played between left-winger Patrick Maroon and right-winger Leon Draisaitl. While Draisaitl was always tabbed for greatness, Maroon was a reclamation project who found an immediate connection with McDavid upon joining the Oilers in February of 2016. McDavid's ability to improve the fortunes of those around him is certainly not lost on Maroon, who more than doubled his previous career high for goals when he netted 27 this past season.

"I want to play there," he told Sportsnet.ca of riding shotgun with McDavid. "That's one thing I really want to do is continue to play there [and] stay in this organization."

McDavid's 70 assists in 2016–17 speak to his incredible ability to find open teammates,

though he's certainly capable of finishing plays himself. By netting 30 goals this past year, McDavid became just the third player since Jaromir Jagr in 1998–99 to hit both the 30-goal and 70-assist plateaus in the same season (the other two are Crosby, who's done it twice, and Evgeni Malkin).

With the individual hardware already piling up, McDavid will surely double down on his goal of ending a nearly 30-year championship drought in Edmonton. The Oilers took huge strides under their sophomore leader this past season, earning their first playoff berth in 11 years. A young Edmonton club knocked off the veteran San Jose Sharks in round one before pushing a very strong Anaheim Ducks squad to seven games in round two. McDavid seemed to be hitting his stride in that series, netting three goals versus the Ducks.

"Obviously it's going to take some time to get over it," he said of the loss. "But I think there are a lot of positives we can take from this year."

Very true. And for Oilers fans, there's absolutely no doubt which one tops the list.

2017

PENGUINS REPEAT AS CHAMPS

The Pittsburgh Penguins and Nashville Predators exited Game 4 of the 2017 Stanley Cup final knotted at two wins apiece. From an outsider's perspective, the series, up to that point, could have been considered even. But like the dead catfish hitting the ice in Tennessee, this Cup final was a little unexpected — and certainly odd.

For the Predators franchise, making it to the Stanley Cup final was another cleared hurdle in a postseason full of firsts. After squeaking into the playoffs with the final playoff berth in the Western Conference, the Preds shocked the top-seeded Chicago Blackhawks — a team that had tormented Nashville in recent springs — with a series sweep.

When Nashville advanced to the conference final, it marked the franchise's furthest foray into second-season hockey. The man who put the club together, GM David Poile, was also in largely unfamiliar territory. In 35 years on the job — 15 with the Washington Capitals and 20 more with Nashville after he was hired to run the club when it was founded in 1997 — Poile had seen his squads make just one final-four appearance. And when the Preds downed the Anaheim Ducks to clinch a Cup-final berth, it was Poile's first-ever trip to the season's last series. Known — and sometimes ribbed — for his reserved personality, Poile had taken bold steps in the previous year to improve the Predators. He sent the granite-jawed face of the franchise, Shea Weber, to the Montreal Canadiens for effervescent star P.K. Subban and snagged No. 1 center Ryan Johansen from the Columbus Blue Jackets in exchange for young star defenseman Seth Jones.

"[Poile] is fearless," Brian Burke, a long-time hockey executive, told Sportsnet.ca. "He's made some huge trades. Meticulous and cautious should not be confused with timid, because this guy's made blockbuster deals. To this day, the riverboat gambler side to David is still very much alive and well."

Pittsburgh, on the other hand, was playing for a championship 12 months after winning the 2016 title. Of the club's 21 players who took to the ice in the 2017 Stanley Cup final, 15 had won the Cup in 2016. Hardly an inexperienced squad — and despite being outplayed through four games, they were hanging around.

The peculiar tone to the year-end matchup was set early in Game 1 when Nashville, hot out of the blocks, stormed the home team and Subban scored what looked like the series' first goal. After an offside challenge and lengthy delay, Pittsburgh came out on the good side of a call that really could have gone either way. With momentum on the home side — in that way that only ever seems to happen in sports — the Predators very quickly saw a potential 1–0 lead turn into a 3–0 deficit. Nashville then turned the heat back up, completely overwhelming the Penguins and not allowing Pittsburgh a shot on goal for an astonishing (and record-setting) 37 minutes. Nashville, however, lost the contest 5–3 and Pittsburgh had all of 12 shots.

"It's wasn't textbook," Crosby said of his team's performance following the victory.

Over the next three games, Nashville largely outpossessed, outshot, outhit and outblocked the Penguins, but a split was the best they could muster — typically airtight goaltender Pekka Rinne looked thoroughly deflated when playing in Pittsburgh. Consider in Games 1 and 2, Rinne allowed eight goals on 36 shots for a .778 save percentage. In Games 3 and 4, in Nashville, Rinne allowed two goals on 52 shots for a .962 save percentage and two Predator victories. It was one of the better Jekyll and Hyde acts in NHL history, and it became increasingly apparent that Rinne needed to show up if Nashville was to have a fighting chance.

Also apparent was that Nashville, playing

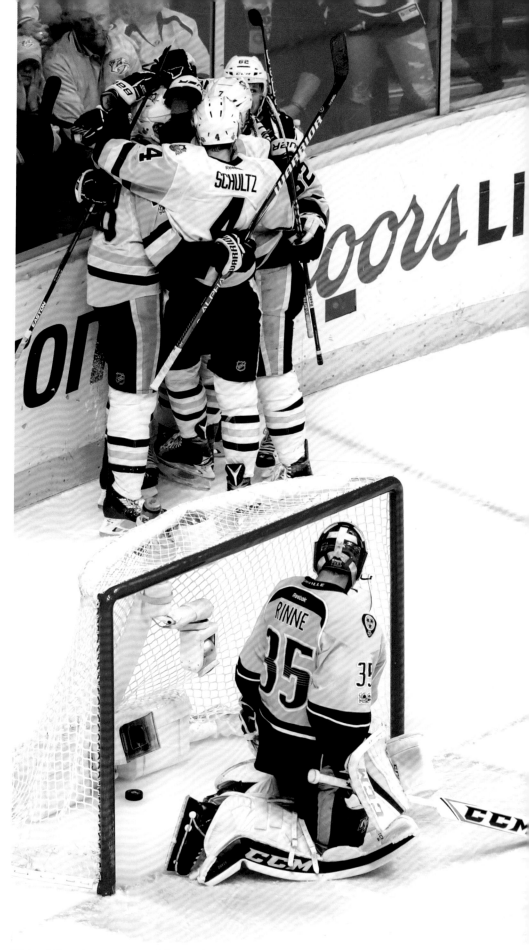

Pittsburgh Penguins teammates celebrate a third-period goal by Patric Hornqvist.

Nashville's Colton Sissons puts the puck past Pittsburgh's Matt Murray. The goal was disallowed because a whistle was blown.

	PITTSBURGH	CHICAGO
STANLEY CUPS	3	3
STANLEY CUP FINAL APPEARANCES	4	3
CONFERENCE FINAL APPEARANCES	5	5
PLAYOFF WINS	91	76
PLAYOFF GAMES PLAYED	158	128
REGULAR-SEASON WINS	536	511

without Johansen since he was lost to thigh surgery following Game 4 of the semifinal series, was going to need role players like Frederick Gaudreau, Colton Sissons and captain Mike Fisher to continue their stellar play.

And then there was Sidney Crosby. Although the Penguins megastar — who missed a game earlier in the playoffs because of a concussion — had registered four points in the series, there was a sense he still had another gear to hit. He found it in Game 5. The depleted Nashville attack couldn't beat goaltender Matt Murray, Rinne was once again chased from the net and Crosby was everywhere, ending the game with three assists as the Pens won a 6–0 laugher.

Still, there was a sense the Preds might be able to force a decisive contest because they had been so strong at Bridgestone Arena. But the good vibes in Game 6 disappeared early in the second period when a tally from Nashville's Sissons was discounted thanks to a quick and unjustified whistle from referee Kevin Pollock. It was a no-goal bookend to go with Subban's disallowed marker in Game 1, and this time there was no doubt it should have gone on the board. Instead, the teams played on through a tight, scoreless affair until former Predator Patric Hornqvist snuck the puck past Rinne with just 1:35 remaining in the third period. Carl Hagelin's empty-netter just over a minute later made it a lock; Pittsburgh was keeping the Cup, becoming the first team to win back-to-back championships since the Detroit Red Wings in 1998.

Pittsburgh's title was won by a familiar cast of characters, with Sidney Crosby leading the team, Evgeni Malkin winning the playoff scoring race and goaltender of the future Matt Murray sealing the deal after franchise great Marc-Andre Fleury played lights-out hockey for most of the first three series.

With Murray's win, he became the first goalie in NHL history to win the Stanley Cup in each of his first two years in the league — having been thrust into the spotlight as a starter in the 2016 playoffs after Fleury was injured. Prior to those playoffs, Murray had appeared in only 13 regular-season games, meaning the 2016–17 season was his true rookie year. Thus, Murray became the first goalie to win the Cup twice as a freshman.

Murray wasn't the only rookie turning heads. Teammate Jake Guentzel put his stamp on the playoffs by tying the playoff rookie point record of 21 on the strength of 13 goals and 8 assists. (Dino Ciccarelli set the mark in 1981, and Ville Leino equaled it in 2010.) Guentzel's 13 goals put him one off Ciccarelli's record of 14, and his five game-winners set a new mark for rookies.

The title also marked Pittsburgh's third parade of the salary cap era (2009, 2016, 2017), the same number of championships won by Chicago in that span. The tiebreaker, if we're debating dynasties, goes to the Penguins franchise for being able to repeat as champions.

As for Crosby, he wound up being a runaway Conn Smythe winner. A season that started with the 29-year-old captaining Canada to top spot at the World Cup ended with him adding another feather to his highly decorated cap.

"In Sid's case," said Penguins GM Jim Rutherford during the celebration, "I think now we can talk about him being in those top two, three, four guys of all time."

INDEX